THE LIBERAL MOMENT

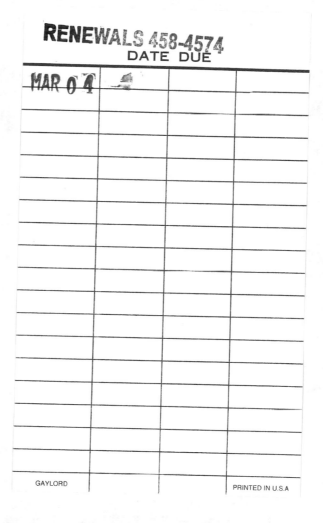

NEW DIRECTIONS IN WORLD POLITICS

John Gerard Ruggie, General Editor

THE LIBERAL MOMENT

✳

Modernity, Security, and the
Making of Postwar International Order

ROBERT LATHAM

COLUMBIA UNIVERSITY PRESS   NEW YORK

Columbia University Press
Publishers Since 1893
New York   Chichester, West Sussex
Copyright © 1997 Columbia University Press
All rights reserved
Library of Congress Cataloging-in-Publication Data
Latham, Robert, 1956–
    The liberal moment : modernity, security, and the making of
postwar international order / Robert Latham.
        p.   cm. — (New directions in world politics)
    Includes bibliographical references and index.
    ISBN 0–231–10756–0. — ISBN 0–231–10757–9 (pbk.)
    1. Europe—Politics and government—1945– 2. Liberalism—Europe—
History—20th century.   3. Cold War.   I. Title   II. Series.
    D843.L287 1997
    320.51'3—dc21   96–53164
                                                                 CIP

Printed in the United States of America
c 10 9 8 7 6 5 4 3 2 1
p 10 9 8 7 6 5 4 3 2 1

NEW DIRECTIONS IN WORLD POLITICS
John Gerard Ruggie, General Editor

To Dalia Kandiyoti, who both inspired and transformed

CONTENTS

✾

ACKNOWLEDGMENTS

❋

A great deal of this book would not have been possible without the help of Aristide Zolberg and Ira Katznelson. Through them both I learned to appreciate the many advantages of joining history, social theory, and normative concerns in a single intellectual framework. They inspired me to keep my eye on the big picture even while I toiled among the details.

This book has its origins in a dissertation completed at the Graduate Faculty of the New School for Social Research. Material for chapter three appeared in an earlier version in an article titled "Liberalism's Order / Liberalism's Other: A Genealogy of Threat," in Alternatives Vol 20, No. 1 (Jan–March 1995). A very small portion of chapter four appeared in an article titled "Democracy and War-Making: Locating the International Liberal Context," in Millennium Vol 22, No. 2 (Summer 1993). Many colleagues and friends at the New School have read and commented on parts of this study. Some of these fellow travelers include Kim Geiger, Andy Grossman, Andrew Schliewitz, and Michelle Stoddard. I would especially like to thank Orin Kirshner and Cathy O'Leary. At different times over the years they both shared an office with me. As a result, they suffered through countlessly aired doubts, and yet remained willing to offer generously their advice.

I would also like to thank the citizens of the Center for the Study of Social Change at the New School. They offered me the opportunity to present portions of this project in their regular seminar on State Formation and

Collective Action. Charles Tilly inspired me to organize my thoughts and sharpen my arguments in innumerable ways. Roy Licklider and Jeff Goodwin provided wise counsel at decisive moments.

Michael Hogan offered helpful comments on significant parts of this study. His superb work on crucial aspects of the "liberal moment" has been a great inspiration to me. I have also greatly benefited from the excellent counseling of Lee Sigal, Steve Smith, and R.B.J. Walker.

Financial support for some of the research upon which this book is based was provided by the Harry S. Truman Library. The New School for Social Research helped financially in countless ways. I also benefited from financial support from the MacArthur Foundation through the program on "The Domestic Consequences of Global Leadership and Their Implications for American Democracy" that it funded at the New School. And the Social Science Research Council, recognizing that one needs to be an active scholar to help organize scholarship, offered time and modest professional development funds to help this project along. David Featherman and Kenneth Prewitt as presidents of the Council were always mindful of the connections between active scholarship and effective organization and administration. The Committee of International Peace and Security with whom I have worked at the SSRC, especially under the leadership of Lawrence Freedman, provided a superb model for combining intellectual integrity with creativity. And I especially appreciate the help of Steve Heydemann, who has been a challenging and thoughtful colleague in matters intellectual and administrative.

I would also like to thank Kate Wittenberg Editor in Chief of Columbia University Press for supporting and contributing to this project through all of its different stages. The advice and criticisms of the panel of reviewers she assembled shaped this study in decisive ways.

Editorial assistance was provided by Allison Lichter and Jeff Wengrofsky, both of whom brought their own creative intellectual views to the project. The book gained from the copyediting of Leslie Bialler at Columbia University Press.

Finally, I am deeply indebted to Dalia Kandiyoti, to whom this book is dedicated. She gave profound intellectual inspiration, practical advice, and emotional support without which this work would surely not have come to fruition.

Robert Latham
March 1997

THE LIBERAL MOMENT

Introduction

Historical shifts and ruptures can shape political and social thought in powerful ways. During the Second World War such thinkers as John Maynard Keynes, Karl Polanyi, and Joseph Schumpeter looked out upon a world opened up to a new and profound range of possibilities—some heartening, others disturbing. At the same time, the Council on Foreign Relations organized a massive, multivolume study of potential postwar outcomes (*The War and Peace Studies of the Council on Foreign Relations, 1939–1945*). Today, the effort to think through the possibilities of reshaping international life in the context of recent shifts and ruptures in Europe and elsewhere has been far more modest. It is unfair to compare the transformative dimensions of the end of the Cold War to those of World War II. Nonetheless, it is remarkable that the range of recent scholarly and public debates has been mostly limited to questions about liberal democracy and markets, issues that, while highly relevant, are narrow in comparison to the questions raised by Polanyi and Schumpeter in their own historical moment. What is even more remarkable, this has occurred when so many scholars have consciously tried to distance themselves from the widely circulated macro-analysis of "what might be"— Francis Fukuyama's *The End of History*, told as a story of liberalism's triumph. Although concerns with democracy and markets have been tempered with substantial research on nationalism and ethnicity, the latter has not generated any macrohistorical vision of what is at stake in the end of the Cold War that can compete with democracy and markets, despite the efforts of thinkers such as Samuel P. Huntington in his controversial essay, "The Clash of Civilizations?"

Thus, whichever way historians choose to look back on the nineties, few will be able to ignore how, in the span of just a few years, new life was breathed into the centuries-old liberal tradition. The impetus for this book is a deep sense of caution about this recourse to liberalism. Above all, outside of the way liberalism shapes practices, principles, institutions, and political and moral arguments in some states and societies, little seems to be known about how liberalism affects political and social life when viewed from a global perspective. I recognize that we may not know much more about other political forms such as state socialism, but these alternatives are no longer very high on peoples' agendas.

Like so many others, my caution is fueled by my experience as a young U.S. citizen growing up with the Cold War, the Vietnam War, the sixties, and a deeply racist society. I wondered how so many apparently illiberal and violent outcomes could be so deeply inscribed in the fabric of what seemed to be the most liberal of societies. My first instinct was to dismiss such suspicions—perhaps in a fit of cognitive dissonance—with the conclusion that there were illiberal forces in the world and liberal societies could not help but contend with them. But this conclusion left me unsatisfied. I knew that it rested on the assumption that there was some way to separate liberalism from supposedly illiberal forces. Indeed, if liberalism was a significant force in the world, it could not help but be involved in the emergence and shaping of important events and developments, however distant from the just intentions of liberalism they appeared to be. Partly, I had come under the influence of Max Horkheimer and Theodore W. Adorno's *Dialectic of Enlightenment* in which the Enlightenment was taken to task for producing and organizing rationalized violence of previously unseen dimensions. Although these authors considered liberalism to be a facet of the Enlightenment, their work could be only a point of departure since it ultimately directed readers to the connections between the Enlightenment and social forces and actors clearly antithetical to liberalism (i.e., fascism).

Given this background, it was easy for me to set my sights on the intersection of liberalism—its practices, doctrines, and institutions—with social and political forms associated with the organization of violence. Once there, I chose to focus on the international realm, which meant that the great machinery of organized violence, military power, would occupy my attention. This choice was especially driven by the observation that, in our contemporary recourse to liberalism discussed above, the international community has dedicated considerable energy to finding new ways to structure security relations after the Cold War along liberal lines. Of course, some readers may accuse me of stacking the deck against liberalism in that the international environment is so hostile and certainly nowhere near as thickly constituted—regarding identities, cultures, and relations—as a domestic society. But it is exactly in this type of environment that connections can be rendered more clear to the analytical eye, as long as the possibility of unfair attribution is kept keenly in mind.

My international focus was also driven by my perception that it has only really been since the Second World War that Western scholars have been able to write about "global liberalism" or "liberal world order" and expect a reasonable, if not automatic, understanding of what is meant by these terms. Such expressions were not generally used in the nineteenth century; a hundred years ago, they would likely have been met with puzzlement. In the nineteenth century, in some quarters of the West, terms such as "liberal state," "liberal society," "liberal trade," and even "liberal foreign policy" would readily elicit meaningful recognition. "Liberal order," if anything, would have been understood in the context of domestic society and not the international realm. Indeed, the predominance of the domestic face of liberalism, which continues even today, is evident in the many treatments of liberalism that have been written from the perspective of individual nations.[1]

In part, the ability to talk about a liberal world order reflects the very development of the field of international relations, which has made international order a central concern. It also reflects the belief of state policymakers in the West that at the conclusion of large-scale twentieth-century wars a far wider range of issues had to be considered than were ever imaginable in the important peace settlements of the nineteenth century. Former Secretary of State Dean Acheson understood that he was "present at the creation" of far more than new military-strategic relations among states.[2]

This book is an attempt to probe the connections between those strategic relations and the practices, principles, and institutions associated with a liberal West that policymakers such as Acheson thought were at stake at the end of the Second World War. An underlying premise of the study is that for far too long international thought has not taken seriously enough the extent to which forms of social existence associated with the liberal tradition have been intertwined with the military-strategic dimensions of international political life. While there might be other ways to explore the plausibility, depth, and varying manifestations of this intertwinement, I focus on the outbreak of the Cold War. The Cold War represents a superb historical laboratory for drawing out lessons about the impact of Western liberalism on international political life and the possible connections between liberalism and military force. That is because, in the post-World War II period, Western liberalism experienced its most extensive reach at the same time that security became an especially acute feature of international relations. Moreover, it was especially in the immediate postwar years, roughly between 1945 and 1950, that decisive actions and events shaped the contours of international political life for decades to come. Studying this period has the advantage of directly confronting a crucial turning point in the history of the liberal tradition: the construction of a liberal order that was more comprehensive and international in scope than any previous attempt to bring liberal doctrines and principles to bear in the making of international political life. This effort, together with the powerful conjunction of historical forces engendered by the Second World War, created a unique liberal moment. I fixed my gaze on this period, in the hope that its formative events would help me to draw out insights about liberalism understood in a global perspective as well as to offer a new interpretation of the beginnings of the Cold War.

A broad outline of the argument is as follows: Beginning with the Second World War, state policymakers in the West, under U.S. leadership, endeavored to build institutions and relations to order their postwar international realm. The social and ideational fabric upon which that construction effort was based was liberal modernity as it had emerged in the West. The boundaries of the order pursued cut across the Americas, Europe, and Asia, incorporating various states, liberal and nonliberal, initially including the Soviet Union. This effort to make an international liberal order would not only create conditions and forces leading to the emergence of the Cold War, but would also generate international political dynamics that shaped the militarization of the West. The aspects of militarization in which I am interested revolve around the process by which military-strategic issues, relations, and institutions come to constitute an increasingly predominant dimension of the overall international political life of a set of states and societies.

The outline just presented, however, is not meant to capture the many lines of analysis, theory, and interpretation developed in the ensuing chapters. As I see it, Western militarization—and the emergence of the Cold War—did not rest on any one factor, but rather on a constellation of forces, processes, and tensions formed by the unique relationship between strategy and liberal order-building. If there is any single common denominator to the different elements in this constellation, it is in the play between freedom, order, and military power. I argue that because military force is, as Michael Mann describes it, the most "concentrated-coercive" social form,[3] it can provide order at the international level through institutions and relations that minimally constrain the liberty of actors including states, democratic publics, corporations, groups, and individuals to set the terms of their own existence in liberal modernity. Order achieved through military-strategic relations will create a far less institutionalized legacy, require less public consent, and intervene in far fewer areas of liberal practice then broad-based political institutions of international governance that might otherwise emerge to sustain order. In other words, with military force constituting the predominant form of social control at the international level, more thickly institutionalized political relations of governance can be avoided, and a certain degree of relative autonomy for actors in the international system can be preserved. We might think of the way military force mediated between autonomy and governance in the context of international liberalism as a form of "embedded militarization." That is, militarization unfolded within and in response to the broader social and political fabric of an international liberal order.[4] Security structures and outcomes were not disembedded from the life of that order, but instead flowed from it.

It is not that states in liberal order are any more or less likely to rely on military relations than states in other contexts such as the socialist order that the Soviet state eventually built in Eastern Europe. I do not carry out a comparative study of the military dimensions of various orders. Nor is my goal to suggest that in the liberal order established in the mid-twentieth century military force protected or secured the relations and the states bounded within it—a point that would readily be accepted by any of the most liberal of thinkers. Rather, I explore the extent to which the forging of military relations and power grows out of and is an important element in the political dynamics *internal* to liberal order.

While I will discuss in greater detail the method, design, and approach that underlies this study, some initial clarification is in order. I do not uncover any new substantive information about what happened in the early Cold War period. Nor do I establish a set of theoretical propositions and then informally test them by marshalling historical data. Instead, I build an *interpretation* of Cold War history, viewed through the lens of U.S. foreign policy. The use of the term "interpretation" cannot be taken for granted. Its use implies a mode of analysis that is distinguishable from the causal explanation that is so often considered synonymous with a positivist approach. Since analysis in the field of international relations has generally taken a positivist attitude in the postwar period, any departure from that attitude cannot be innocent.[5] At the same time, the hermeneutical or interpretive turn in the social sciences has a considerable history which cannot rightfully be ignored. This is not the place to retell the history of hermeneutics, nor to rehearse the debate between the interpretive and scientific approaches to social knowledge, but I will make clear what type of interpretation I am doing and at the same time confront the issues raised by the scientific tradition by briefly considering Max Weber's concept of "explanatory understanding." Hermeneutics, as the "art of understanding texts," was increasingly systematized in the nineteenth century and applied in sociological, historiographical, and psychoanalytical contexts.[6] Social action, historical periods, and life histories came to be viewed as texts subject to interpretation.[7] Weber was quite aware of the hermeneutical tradition that was especially strong in his own Germany. He sought to show how an understanding (*Verstehen*) of the meaning or significance of action for agents could yield knowledge about the motives generating such action. Such knowledge would, thus, provide a causal explanation of that action.[8] This explanation could then be subject to verification along scientific lines, either in statistical terms, as instances of a general hypothesis or law, or in logical terms, as part of a theory subject to logical proof. Until that testing takes place, the interpretation that gives us an understanding of action "must remain only a particularly plausible hypothesis."[9] In this way, Weber sought in principle to join science and interpretation.

In practice, however, Weber mostly worked in the realm of building meaningful contexts for social action, such as the rise of capitalism. Placing his stated concerns with scientistic verification aside, can his corpus be understood as being guided not only by the pursuit of interpretations that explain, but also by explanations that interpret? In an "interpretive explanation" (in contrast to Weber's "explanatory understanding") an analyst makes an argument about the logic of forces bearing on social or historical outcomes and developments. This logic gives meaning and significance to these outcomes and developments. What we are doing in interpretive explanation is employing explanatory schemes that show why things have become what they are, which thereby sets up frameworks of meaning for a given historical period or complex of social action. That is, identifying forces and illuminating how they are linked and impinge on one another creates particular types of what Clifford Geertz calls "intelligible frames" and, thus, assigns significance to certain relations and phenomena. To a great extent this is what many historians do, and it is what Weber did in his exploration of the impact of religion on the rise of capitalism.

This way of framing the relationship between interpretation and explanation does unhinge causality from the type of scientific verification Weber was after. But this does not mean that we can forego the question of the validation of interpretations. Looking to the hermeneutical tradition, thinkers such as Jurgen Habermas, Charles Taylor, and Paul Ricoeur have emphasized that arguments and judgments about the plausibility of competing interpretations constitute a process of validation that is never complete.[10] An interpretation can be judged to be sensible or plausible because of the way it puts together historical elements and facts, tells a story about the unfolding of events, or sheds new light on the configuration of social and political relations.[11] An interpretation may be judged to be implausible because it gets the story wrong, especially by missing things. Thus, the comprehensiveness of an interpretation matters.

Two related goals of this study justify this interpretive approach. One goal is to identify and explore the connections that emerge in a broad spectrum of processes and outcomes relating to the rise of the Cold War and to flesh out the intersection of liberalism and military force within which the U.S. state played a crucial role. The second goal is to gain some insight into the tensions that have shaped postwar history, which might tell us something about the international face of liberalism more generally. I have tried to render my interpretation plausible by engaging and evaluating the specific history of the early postwar period. I appraise other interpretations of the Cold War and the relation between liberalism and military force. If I were to make any single comparative claim, especially against the approach that has dominated U.S. international relations—realism—it is that the interpretation offered here is more comprehensive. Thus, I hope the reader will judge the merit of this study on the basis of its ability to raise questions about important dimensions of international political life and its history that have received little attention in the past and that have not been tied together before in the ways they are here.

In chapter 1, I specify what is meant by the terms liberal modernity and liberal order. I suggest how these social forms can be placed in an international perspective and lay out the advantages of viewing modernity through the lens of liberalism rather than capitalism or some other historical context. Although this will take the argument in an initially abstract direction, the establishment of a clear understanding of both liberalism and order is necessary before the analysis can move forward. The purpose of this chapter is to demonstrate how liberalism constitutes a historical context that has shaped the contours of modern international life along five dimensions: open economic exchange, domestic market relations, the liberal governance of the polity, individual and group rights, and the right of collective self-determination.

In chapter 2, I probe the initial phases of what I call the "liberal moment," arising above all out of the Second World War. I develop the basic elements of a conceptual infrastructure for interpreting the change surrounding this period. Especially important is a consideration of the specific conditions associated with U.S. liberal hegemonic agency. What forces drew the U.S. into its hegemonic role? How was the character of the U.S. presence in the international realm shaped by its identity as a liberal state? How was the course of action open to the U.S. limited by the complex web of actors and interests inside and outside the U.S. state? Much relevant political debate in the U.S. revolved around the question of how extensive the U.S. international commitment would be in political, economic, and military terms in the postwar period. This chapter also situates the argument in the context of other interpretations of the period in the fields of international relations and diplomatic history.

In chapter 3, I push the substantive exploration of the postwar period further. I start by asking how international, as opposed to domestic, order is actually created, and look into the relevance and possibilities of international community that existed at the time. I go on to consider the formidable task of defining and constructing liberal relations under U.S. leadership. I also analyze how the Soviet Union shaped the liberal order-building process and the ways that a central tension in that process emerged out of the endeavor to incorporate the Soviet Union into the international liberal order. I identify the tensions among liberal states that contributed to the growing Cold War confrontation and probe the dynamics of relations between the U.S., Europe, and the non-Western world. I examine the deepening of the Cold War into spheres of influence as well as the feasibility of alternatives to this outcome. Finally, I argue that it is only against the backdrop of a liberal order-building project that we can understand the perception of U.S. policymakers—and later commentators—that increasing international political tensions and intervention in Europe were a response to a cascade of failed policies and institutions operating in the first couple of postwar years.

The adoption of specific strategies for building a liberal order were organized under the general rubric of containment, which reflected, as I argue in chapter 4, both the dynamics of liberal relations and the liberal contours of U.S. agency. That is, the strategic doctrine of containment can be understood as a specifically liberal political form. There was a decidedly economic emphasis to containment early on and the question is: how did it so rapidly become militarized? What was the significance of the strategic system of military bases being constructed at the time? How did economic commitments engender military ones? In chapter 4, I also explore the political and strategic impact of incorporating nonliberal states and societies within liberal order. I move on to focus on how the limits placed on the formation of U.S. hegemonic agency contributed to militarization. Was the commitment, under the containment doctrine, to economic over military security in part undermined by the minimal institutional forms constructed as the means for the exercise of U.S. agency and the facilitation of liberal relations? The relationship between political and economic integration, the formation of NATO, and a search for a workable framework for cooperation is also considered. I ask as well whether there is something unique about how threat and fear is manifested in liberal order. And finally, I address the question of whether there is something in the character of military force that makes it well-suited to the construction of liberal order.

I draw out some of the lessons about liberal order and U.S. foreign policy in the fifth and concluding chapter. To do so, I recall basic dilemmas and paradoxes of international agency in the context of liberal modernity. Especially important is the tension between forces that pull liberal states toward inaction and those that push them toward overreaction. Finding a middle ground between these two extremes will be difficult for a U.S. state that will likely remain an international leader into the twenty-first century. But that ground may provide the basis for a more effective, if not more just, foreign policy.

This book has been written from a perspective that embraces many of the values and practices associated with the liberal tradition including: equality, democratic decisionmaking, peaceful conflict resolution, and political and social rights. Yet the study implies that post-World War II international liberal order as it has been realized so far may not be the best form for pursuing these values and practices. Like many scholars who are critical of how political and social life is currently constituted on a global scale, I am uncomfortable advocating neo-Marxist social visions as an alternative, and I am deeply ambivalent about looking only to the liberal state as the form of polity through which just political outcomes can be pursued. This study has convinced me that the field of international relations needs, above all, to reflect on what are taken to be the starting points for thinking through the terms of international political life at the end of the twentieth century, and at least to question whether that life should include a commitment to liberal order or not. It is hoped that in some way the analysis that follows can contribute to these efforts.

I

❉

"A Certain Overlordship"
Locating the International Liberal Context

Liberal Modernity

It is still too early to tell whether what has commonly been taken in the West to be a surge of commitment in Eastern Europe and the former Soviet Union to the organization of social and political life along liberal lines will hold. It is not clear how seriously this organization will penetrate societies in the region or whether it will sustain any deep popular support. Nonetheless, the shift in values in the former Soviet-bloc countries toward the Western liberal tradition on an historically unprecedented scale has received a great deal of attention from scholars and commentators.[1] This sense of great change was reinforced by the new forces of democratization and privatization that emerged in the 1980s in regions as diverse as Latin America, the Middle East, and East Asia.

In general, these developments have been viewed through the lens of liberal democracy, a perspective that, according to Tony Smith, joins two longstanding traditions, liberalism and democracy.[2] Liberal democracy represents a cluster of principles and practices that organize a state and society. This cluster includes the holding of free, competitive, and broad-based elections; the restraint of state power vis-à-vis a relatively autonomous civil society; and the commitment to equality, tolerance, and the rights of groups and individuals. Within the field of international relations, the inquiry into the scarcity of war between liberal democracies has placed such states and societies at the center of what has become an increasingly popular research program.[3] Liberal democracy is certainly a useful concept for the analysis and comparison of distinct types of states and societies. But the concept in itself does not tell us much about the wider historical context of which it is a part, namely, liberal modernity. The task of this chapter is to probe the character and breadth of this historical context and its relationship to international order. By doing so, I hope to demonstrate that this historical setting is a productive starting point for thinking about twentieth-century liberal order in a global perspective.

To begin with, broad historical contexts have entered the study of international relations in roughly two forms. One is neo-Marxism. Analysts in the neo-Marxist tradition embed their analysis of international social and political life in the broad historical context of capitalism, which encompasses ideology, culture, and modes of social and material organization. Because it clearly sets analysis in a global perspective, the work of sociologist Immanuel Wallerstein has had significant resonance in the field of international relations. Wallerstein's notion of a "world capitalist system" places capitalism as a macro-historical fabric in a specific geopolitical setting. In that setting, differences between core areas, composed of leading states and societies, and the rest of the world, composed of weak peripheral regions and less weak semi-peripheral regions, generate large-scale global economic, political, and cultural dynamics.[4]

Historical contexts have also entered the study of international relations in a form that has no ready label. It, nonetheless, can be distinguished by its focus on historical changes in the way societies and polities are organized. Although capitalism is recognized in this form as an important force, it is less central to analysis than it is in neo-Marxism. The institution of sovereignty is more central. For example, John Ruggie points to the transformation in Europe of polities from medieval to modern forms within which different modes of legitimating rule and authority have had important implications for the constitution of sovereignty as a practice and institution.[5] Stephen Krasner also explores the differences between the medieval and modern worlds in order to argue that the institutionalization of sovereignty followed transformations in political and economic practices.[6] And R. B. J. Walker places the entire tradition of international relations in the context of a modernity within which political community and identity are deeply invested in the bordered nation-state.[7]

By distinguishing two forms of concern with large historical contexts I do not want to imply that analysts are forced to choose between exclusive perspectives. Robert Cox has probably gone farthest in synthesizing both forms of concern through his concept of "historical structures." In this construct, material capabilities, institutions, and ideas interact to create a "framework for action," which is a "context of habits, pressures, expectations and constraints within which action takes place."[8] Cox's synthesis of the two forms emerges from his interest in learning about capitalism *and* international relations rather than only the former.

More generally, both forms share a concern with the implications of the emergence and development of modernity. Neo-Marxists have focused on the study of a profound dimension of modern existence, capitalism, while the international relations theorists have tried to trace some of the forces determining the practice and understanding of modern world politics. As an especially broad-based and comprehensive historical context, modernity refers to a complex of collective practices, shared ideas, and forms of organizing social existence with unique historical consequences including nation-states, modern cities, industrial societies, and global markets. Few would dispute that Max Weber and Karl Marx captured important dimensions of modern existence, including its organization of social relations, based on rational design. Both theorists appreciated that modern life threw open nearly every aspect of social existence to reformulation and reorganization. They also were keenly aware that this openness was not necessarily a matter of liberation: for Weber there was the "iron cage" of mechanistic and spiritless rational organization and for Marx there was the development of class exploitation and alienation.[9]

Modernity has so many dimensions and facets that it defies any single depiction and it certainly is not subject to definition. To try to so encapsulate it would be like trying to contain half a millennium of history on a notecard. There are two further complications. One is that it would be deceptive to think of modernity as the totality of post-medieval existence even in the West, although it certainly is an extremely predominant dimension. There are cultural forms and identities (e.g., fundamentalist religion) that are distinguishable as nonmodern, despite the obvious imbrications with modern existence.

The other complication is the sheer heterogeneity of modernity. If we consider the various forms that modern existence has taken in different contexts—in socialist and fascist societies, in the Third World, and in the West—it becomes obvious that modernity is variegated. That is, there are not only different historical periods to modernity, but also different ways of being modern. These different ways involve ideology and identity as well as modes of practice and organization. Where one author has recently identified what he calls "reactionary modernism" in Germany's Weimar Republic, another has discerned an approach to the relation between tradition and modern technology in India that is far different than in the West.[10] These forms are not deviations from some norm of Western modernity, but rather different registers of being modern. S. N. Eisenstadt points to "the uniqueness of the civilization of modernity and . . . the great variability of the symbolic, ideological, and institutional responses to it."[11] It is far from clear what all these variations share. But one common element is the recognition that an important dimension in the making and sustaining of modern social existence is the enduring possibility of the purposive organization and reorganization of forms of large-scale human agency associated with such phenomena as rational administration, mass movements, and scientific endeavor. This organization can be experienced as a Weberian "iron cage" of an over-rationalized existence; or as the flux and volatility, expressed in the writings of the poet Charles Baudelaire, of a world in which everything is subject to organized revision and remaking.[12]

Within that variability lies liberal modernity. If we understand modernity to be a very broad and comprehensive macro-historical fabric, or what Eisenstadt calls—perhaps unfortunately—a "civilization," liberal modernity represents a mode of fashioning and sustaining aspects of social and political existence within that fabric. Thus, in any given geographic region, liberal modernity exists alongside of and intersects with other aspects of modernity, including capitalism, or capitalist modernity, and industrialism, or industrial modernity.[13] Indeed, besides its value in making clear that liberalism is not just a body of doctrine or a set of principles but a way of being modern, the term liberal modernity makes it possible to place liberalism and other organizational forms within the same macro-historical fabric.[14] Capitalist modernity, explored so thoroughly by Marx, is the broad body of social relations, such as those between workers and capitalists, structured by forms of political and economic organization such as the state. Liberal, as distinct from capitalist, modernity represents the particular shaping of the political and social entities or spaces in which one lives through practices, principles, and institutions associated with liberal governance, rights, markets, and self-determination. These two forms of modernity, despite their close historical proximity, have different ontologies. Whereas capitalist modernity refers to material and organizational forces such as those associated with the circulation of commodities and its manifestation in the social and political life of towns and cities (e.g., in the political domination of certain classes over others), liberal modernity refers to the patterning of that social and political life through a broad body of doctrines and practices. It therefore makes a great deal of sense in the case of capitalist modernity to apply the term "system" to describe the interaction of different actors and entities that emerge within the capitalist fabric. But it makes less sense to do so for liberal modernity (however, as we shall see, the term "order" is a different matter).[15] While liberal practices such as multilateral trade might shape the identity of the capitalist economic system, it is only in the sense of there being coherence among elements that we can speak of dimensions of liberalism forming a system in their own right.

We can also differentiate between a capitalist state and a liberal state. The former refers to a state operating in—and even for the development and protection of—capitalist relations, while the latter refers to a state that is organized and shaped by liberal doctrines and practices.[16] In the case of markets the contrast is equally evident. As Karl Polanyi made clear, markets in modernity are politically constituted economic spaces for trade and exchange within and across polities.[17] Whereas liberal doctrine and principles and liberals themselves have shaped how those markets are constituted (i.e, their character and status within a given polity, especially freedom of contract), capitalist relations comprise the wider economic framework within which markets operate regarding production, consumption, and the generation of economic agents. While both states and markets existed long before the advent of capitalism and liberalism, liberalism transformed states and markets in distinct and decisive ways. In some respects, the difference between the two might sound like the classic distinction between sub- and super-structures. But such a view misses one point: capitalist modernity has a political dimension that can—but need not—be liberal in character, and that—however deeply intertwined it is with capitalist modernity—the vast body of liberal doctrine and practices constitutes a distinct dimension of modern social existence. (There is little to be gained from debates about the relative autonomy of these social forms.)

The relationship between markets and liberal modernity illustrates why the latter is a far more comprehensive qualifier of modernity than the term liberal democratic. Liberal modernity refers not just to a type of polity, but also to the relations between polities and other social actors in the context of international trade and politics; the movement of people; and the exchange of ideas and identities (e.g., cosmopolitanism). Liberal modernity thus has a distinctly international dimension which is not captured by the construct, liberal democracy.[18] Moreover, liberal modernity also conveys the sense of there being a macro-historical space within which a way of organizing social existence—usually referred to as "Western"—has unfolded. Karl Deutsch was really writing about liberal modernity when he pointed to the "combination of incomes, welfare services, and individual liberties that makes up much of that 'Western' way of life which is so often felt and referred to but which seems so hard to define."[19] Recent advocates of Deutschian analysis call this type of phenomenon a transnational "social environment."[20] The point is that being liberal democratic situates an individual, group, state, or society in a complex but identifiable transnational historical context that is liberal modernity.

Liberal modernity is also more comprehensive because the doctrines, agents, and institutions traditionally emphasized in liberalism bear on a far greater range of social existence than simply political governance, which is the paramount focus of liberal democracy. Central to the making of liberal modernity are not only markets, but also civil societies, encompassing religious organizations, cultural institutions, intellectual endeavor, and the status of modern individuals vis-à-vis their autonomy and rights.[21]

While it may be tempting to refer to this macro-historical fabric as Western—rather than liberal—modernity, to do so would be a mistake for two reasons that should already be obvious. One reason is that, although there is no disputing the centrality of the West in the formation of liberal modernity, it has not been the only region, understood in historical, geographical, or social terms, where it has emerged. The most potent examples are countries along the Pacific Rim whose liberalizing markets have recently received considerable attention. By identifying as westernized those states and societies in myriad regions that have liberal dimensions, one, in effect, makes claims that these regions have become like the West when they in fact have their own regional and historical identities.

The second reason why Western identity is problematic is that liberalism, as I have noted above, is not the West's only legacy. Fascism, right-wing authoritarianism, and state socialism are nonliberal, but clearly Western, forces. It is a one-sided but not infrequent error to associate the West exclusively with the liberal tradition, an error that ignores an important body of historical information that is beyond the scope of this study.

Just as any conception of the West—or for that matter, as we saw, modernity—cannot be reduced to a single mode of organizing social existence, liberal modernity itself has been subject to considerable variation. States and societies forming part of the fabric of liberal modernity organize their relations, construct their institutions, and articulate their doctrines differently. Further variation emerges on the historical plane in the ways that relevant practices, principles, and institutions change over time and at different speeds, depths, and degrees and appear in different combinations in the social spaces where liberal modernity has made itself felt.[22] Even within the geographical West, there was significant variation in the way that liberalism appeared on and off the European continent.

Despite the complexity and variation in liberal modernity, its formation has not been a completely unstructured process. It certainly would be disingenuous in the face of the variability of liberal modernity to posit any core themes, especially since each national tradition will have its own set of arguments about its sense of a core.[23] Short of identifying core themes, there is something that makes principles and practices such as public debate hang together in what can be understood to be a family resemblance, in the Wittgensteinian sense, as the elements of liberal modernity.[24] That "hanging together" happens because the social action that goes into the formation and transformation of liberal modernity—and the transnational social environment that is associated with it—historically has been organized around five distinct elements: open international economic exchange, domestic market relations, the liberal governance of the polity, individual and group rights, and the right of collective self-determination.

These are the predominant mediums through which liberal modernity and the macro-historical entities associated with it—states, civil societies, markets, and the liberal dimensions of international society—are shaped. While we may associate liberal modernity with all sorts of doctrines and practices, such as religious freedom and economic redistribution, these five elements are distinguishable as the building blocks of liberal social existence as it has unfolded in the international realm. They are not simply means to pursue liberal values (e.g., liberty and equality), although this is one way for actors to engage them. Each element as a medium is more than a channel or mechanism for the pursuit of liberal values. It is also a constitutive element itself in the formation of liberal social spaces. For example, the establishment of a body of individual rights under constitutional protection is an important dimension in the making of a liberal state.

A variegated body and history of practices, principles, and institutions began to form in the nineteenth century around each of these mediums, through the effort of countless agents in all sorts of national and historical settings. Regarding liberal governance, for instance, liberals in Europe struggled to establish constitutional government in various forms, inventing and borrowing different doctrines and practical blueprints from neighboring states and societies.[25] While each medium may take a particular form in a given state and society, it is possible to take an analytical step back to view the body of phenomena associated with a given medium that exists across the entire geographical and social reach of liberal modernity (e.g., one could look at the various ways that markets have emerged across different societies). Each body can be thought of as constituting a distinct domain of liberal modernity. Through this heuristic leap we learn how the great variation that marks liberal modernity is loosely structured. By viewing liberalism in global perspective this way, we gain an analytical window on the shifts, ruptures, and transnational migrations of doctrines and practices occurring across the historical and spatial fabric of liberal modernity. But most important of all, the domain analytic maps the broad social environment out of which international liberal order and its tensions are formed.

The Domain Analytic

Domains are analytical constructs. They provide a basis for grasping the diverse and transformative elements of liberal modernity from a vantage point that is transnational and transhistorical. As a heuristic device the domain analytic rests on the assumption that at any given moment in time, we can look out across the geographical and social fabric of liberal modernity and discern the different ways in which a given medium, such as rights, takes form in specific societies. It is also assumed that the practices and discourses that emerge in different societies influence one another and share an intertwined history.

At first glance, domains might resemble issue areas.[26] Issue areas emerge around the perceptions and the directed action of agents regarding a given problem or policy area. The environment and nuclear nonproliferation are two examples. Like domains, issue areas can comprise practices, principles, and institutions centered about a given issue. Similarly, the policies and perceptions of actors shaping liberal modernity can play a part in determining the dimensions of a domain at any given point in time. But where issue areas and domains differ is in the nature of the object around which they form and the context in which they are embedded. For issue areas, the objects are specific areas of action in the context of the current international political and social life of a group of actors. Domains, as we have seen, emerge around mediums such as liberal governance that shape, to varying degrees, the form of existence for a given state and society. Each domain represents an area of human struggle and a constellation of goals regarding the character of human existence in and across states and societies bearing on human rights, democracy, market life, and the right to an independent political community. Despite their different character, issue areas and domains can be imbricated with one another in important ways.

One example is the intersection of the issue area of international human rights with the domain of liberal rights. At Helsinki in 1975 the Final Act helped set in motion civil challenges to the extremely weak record on human rights in Eastern Europe (e.g., Charter 77) and the Soviet Union. On the one hand, these challenges shifted the way policymakers understood the stakes in the Helsinki accords as an element in the issue area of human rights. On the other hand, the reach of the domain of liberal rights was expanded eastward, however superficially. In that expansion, a new set of actors emerged to forge new forms of struggle to establish rights associated with liberal modernity in societies that had hitherto been only marginal elements in that domain.

For others, the domain analytic might resemble Michael Walzer's attempt to view liberal society in terms of multiple spheres. He has argued that liberals in modern society have struggled to establish separations or walls between spheres of life, from the market to the political community.[27] In contrast to domains, Walzer's spheres operate within a single national community. Liberal domains exist within the context of a transnational social environment with a variety of national communities. Consistency, regularity, and coherence are much less likely to emerge in this context. Moreover, since domains operate within and across national spaces, there does not exist a central authority such as a state, which for Walzer serves as "the agent of separation and defender, as it were, of the social map."[28] Domains simply lack clearly identifiable borders and consistent principles of operation.[29] Thus, elements of each domain overlap in the complex web of liberal modernity (e.g., liberal rights are clearly embedded in liberal governance). This overlap is inherent in the nature of liberal modernity.[30]

Finally, some readers will correctly see parallels between domains and the analyses Michel Foucault undertook of the "several fields" of "fundamental experience: madness, illness, death, crime, sexuality, and so forth."[31] His studies trace the ways that modern life is shaped by specific bodies of knowledge, discourse, and practices as well as relations of power that have emerged around these fields of experience. Such bodies, in effect, constitute domains. But Foucault purposely avoided making any connections between the domains he explored and the broader macro-historical entities such as modernity, the state, and civil society.[32] In contrast, the liberal domains described below are explicitly linked to the constitution of liberal modernity and order.

The substance of Foucault's domains were transformed as a result of ruptures, inventions, and shifts in discourse, knowledge, and practices.[33] Along these lines, I would argue the only way we have of determining if a domain exists is the ability to trace a distinct trajectory of transformation regarding the objects, actors, principles, discourses, and practices that form around a liberal medium across different time periods. One need only think of the transformation of international economic exchange from its nineteenth- to twentieth-century forms, as international institutions proliferated and the nature of regulation and multilateralism underwent considerable change.[34] The driving force behind transformation in all of the liberal domains is conflict between actors who are struggling to contest and define the dimensions of their political and social life.

It might be theoretically possible to write a history of all the practices, principles, and institutions that have to date formed the substance of a given domain as manifested in different national settings. Obviously, such a task can be conceived of only in the abstract. But the idea of such a history suggests an additional route I can take toward further clarifying what domains are: to provide a brief sketch of the content and history of the five liberal domains.[35]

The Domains of Liberal Modernity

Liberal domains did not emerge until the nineteenth century, despite clear historical precedents.[36] Two factors mark this emergence: The first is the spread of liberal practices, principles, and institutions across different national spaces, which was reflected in a multiplication of the number and type of liberal actors, including corporations, national movements, and associations. Prior to the nineteenth century, only Britain and the U.S. had experienced this type of advance in any significant way (the revolutionary transformation of France notwithstanding). The second factor is the extent to which liberal practices, principles, and institutions became differentiated by area, each with its own identifiable set of actors, doctrinal history, and categories of social action and objects. Such a formation is signalled by the very ability of actors such as states or political movements to develop policies and doctrines about specific areas of liberal practice, such as free trade or constitutionalism, which simply did not exist in previous eras.

In the sketches that follow I concentrate on the emergence of domains in western and central Europe in the nineteenth century and generally ignore the U.S. I do this because the multiplicity of states in the European region and their interconnections in that century provide a more illustrative basis for noting the international historical transformations in each domain. The U.S. simply was not a significant factor in the regional dynamics of Europe until the twentieth century. Even with this concentration on one, albeit crucial, region in the making of liberal modernity, I can do no more than skip across the surfaces of each domain.

Open International Economic Exchange

While international trade—conducted sometimes under relatively "free" conditions—has had a long and illustrious history, prior to the nineteenth century, the doctrines and practices associated with multilateral exchange and the relatively free movement of goods and capital across state boundaries would become a notable part of the life of states and societies only then.[37] No other domain is more closely associated with the international dimensions of liberal modernity than open international exchange. It is the one domain that most clearly ties states and civil societies into a complex network of international political-economic relations. Such a network expands the economic freedom of market actors and limits the restrictions to that freedom inherent in state-defined borders. Beyond this, an open international market constitutes a macrohistorical entity of enormous proportions that is deeply grounded in the liberal tradition.

The influence on liberal doctrine of English political economists such as Adam Smith was profound in the first industrial nation, Britain.[38] Smith's theory of free trade departed from its predecessor, that of mid-eighteenth century French physiocrats, by emphasizing the firm as the center of economic action. Smith's insights found further expression in the Manchester School which began to emerge in the 1820s. Elsewhere in Europe, liberal adherents to the doctrine of free trade and exchange were more slow in coming, despite the efforts of writers such as Say and Bastiat in France, and Karl Heinrich Rau and Prince Smith in Germany.[39]

In practice, even the mercantilist era was marked by significant economic interdependence.[40] Numerous pre-nineteenth-century precedents to the free trade era can be identified, including the 1786 Eden Treaty which relaxed tariffs between Britain and France. Even after the Napoleonic Wars, free trade policies existed among the small states and free cities, including the northern provinces of the Netherlands, Hamburg, Bremen, Frankfurt-am-Main. States such as Switzerland, Rhineland-Westphalia, and Saxony on the whole held to liberal tariff policies.[41] After 1815 it was Prussia, not Britain, that had in many significant ways the most liberal tariff policy among the larger states in Europe.[42] Despite some moves toward liberalization in the 1820s, it would take among other things the political pressures of the Anti-Corn Law League to usher Britain into a truly free trade stance. Other such movements sprang up on the Continent. With the emergence of the free trade era marked by the Cobden-Chevalier Treaty of 1860, France would sign trade treaties with Belgium, the Zollverein, Italy, Switzerland, Sweden, Norway, the Netherlands and the Hanse towns, Spain, Austria, and Portugal. Although Britain had little to concede in a trade treaty after its unilateral liberalization of the 1840s, it managed to sign treaties with Belgium, Italy, the Zollverein, and Austria. Because of the emergence of the most-favored-nation clause these treaties laid the basis for multilateral trade, a central aspect of exchange in the twentieth century.

In the final three decades of the nineteenth century a multilateral payment system formed that was an important component of the multilateral trade system. Its features included the convertibility of currencies and a complex pattern of payment balancing including colonies and the United States.[43] Facilitating this exchange was the stability of Britain's sterling currency. Although sterling was backed by gold since the 1820s, in part explaining the currency's stability, it was not until the last decade of the nineteenth century that a monetary system based on the institution of the gold standard would come into full fruition, when all the major European states abandoned silver and adopted gold as their exclusive standard.

In mid-century, movement in a whole range of spheres opened up. Movement involving waterways, capital, labor, businessmen, and communications all became much easier. In addition, Britain as well as France and the Netherlands had opened up trade access to their colonies. Most of the international organizations in the period were dedicated to standardizing this new movement, regulating railroads, canals, telegraphs, the mails, and even fishing.

Although the 1870s saw a multilateral payments system emerge in full form, the decade has nevertheless been associated with the return to protectionism. While most European states moved toward protection in the last decades of the nineteenth century (Britain, the Netherlands, and Denmark are the exceptions), trade flows remained open. Even in the height of the free trade era there already were protective measures built into the system, and in the protectionist retrenchment many of the elements of free trade were not abandoned.[44] Indeed, the most-favored-nation principle remained more or less in effect. Thus, rather than signalling the closure of the domain of open international exchange, the move toward protection reflected a shift in its practices. Such a shift also included restrictions on the movement of labor and the return of colonial preferences.

Despite the numerous inroads of economic nationalism, occurring especially toward the end of the nineteenth century and the first half of the twentieth century, and the severe contraction of the interwar years, the Bretton Woods Conference in 1944 invented institutions (i.e., the World Bank and the International Monetary Fund) to facilitate exchange in novel ways. As a result, liberal multilateral exchange was placed on a new plane in the post–World War II period.[45]

Domestic Market Relations

Liberals traditionally have taken the principles and institutions that organize material life in a given society (i.e., national economies) to be decisive for the pursuit of liberty. One reason is that so many dimensions of life are drawn up into the organization of economic relations. Markets, domestic as well as international, are not only a medium for the operation of the pluralized system of economic relations we know as capitalism, but are also expected to mold the organization and administration of material life into a form that expands the autonomy of individuals and groups. The end of mercantilist restrictions and the powerful potential of "economic man" were seen as opening up choices over movement, consumption, exchange, and work that were not dictated by custom or state power, but by interest and the logic of following one's own nature into the division of labor.[46]

It is true that prior to the nineteenth century much of northern Europe had been organized into states whose territory contained an identifiable realm of economic activity that could be taken for a national economy. While these states and societies traded extensively with one another, part of the genius of *The Wealth of Nations* is the recognition that each national sphere would benefit by forming itself into a national market drawn up into an international market that is organized according to an international division of labor. The national market economy represents a social space, reproduced on an international basis across political territories, within which individuals and groups (namely, firms) can achieve freedoms in their economic activity.[47] With the market's ascendance in the first half of the nineteenth century "economic liberalism" became a significant aspect of the doctrine of every liberal movement in Europe, even though in countries on the Continent, such as Germany, liberals embraced market ideology uneasily.[48] Indeed, as Polanyi shows, by the end of the century economic liberals came to believe that markets were self-regulating entities that had taken on a life of their own vis-à-vis the societies and states within which they were embedded.[49]

The emergence of domestic market relations was really a twofold process, involving the formation of a market on a national basis and the liberalization of economic activity more generally. Both aspects depended on state action to various degrees. Britain, as might be expected, led the way in the formation of national markets. Although it remained a pre-industrial market and still had neither efficient transport systems such as canals nor legal machinery for the freedom of contract, as early as 1750, Britain could be counted as having the beginnings of "a monetary and market economy on a national scale."[50] Markets in France, in contrast, remained fragmented and "scattered" well into the nineteenth century. Its financial system was limited on a national basis and did not begin to experience significant reform until 1848. Major financial reforms only came in the 1860s, which is when rail construction began to unify the market more generally.[51] Napoleon III reorganized the railroads and encouraged the creation of two banks as sources of credit for public and private enterprises.

Viewed retrospectively, from the standpoint of the national markets that emerged with unification, both Germany and Italy suffered from their long history of political fragmentation. Although Germany, prior to unification, did make a serious effort to build a national market through the Zollverein. The geopolitical situation of Italy, being under the thumb of Austria, precluded such efforts. But the accomplishments of the German states under Prussian state leadership should not be exaggerated. Despite the formation of the Zollverein in 1834, it was not until well into the 1850s that anything approaching market formation occurred. Indeed, it was only in 1857 that currencies were placed on a common basis.[52]

The second aspect of national market formation, the process of liberalization, represented the effort of states and societies to shed their feudal restrictions in industry and agriculture. In the last decades of the eighteenth century both Britain and France attacked the power of the guilds which controlled a person's choice of occupation and freedom of movement. While in Germany guilds would be stripped of their powers by the 1840s, in Italy they were not finally abolished until the mid-1860s. Other forms of liberalization included the abolition of internal tolls and duties, the removal of restrictions on interest rates and, most notably, the legalization of the joint-stock company, which limited liability and opened up the possibility of firms freely incorporating without being wholly dependent on special authorization from the state.[53] Once again Britain led the way in this area in a process of legalization beginning in the second quarter of the century. Other countries legalized the joint-stock company between the 1860s and 1890s.[54] In the sphere of agriculture the most obvious set of reforms involved the abolition of serfdom. Also of importance was the abolition of restriction on land purchases, which in Prussia, for example, was limited to nobles until the reforms of the 1820s.

It is well known by now that the state's role vis-à-vis market relations has gone far beyond that of clearing the way for economic freedom and security. Adjusting and regulating market processes and outcomes so that the capabilities of the disadvantaged are facilitated has become a common practice of liberal states in the twentieth century. The progressive doctrine that helped articulate this role within the liberal tradition emerged toward the end of the nineteenth century among a new breed of liberals in Britain. One of their major spokesmen, L. T. Hobhouse made the claim that "the State is vested with a certain overlordship over property in general and a supervisory power over industry in general, and this principle of economic sovereignty may be set side by side with that of economic justice as a no less fundamental conception of economic Liberalism."[55] In Europe the development of this sovereign regulatory and planning state was driven in no small measure by the demands of the disadvantaged themselves, who had also helped propel the democratic organization of the state.[56]

Liberal Governance of the Polity

As Hobhouse's statement makes clear, an increasing range of modern life became subject to the governance of states across western societies. Of course, the nature and scope of state power in the liberal tradition is a well-known and longstanding issue. A limited executive power, a robust assembly of representatives, and a well-defined set of political or civic rights all established on a constitutional basis has figured in most liberal versions of governance.

The choice of the term "liberal governance" to describe this medium of liberal modernity is not without problems. First, there is the question of the status in liberal modernity of the republican tradition, which clearly has been a force in the making of constitutional government. Among the many dimensions of republicanism there is government divided sufficiently between forces and interests to effect checks and balances; popular sovereignty that ultimately provides the governed with leverage over the governors; and a commitment to the public good on the part of all citizens through which their own freedom is made more secure.[57]

While republicanism represents a distinct doctrinal and political tradition, the practices and principles associated with it (e.g., relatively autonomous branches of government) have in the twentieth century melded into the liberal state-building process and liberal modernity more generally, although it was sometimes at odds with the nineteenth-century liberal tradition. Even doctrinally, as Quentin Skinner points out, "the ideals of classical republicanism had largely been swallowed up by the rising tide of contractarian political thought."[58] Nonetheless, it remains possible today to identify the republican dimensions of contemporary liberal modernity.[59]

Second, there is the question of democracy. The term liberal governance is meant to avoid any connotation that democratic practice, associated with a wide franchise and competitive elections, was an inherent feature of the liberal state.[60] It is true that liberal states became increasingly democratic in this sense in the last decades of the nineteenth century. Indeed, in twentieth century it is no longer possible to identify a liberal state that is not also democratic. However, to see liberal states on some inevitable march toward democratization is at best teleological. This is not to say that the liberalization of governance did not open pathways toward democratization in both political and cultural ways.[61] Rather it is to assert that there is no *necessary* linkage between the two and that governance can be liberal without an explicit trajectory of transformation toward democracy being present at a given historical time.[62] Britain was a liberal state prior to the 1832 reform act by virtue of its enforcement of individual rights and middle-class representation at that time and not by virtue of its status as a proto-democracy.

It has been widely recognized that liberal thinkers and movements resisted democratization and even republicanism. The chief fear expressed was that an unruly mass would violate the myriad rights of individuals which liberals had fought for in their struggle with absolutism. Moreover, the constitutional guarantees of liberties protected under the limited monarchies that liberals helped to construct in countries such as Britain and post-1830 France, were felt to be vulnerable to republican forms of governance.[63] Liberal political actors and the monarchial forces they cooperated with inherited or constructed a host of restrictions on the possibilities of mass democracy. Besides the most familiar franchise restrictions based on property, gender, or education, there was the empowerment of the upper legislative houses, the avoidance of the closed ballot, unpaid representatives, and voting weights biased toward privileged districts.[64]

The emergence of liberal governance in Europe was generally uneven. It reflected the spread of the interrelated developments of constitutionalism, parliamentarism, and ultimately democracy. These first two developments were manifested in the efforts of liberals to limit monarchies, above all, through the power of legislative assemblies.[65]

Outside of the unique political precedents set by the French and American revolutions, only Britain had managed to achieve such limits on monarchial authorities as early as the late eighteenth century. Although in the first half of the nineteenth century other pockets of constitutionalism and parliamentarism could be found in such places as the Netherlands and some of the German states, for the most part only Britain, Belgium, and post-1830 France stood out as liberal states prior to 1848. In the wake of the failed revolutions of 1848, constitutions emerged in many continental states. However, the power of the lower chambers remained limited. Denmark was an exception and the Netherlands managed some expansion of parliamentary power in that wake.[66] After the reactionary period of the 1850s, many states underwent significant liberal reforms in the 1860s including Britain, Prussia, Austria, and Sweden. In that decade even Louis Napoleon liberalized aspects of his regime.

It was in this period that the suffrage began to widen in many states and we can begin to speak of democratization in earnest. Although the U.S. had led the way by the 1840s, both France and Switzerland had achieved universal male suffrage by the 1850s; Prussia did so in 1867. In the 1870s Denmark would also move toward a relatively wide franchise. Britain, on the basis of its reform act of 1867 enfranchised only about 30 percent of its adult males. Belgium was also slow in this regard: in 1894 it raised suffrage to 37 percent of males. Other states also moved toward universal suffrage at the end of the century, achieving it by the time of World War I.

In general, the liberal states that emerged in Europe through the nineteenth century became important forces in the mapping out of all sorts of liberal relations. Although these relations existed mostly in the context of discrete territorial states, viewed from an aggregate international perspective, liberal modernity has little meaning without there being at least some such spaces inscribed in the international realm. Moreover, the possibility of the emergence of those liberal relations which are more easily associated as a part of international relations proper, such as international exchange, is made more remote without the agency of one or more liberal states.

Individual and Group Rights

In each domain described so far individual and group rights have been essential elements. Markets rest on rights to property, contract, and movement. And contemporary political theorists such as Robert Dahl take civil and political rights (e.g., to free expression and association) for granted in the operation of even imperfect forms of liberal democracy.[67] Indeed, rights are so omnipresent within the manifold dimensions of liberal life that their standing as a medium of liberal modernity is in need of little explication. Like markets and liberal governance, rights were not an invention of the nineteenth century. But with the rise of the constitutional state an institutionalization of rights occurred that marked a distinct shift in the relationship between the state and its citizenry. Although there are numerous ways to characterize liberal rights, Jürgen Habermas has done so in a manner that captures the impact of this domain on the political life of nineteenth-century liberal modernity:

A set of basic rights concerned the sphere of the public engaged in rational-critical debate (freedom of opinion and speech, freedom of press, freedom of assembly and association, etc.) and the political function of private people in this public sphere (right of petition, equality of vote, etc.). A second set of basic rights concerned the individual's status as a free human being, grounded in the intimate sphere of the patriarchal conjugal family (personal freedom, inviolability of the home, etc.). The third set of basic rights concerned the transactions of the private owners of property in the sphere of civil society (equality before the law, protection of private property, etc.). The basic rights guaranteed: the *spheres* of the public realm and of the private (with the intimate sphere at its core); the *institutions* and *instruments* of the public sphere, on the one hand (press, parties), and the foundation of private autonomy (family and property), on the other; finally, the *functions* of the private people, both their political ones as citizens and their economic ones as owners of commodities (and, as "human beings," those of individual communication, e.g., through inviolability of letters).[68]

Each country in Europe had its own trajectory of development regarding rights. Whereas Britain led the way by establishing a firm civil rights tradition in the first few decades of the century,[69] states on the Continent tended to achieve their rights in fits and starts. After 1830, Western European states at times not only caught up to, but sometimes surpassed, the British record on rights. With regard to the right to form unions and to strike, for instance, Britain experienced, as did other countries, a slow process of development. Although Britain had repealed its Anti-Combination Laws in 1824, it would not be until the middle of the 1870s that full system of recognition of labor's rights would emerge. While workers would have to wait until 1884 in France for the equivalent, Belgium and northern Germany offered significant forms of recognition in the 1860s.

This is a very domestic-centered story of a domain that actually spans the domestic and international realms, justified, perhaps, by the limited impact of the latter in the nineteenth century. In the international realm, what can be understood as the rights of groups and individuals took shape in a much more limited form. Among international legal scholars, it is generally believed that in the nineteenth century the broad array of rights denoted now by the term 'human rights'—which subsumes the nineteenth-century liberal rights discussed above and includes civil (e.g., personal and economic), political, cultural, and social rights—were not codified into international law in any serious fashion.[70] However, in the international realm there were important precedents. European states sought in a number of instances to protect the status of minorities, to ensure religious toleration, and to end the slave trade.

Treaties, often between a European and non-European state, announced commitments to ensure "safety, life, liberty, dignity and property of foreigners."[71] These rights helped define what a "civilized nation" was and set the terms of exchange and movement which were of concern to thinkers such as Immanuel Kant.[72] They can be viewed as the precursors to the broader category of international human rights associated with the post-World War II period.[73] The understanding of international human rights circulating today incorporates the body of rights that have traditionally been defined and enforced at the domestic level with a whole new range of rights bearing on culture, social identity, and security.

Right of Collective Self-Determination

It is because of its unique status as an important constituent in the normative and institutional framework of international society that the right of collective self-determination can be distinguished from the rights discussed above as a medium of liberal modernity. The practices, principles, and institutions associated with self-determination have traditionally formed around the legitimation of claims made in the name of collectivities to establish and maintain independent states for self-governance. It is the only area of social action in the international realm where there has been the type of struggle against authority and power that has marked the course of many liberal movements in the domestic sphere. This became apparent in the first half of the nineteenth century when self-determination was manifested as a national struggle against empires such as the Ottoman one.

The linkage between liberalism and self-determination is not just predicated upon the politics of struggle. There is a much deeper doctrinal tie emerging out of the near universal association of the nation with self-determination. Liberals, most notably John Stuart Mill, saw nations as the most viable vessels of human progress. Nations were viewed as a social space within which to perfect each society and hence the entire fabric of European civilization. Mill claimed in *Representative Government* that in the context of a state made of multiple nationalities "[f]ree institutions are next to impossible."[74] Self-determination was therefore justified as the most desirable means toward the end of a free state, in that the very struggle for independence was one of freedom against tyranny.[75]

In practice, the link between free institutions, the nation, and self-determination was not inevitable. The only international practice associated with self-determination to emerge in the nineteenth century was the plebiscite. Its first application—under the auspices of the French revolutionary state in the papal enclaves of Avigon and Venaissin, as well as in Nice and Savoy—served to justify annexation on the supposed basis of popular sovereignty and did not yet involve national aspirations. Other plebiscites in the century included the one held in Moldavia and Wallachia in 1857. That plebiscite was "the first time in history that an international congress of great powers postponed their action until they could ascertain the desire of the inhabitants themselves," although the results were not honored by those powers.[76]

Although there were some instances of struggles for independence prior to the end of the Napoleonic Wars that had a national character, among them the Serbian revolt in 1804, the Vienna Settlement of 1815 generally ignored the question of national claims to statehood.[77] What we now call Belgium, for instance, was annexed to the Netherlands after the Napoleonic wars with little concern for the sentiments of the population. The Greek War of Independence in the 1820s was perhaps the most notable early instance of a struggle for national self-determination. It was taken up as a cause by liberal movements across Europe, leading to such organizations as the London Greek Committee. In the period between the independence of Belgium in 1831 and the creation of the German Empire in 1871, national self-determination became for the first time a factor helping to shape political outcomes in Europe.

However, as Eric Hobsbawm points out, liberal support for the principle of nationality was never universal in the first place: it was meant to apply to those collectivities judged to be viable nation-states on cultural and economic terms.[78] The continued existence, legitimated through the Concert order, of the Austrian, Russian, and Ottoman multinational empires placed a check on the possible success of national movements, which multiplied in the second half of the century. The British state refused to aid Hungary's bid for independence from the Austrian Empire. In Germany the newly established liberal Frankfurt Assembly in 1848 expressly failed to make any moves toward ending the partition of Poland. The fate of Schleswig and Holstein in the 1860s clearly was set without regard to national self-determination.[79] By the time Europe entered the post-German unification period there were few changes in the map of Europe, except in the case of Norway and the Balkans. Concurrent with the waning salience of self-determination as a force in international politics in the last decades of the century, there was a shift in the character of nationalism toward the right, signaled by a greater emphasis on cultural difference and exclusion. In such a shift a wide basis of transnational support for national movements, except for one's own, was unlikely to emerge.

A new set of forces capable of setting self-determination on a different course in the twentieth century would emerge only with the first World War and the subsequent need to articulate a legitimate war settlement that could deal with the collapsing empires in the region. It is well known that national self-determination received more universalistic expression and application in the 1919 Paris Peace Conference than it ever did any time in the nineteenth century. In this period self-determination was still associated with the claims of *national* collectivities. But by the middle of the twentieth century, self-determination became the central principle in the anti-colonial struggles against European empires. These struggles were waged on the basis of *race* and they changed the character of the international realm, as new sovereign states were established throughout the former colonial world.[80]

Although state sovereignty per se is not a constitutive medium of liberal modernity, the operation of markets, international exchange, liberal governance, and rights has depended on it in obvious ways.[81] In the domain of collective self-determination, however, the role of state sovereignty has been far more intricate. Indeed, the right to form a sovereign state has remained central to the principles, practices, and institutions associated with collective self-determination even as the domain transformed across the nineteenth and twentieth centuries. In the U.N. Charter the reference to 'peoples' rather than 'nations' as the subject of self-determination facilitated the claims of states on behalf of the collectivities they contain more than it reinforced the claims of collectivities themselves struggling against oppression. Self-determination had in many ways become in practice a legitimation of the borders and integrity of extant states.[82] This carried over into the process of decolonization where, once a sovereign state was established, "[r]acial sovereignty and ex-colonial boundaries in many cases" had "effectively transformed self-determination into a right of sovcreigns."[83] Liberal doctrine had never really come to terms with the status of state sovereignty in the international realm. In general, liberal discourse on state sovereignty has been absorbed most with the question of nonintervention. Kant, Mill, Cobden, and Mazzini offered various parameters, qualifications, and critiques of the principle of nonintervention.[84] Their concerns were not focused on the sovereign status of the state, but rather on the question of whether intervention and nonintervention lead to what they saw as liberal political outcomes.

Liberal Modernity and International Relations

In conceiving of liberalism as a constellation of domains and as a dimension of modernity I have departed from the traditional treatments of international liberalism in the field of international relations. Most frequently international liberalism is understood to be a type of ideology or doctrine for organizing social action in the international realm, specifically, the foreign policy of states.[85] Understood as such, international liberalism identifies social and political goals for foreign policy that are consistent with the liberal tradition (e.g., equality and freedom). In addition, liberal doctrine can serve as a guide in the construction and maintenance at home and abroad of institutions typically associated with liberal democratic political life (e.g., democratic governance and civil rights).[86] These institutions and the norms associated with them have been central to the recently popular democratic peace approach, which explores the dimensions and causes of the apparent absence of war between liberal democracies.

A second way that international liberalism has been understood in the field of international relations is as a type of political economic system marked by the open movement of goods and capital between a plurality of states and societies. Generally, such a system emerges under the leadership of a liberal hegemon, which can shape the institutions and influence the policies of states in a fashion that creates and maintains openness.[87] In this understanding—typically associated with the study of international political economy—international liberalism represents not only doctrines and institutions, but also a set of relations which constitute a political economic system operating across a wide geographical expanse.

Finally, international liberalism can be understood to represent a distinct approach to understanding and explaining political outcomes in the international realm. As such, liberalism is held up as an alternative to neorealism and Marxism. This understanding stresses a logic of cooperation and inter-dependence based on a distribution of benefits to states and societies through participation in markets, collective security, or any number of institutions affecting outcomes in issue-areas across the international arena.[88]

Each of these treatments deals with specific aspects of liberal modernity. But they all fail to explore the question of the historic status of liberalism as a way to organize social life. The treatments generally take as given the very existence of liberal modernity as a force in international history, either in the form of a repertoire of practices and principles that states can rely on to build institutions and fashion policies; or as a set of logics and doctrines that make sense of aspects of contemporary social existence and world politics. In contrast, I have emphasized liberal modernity's historicity, contingency, and mutability across time and space. I will argue in the next section that liberal order should be understood not simply as the application of liberal principles to organize international relations, but rather as the ordering of this mutable and variegated liberal modernity itself.

International Liberal Order

Ever since Woodrow Wilson attempted to use the settlement of World War I to found an international order based on national self-determination, liberal governance, and international economic exchange, liberalism has been associated with order in the field of international relations. Among the traditional treatments discussed above, the association is most explicit in conceptions of liberal international economic systems (or "orders"). But the link is also apparent in the treatment of liberalism as a mode of analysis, especially when the object of analysis is some dimension of order among Western states, such as the rules and norms associated with international regimes that govern economic relations.[89] Similarly, international order has often been identified as a goal in the foreign policy of the most powerful liberal state in the twentieth century, the United States.[90]

There are two general senses of order evoked in these treatments. By exploring them, I can convey how order and liberal modernity intersect. In the first sense, there is an emphasis on the active "ordering" of relations through sets of mechanisms and institutions that organize international relations and transactions according to principles such as multilateralism. The ordering that is associated with economic systems and the foreign policy goals of powerful states gravitates toward this aspect. Agency, in the form of purposive pursuit and maintenance of order by states, is a key feature here.[91]

The other sense of order is less focused on agency. It is a depictive sense in which patterns of international political life are described. An order can be characterized according to any number of attributes that have been of concern to international relations scholars and policymakers. It can be peaceful, mercantilist, or even just.[92]

Of course, in any given concept of order, both the purposive and depictive senses are likely to be present in varying degrees. Hedley Bull captured this duality in his concept of international order as "a pattern of activity that sustains the elementary or primary goals of the society of states, or international society."[93] The purposive will of states establishes and maintains the "pattern of activity," the depiction of which conveys specific characteristics and goals of an order.[94]

Working with either the depictive and purposive senses of international order begs a crucial question: what is the context out of which the meaning and significance of depictions and purposes are drawn? In Bull's conception, the context for the emergence of order is the common rules and institutions of international society. Order, for Bull, facilitates the existence of that society. In other words, there exists a fabric of social relations within which order emerges. This same sense of ordering and facilitating is employed in Robert Cox's concept of liberal world order. Order exists when states and the system in which they operate in sustain conditions for an "open world economy while refraining from interfering with the operations of . . . economic agents."[95] For Cox, capitalism is the macro-historical context for liberal order, which mechanisms such as an open world economy facilitate. Alternatively, we might imagine that order in itself can form a context. This is actually typical of how global order is now conceived in the field of international relations. James Rosenau tells us that global order "consists of those routinized arrangements through which world politics gets from one moment to the next."[96] Such arrangements include hierarchies of power and rules of interaction. Order understood in this way is itself the fabric of relations that constitute the global realm. It encompasses "every region, country, international relationship, social movement, and private organization that engages in activities across national boundaries."[97]

We need not be so all-encompassing to posit order as a context in itself. Stephen Krasner analyzes North-South relations against the background of "a liberal global order characterized by multilateralism, nondiscrimination, the minimalization of impediments to the movement of goods and factors (with the exception of labor) and the control of such movements by privately owned rather than publicly owned entities."[98] The principles and mechanisms of this order effectively form a context in themselves, based on the power, agency, and the liberal character of the U.S. state and society.

These different perspectives on order and context suggest that, in conceptualizing order, the term "liberal' can be used either to characterize an order that has liberal qualities, or it can denote that international liberal relations have been ordered. In the first instance, mechanisms and patterns of activity such as treaties that order international relations and transactions are identified as liberal. Despite the differences between Cox and Krasner, both hold that mechanisms and principles that can be identified as liberal, such as open exchange, make an order liberal.

I find the second instance a more appropriate understanding of liberal order. To posit liberalism as mechanisms of order, as is done in the first instance, once again treats liberal principles and doctrines as simply a repertoire for states and other actors to draw on at certain historical junctures. It assumes a coherence and consistency—i.e., a readiness to be applied in the shaping of international relations—that is unrealistic. The brief sketches of liberal domains offered above show that this readiness is far from the case. Principles, practices, and institutions such as democracy or multilateral exchange take multiple and contested forms across time and space. If mechanisms and patterns of activity associated with liberalism are to be established on an international basis, then it is the very disparate doctrines and practices of liberal modernity that need to be ordered. An especially acute example of this is found in John Ruggie's concept of embedded liberalism.[99] States in Western Europe, which sought to achieve their own social welfare agendas after World War II, altered the terms of international economic exchange so this could be achieved within emerging liberal trade and finance regimes. As a result, the very character of international exchange had been transformed. What was ordered was international exchange itself, and in the process new principles, practices, and institutions were formed. In this case, the mechanism and pattern of activity that did the ordering was a regime, the "principles, norms, rules and decision-making procedures" regarding a given area,[100] an entity which in itself is not intrinsically liberal.

By positing liberal modernity as the context of liberal order—i.e., the thing that is ordered in a purposive fashion—I do not mean simply to displace capitalism or, for that matter, other dimensions of modernity as contexts. Capitalist modernity is associated with forces such as class differentiation or patterns of capital accumulation which, as I have argued above, are deeply intertwined—and can shape and be shaped by—liberal modernity itself. Indeed, the expansion of a bourgeois class in the nineteenth century and the massing of pools of wage labor in major Western cities are two of many forces that precipitated important transformations in liberal domains (e.g., support for republican and, ultimately, democratic institutions). A history of liberal modernity, which is beyond the scope of this book, would need to trace the historical forces at play in these transformations.[101]

Alternatively, the codification by states of liberal economic rights was decisive for the transformation of capitalism in the nineteenth century. Besides making claims that a liberal order—i.e., an ordering of liberal relations—can have important implications for capitalist relations (e.g., creating conditions for the operation of a market), or vise versa, it is far from clear that something that is a liberal order could actually order capitalist modernity. This would mean that the very existence of wage workers and the commodities they produce—crucial dimensions of capitalist modernity—would have to be drawn up into the machinery of order.[102]

One type of order that does clearly order capitalism in the purposive sense I am talking about—which has to date really appeared only at the level of the state—is a socialist order.[103] In such an order, the system of relations of production is transformed in decisive ways. Of course, short of socialist transformation, mechanisms and patterns of activity traditionally associated with a liberal order—including the actions of the liberal state—can also allow for relations and issues associated with capitalist modernity (e.g., working hours, industrial relations, and financial regulation) to be dealt with by actors in decisive ways.[104] But the key difference is that in a liberal order it is liberal relations themselves that are ordered, whatever the implications for capitalism. Thus, there is a distinction between facilitating capitalism in a functional sense, or even shaping its relations and practices, and actually bringing it into a distinct pattern or arrangement (i.e., ordering) on an international basis. To claim that a specifically international liberal order could do so regarding capitalist modernity, one would have to bracket out the very process of bringing liberal relations themselves into some kind of alignment.[105] The alternative is to make the dubious claim that liberal relations can be both forces of order and subject to being ordered themselves.

The concept of liberal order that is emerging here is purposive and contextual. (It is, therefore, thoroughly modern, in the way I have described it above.) It is one in which dimensions of a heterogeneous liberal modernity are ordered through mechanisms and patterns of activity. There are two ways in which such an ordering can be understood. One is as orchestration, where policies and practices of states and societies in liberal modernity are arranged in a manner that allows for cooperation and coordination and yet preserves heterogeneity. An example of a body of such arrangements has emerged in the OECD (Organization for Economic Cooperation and Development). It is a forum through which the advanced industrial states attempt to coordinate their economic activities and policies. Despite limited impact, the OECD has produced various codes of conduct and attempts at coordinating domestic and foreign policies. These efforts have mostly been about bringing policies into a mutually reinforcing alignment rather than producing a homogeneous model of liberal state practice.

Another way of ordering liberal modernity is the outright construction of practices, principles, and institutions, which can operate across a set of states and societies and which can help constitute the very character of liberal modernity in a given period. The point is that rather than simply orchestrating relations and policies, construction requires the establishment or even invention of new principles, practices, and institutions that shape international and domestic life. Construction is therefore a far more intrusive form of ordering than orchestration. But it need not necessarily imply a diminution of heterogeneity. As the phenomenon of embedded liberalism described above makes clear, it is possible to construct principles and practices that facilitate heterogeneous forms of state and society.

Like many of the concepts introduced above, orchestration and construction are heuristic polarities. In practice, every orchestration involves a construction in the building of the institutional means of coordination. And every common construction involves coordination in that the establishment of common principles and practices will take place in a context of heterogeneity.

In themselves, however, orchestration and construction specify only what is done in ordering liberal modernity. In order to understand how such modalities are realized through the international political relations that form the mechanisms and patterns of activity of order, a second distinction must be introduced. First, there are political relations that constitute arenas for cooperation among actors. Examples of this type of arena include councils of foreign ministers, congresses, and regional organizations (e.g., the Organization of American States). Second, there are political relations that constitute concentrations of agency that can organize and impel actors. Although other examples, among them the UN Security Council, exist, the most significant manifestation of this concentration of agency is U.S. hegemonic leadership, which is a central focus of this study. Again, this is a heuristic distinction: no single institution or macro-historical form can be identified exclusively with either mode of political relations. Cooperative dimensions are associated with both U.S. hegemony and the Security Council.[106]

Compared to some of the other concepts of order discussed above, the one I offer is highly circumscribed. Its scope is international (i.e., between states and societies) rather than global (i.e., the totality of interactions and processes on the planet). And although its context, liberal modernity, encompasses a far deeper range of domestic and international factors than the rules and common institutions between states in Bull's international society, liberal order is not a world order. It does not refer to a single fabric of order applicable to humankind in total. Bull characterized world order, in contrast to his notion of international order discussed above, as "those patterns or dispositions of human activity that sustain the elementary or primary goals of social life among mankind as a whole."[107] And similarly, Richard Falk has been concerned with order that is associated with "a given past, present, or future arrangement of power and authority," that is "able to realize a set of human goals that are affirmed as beneficial for all people and apply to the whole world."[108] On the one hand, the recognition that there are different forms of modernity makes problematic the application of the concept of order to humankind in general, except in the trivial and purely depictive sense of order as the way things are for humankind. On the other hand, the heterogeneity of liberal modernity itself precludes any specification of universal primary or beneficial goals. Of course, any purposive order will be pervaded by goals. In international liberal order, examples include the expansion of international trade or the protection of rights. But these goals are those of agents within the order. They are not universally discernible through the deductions of the analyst of order.

Far more relevant are those conceptions of order that recognize a plurality of coexisting orders in the world. In a conference on conditions of world order held in 1965, it was suggested that there may not be a single world order, but "a set of world order systems."[109] More recently, Hayward Alker, Jr. has mapped out the different configurations and concepts of world order that can both compete with and penetrate one another.[110] Liberal order can be understood to be a zone of order in the global realm, distinct from other orders such as a socialist one. Interpenetration can occur in the areas of trade, communications, and contention over the boundaries of order.

The notion of orders having boundaries (to be discussed further below) raises the issue of how states and societies are actually included in a liberal order. By the post-World War II period, the domains of liberal modernity came to define a substantial portion of the domestic and international relations of the liberal democracies in the Atlantic community. But they also shaped the relations and practices of many states and societies outside of the region, which had become entwined, willingly and unwillingly, with various dimensions of liberal modernity, and as a result were drawn up into the post-World War II liberal order. For instance, for much of the postwar era, Latin American states governed by authoritarian regimes have had market economies and have participated in international exchange. And certainly, as Robert Jackson has pointed out, the assertion of sovereignty claims based on principles of self-determination—which he shows are squarely situated in the liberal tradition—have become particularly important for all sorts of states that are not typically associated with liberal modernity.[111]

Indeed, there is a certain inverse, yet complementary, duality, that marks liberal modernity and the relations that order it. That is, they are *partial* in both senses of the term.[112] On the one hand, liberal modernity can emerge as a presence in states and societies in circumscribed and bounded arenas, such as among the bourgeois classes in leading cities of the Third World. Not only might there be a limited range of liberal practices inscribed in a given state and society, but also whole regions of social existence within that society can be excluded from participation in liberal domains (although the effects of the operation of liberal domains are far more difficult to bound). This was the unfortunate fate of African-Americans for centuries even in so liberal a society as the U.S. On the other hand, those states and societies that have all five liberal domains inscribed in their social fabric are—as we shall see below—constituents of a liberal core. This core, during and after waging global war, took it upon itself to set boundaries, define relations, construct institutions, designate identities, and generally organize and order a constellation of practices and principles located in liberal modernity.

Conclusion

I have asked readers to take seriously the notion that a certain way of being modern is at stake in the organization of states, societies, and international life around the liberal tradition. I have also asked readers to consider how states and societies shaped by liberal modernity might be included in a liberal order that is international in scope. Despite their obvious convergence, liberal modernity and liberal order exist in two different dimensions of historical time. Fernand Braudel has distinguished between the *longue durée*, which he usually associated with those longstanding—especially geographical—structures that constitute part of the permanent historical landscape, and the *conjuncture*, which he understood to be the cyclical patterns and social formations emerging across regions, states, and societies in a given span of time.[113] A similar distinction between the long and medium terms of historical time applies to liberal modernity and liberal order. Liberal modernity resembles a *longue durée*, although it is a far more changeable and socially determined version. It is constituted by the broad trajectory of liberal domains unfolding across the centuries subject to shifts in social forces, ruptures in discourse, and inventions in practices and institutions. Liberal order, in contrast, represents a particular historical conjuncture of power, agency, and systemic relations formed around the principles, practices, and institutions of liberal modernity. Its time horizon is not centuries, but decades.

A historical convergence of liberalism, modernity, and international order occurred in the wake of World War II. This convergence comprised specific historical developments, constructions of agency, and configurations of what has so often been of central concern in international relations: violence and military power. The main task of the chapters that follow will be to untangle the complex web of relations and outcomes that emerged in and through this fateful convergence or liberal moment. That untangling will depend on the construction of an interpretive explanation (described in the introduction) for which the domains of liberal modernity represent a crucial starting point. Together with the dynamics of the liberal moment, they constitute the broad context against which the politics and tensions of liberal order-making can be understood.

2

❋

"Stupendous Forces Are Loose"

Liberal modernity has been crucial in shaping post-World War II international life. To demonstrate how and why I need to craft the basic tools of analysis that will be used to register the various dimensions of that influence. This chapter will be devoted to introducing these elements and considering more generally how they build on as well as depart from other analytical traditions relevant to understanding the contours of the postwar period. I will begin with a discussion of the concept that constitutes the title of this study: the liberal moment.

The Liberal Moment

For more than forty years what has often conveniently been referred to as the "settlement" of the Second World War has been central to the study of contemporary international political life.[1] Although scholars have taken the tumultuous developments of the 1970s and the more recent events associated with the ending of the Cold War in Europe as important points of departure for research, the immediate aftermath of World War II remains for many a baseline point of reference for the analysis of international political life in the second half of the twentieth century. In general, the ending of the Cold War did not represent a wholesale overturning of the structures and relations that emerged after World War II. If anything, it reinforced what is understood to be central to the settlement of the Second World War: a system of multilateral economic exchange and the international leadership of Western powers. At the same time, the end of the Cold War appeared to offer new hope for the principles and institutions of universalistic dimensions associated with the settlement of World War II, embodied most clearly in the UN.

The longstanding resonance of the concept of a post-World War II settlement should be no surprise given the relatively extensive geographical scope, institutional architecture, and range of issues and relations associated with it. The depth and scope of the negotiations and institutional constructions constituting the settlement of World War II is indeed impressive relative to its most recent predecessor, the settlement of World War I. In 1919 the focus was mostly on Europe, an especially probable outcome given the locus of the war and the relatively unshaken commitment to imperial continuity and spheres of influence. While in 1945 a European focus was retained, the war in Asia and the challenges to the European empires, among other things, guaranteed that considerable effort would be made to negotiate the future of the rest of the world in ways that were unimaginable in 1919. Also after the First World War a far more circumscribed institutional foundation was laid within which there were, relative to 1945, more limited options for the construction of practices and orchestration of policies that are central to the making of liberal order. As one recent study of international organizational life since the nineteenth century put it, the "GATT, the Bretton Woods organizations, and the other institutions of the UN system finally began doing what the League never did."[2] In both 1945 and 1919 more than economic relations were subject to ordering. But in 1945 an unprecedented international politico-strategic and normative infrastructure was established for, among other things, the multiplication of sovereign states across the globe; for the construction of machinery that would codify and institutionalize human rights as never before; and for the establishment of a military system whose scope was the most extensive in history.

The relative magnitude of the two twentieth-century transitions of 1919 and 1945 has not been the only point of comparison. Concern over the relative degree of stability and sustainability of these two settlements has, if anything, been at least as central as their relative scope.[3] The implications of the collapse of the post-World War I settlement for the future began preoccupying leading international thinkers such as Karl Polanyi and E. H. Carr even before the outlines of a post-World War II order became visible. Carr's title, *The Twenty Years' Crisis, 1919–1939*, starkly announced his view of the viability of the settlement of the First World War. For him, the "characteristic feature of the crisis . . . was the abrupt descent from the visionary hopes of the first decade to the grim despair of the second, from a utopia which took little account of reality to a reality from which every element of utopia was rigorously excluded."[4] Those visionary hopes were tied to nineteenth-century liberal principles such as the belief that trade could render international relations more peaceful. According to Carr, these hopes simply did not account for the dynamics of power politics.

Polanyi also pointed to the relatively swift breakdown of an order in which a nostalgic longing for a return to the perceived stability of the nineteenth-century gold standard—which could be sustained only for a few years—was combined with vain hopes of institutionalizing peace through the League of Nations.[5] Running headlong into economic depression, a relatively isolationist U.S., the collapse of liberal democratic regimes, and increasingly aggressive and antagonistic foreign policies, the states of the West who were the victors of World War I were hard put to locate an Archimedean point from which to sustain the political relations worked out in treaties such as Versailles and Locarno.

In this discussion it is somewhat inaccurate to employ the term settlement and to use the fixed yearly points of 1945 and 1919 to describe the agreements and structure of relations negotiated in the aftermath of the world wars of the twentieth century. The concept of a war settlement conveys a sense of coming to terms with the outcome of war through great treaties such as Westphalia (1648), Utrecht (1713), or those signed in the aftermath of the Napoleonic Wars. It is therefore rather mechanical—i.e., a dimension of war itself—and implies that matters can actually be settled. This certainly was not the case in the interwar years as conditions undermined agreements and relations across the 1920s and 1930s. It is also difficult to apply to the post-World War II period, since so much of international relations was contested for years afterward. We can use the term to describe what war belligerents might understand to be their task upon defeat or victory, namely, shaping a peace. But relying only on the term "settlement," risks underplaying the extent to which the project of making a peace is about constructing an international order of a particular form and character. In this sense the concept of war settlement has an air of neutrality regarding the substance of such a construction that is deceiving. It is profoundly underspecified.

This underspecification applies not only to the making of peace, but also to the ramifications of war, which itself is not a neutral and self-contained process with implications only for its victims and belligerents. To a great extent the ramifications of war have been thought of in the field of international relations in terms of the way belligerents might be able to effect large-scale shifts in configurations of power and relations through hegemonic or global wars. In Robert Gilpin's *War and Change in World Politics* we are shown how a given state, gaining status as an international leader as a result of hegemonic war, can prompt changes in the character of an international system, making it, for instance, more or less liberal. This formulation underplays the extent to which wars in themselves can effect social, cultural, and political transformations. In recent decades a current of political sociology, associated especially with Charles Tilly and Theda Skocpol and inspired by Max Weber and Otto Hintze, has explored the ways that war and military organization have affected state-formation, revolution, and even regime-type.[6] The same concerns with the transformative impact of war have not escaped the notice of historians such as William McNeill and Arthur Marwick.[7] While Gilpin is well aware of this impact he mostly links it to the rise of the nation-state as a preeminent political form in international life, rather than the more specific system changes associated with large-scale warfare.[8] This is actually in line with the political sociology literature in that its primary focus is the influence of war on individual states in a comparative perspective. What has not received the same type of theoretical treatment is the impact of war on transnational social environments, encompassing not only a range of states and societies but also the social and political linkages among them.[9]

I do not intend to offer here an elaborate exploration or even theoretical model of transnational cultural, social, and political transformations effected by war.[10] But I would like to focus on one way to think about such transformation that bears directly on the post-World War II transition and the formation of a liberal order: that is, through the concept of a historical moment. The Depression, the aggressive expansion of fascism, and finally the world war itself were historical experiences that ruptured and even shattered policies, governments, and, of course, many lives. This rupture is what lends credence to the sense of urgency of which Polanyi wrote and to Carr's choice of the word "crisis" to describe the interwar years. Carr, in fact, cites a passage written by British Foreign Secretary Anthony Eden in 1938 that Carr believed expresses the "impression made on the ordinary man":

> It is utterly futile to imagine that we are involved in a European crisis which may pass as it has come. We are involved in a crisis of humanity all the world over. We are living in one of those great periods of history which are awe-inspiring in their responsibilities and in their consequences. Stupendous forces are loose, hurricane forces.[11]

Even discounting the tone of a propagandistic call to arms inherent in this passage, we can note the sense of rupture that underlies Eden's phrases, a sense that makes it possible to speak in these exaggerated terms without appearing ridiculous.

The responsibilities and consequences Eden invoked refer to the things that must be done to respond to great crises that fall outside the routine policies and forms of agency that we associate with the mundane workings of states. On one level, the rhetoric of heroic action always lies nearby when things are put in these terms.[12] The speeches of FDR, Churchill, and Stalin in this period were full of this rhetoric. On another level, underlying Eden's words is the tension between: periods of history when the relatively routine structures, orders, and relations generally transport us from one week to the next; and periods—or even episodes—when these routines tend to fall away or are smashed, creating the opportunity for the construction of either new relations and structures or the reestablishment of old ones in relatively new terms.[13] The second type of period is what I mean by a historical moment.[14]

In one form or another, the basic distinction between order and flux inherent in the above duality has appeared frequently in the thought of major Western thinkers. Friedrich Nietzsche in his exploration of classical Greek culture in *The Birth of Tragedy* distinguished between Apollonian ordered forms and Dionysian celebratory bursts of energy, and bemoaned the absence of the latter in his own time.[15] Emile Durkheim contrasted the protective religious force of "physical and moral order" with the "evil and impure powers, productive of disorders," which "correspond to the two opposed states through which all social life passes."[16] Sigmund Freud differentiated the unorganized energies and instincts of the id from the severe, censoring prohibitions emanating from the superego.[17] And Max Weber wrote of charismatic leaders who as revolutionary forces could unhinge social orders and stand "outside the realm of everyday routine."[18] In the post-World War II period, Henri Lefebvre pointed to the experience of moments when all things appeared possible which he applied to revolutionary ruptures such as the Paris Commune and the French student movement of May 1968.[19] The anthropologist Victor Turner explored the possibility that groups could move from ordered and structured relations to situations described as anti-structural in which order breaks down and ambiguity and reversals set in.[20]

These lines of thought are all highly complex and can be equated only at the most superficial levels. But together they show that the opposition of flux and order has been a longstanding thematic in the conceptualization of modernity. I wrote of flux in the last chapter as a vital element in the experience of a modern existence facing the enduring possibility of reordering and remaking. Weber, Lefebvre, and Turner point to the possibility of communities entering into states of flux at historic junctures when disorder and the opportunities of reordering becomes possible. It is especially here that I see the opposition of flux and order as applicable to the post-World War II transition as a specific historical moment.[21]

By using the term flux to describe conditions in a historical moment I do not mean to imply that when a community enters a transformative period its historical contexts of meaning, power, and hierarchy are abandoned. Turner argues that groups return from periods of anti-structure to their structured forms of life, but that life may be transformed to varying degrees. Charles Maier has considered the ways that in the aftermath of both twentieth century world wars, familiar ideas about social organization reappeared, longstanding economic problems resurfaced, certain elites returned to power, and key class relations were reconstituted, however much on new grounds.[22] Indeed, it would make little sense to designate the period surrounding the Second World War as a *liberal* moment if the continuities with the liberal past described in the last chapter did not exist.

My identification of this moment as liberal calls for three clarifications. First, this identity rests on the proposition that events, developments, and conditions of this period helped precipitate an ordering of liberal modernity that otherwise would have been highly unlikely, given the fate of liberalism in the 1930s. As I will explain below, war-making became liberal order-making. New forms of agency, domestic and international, emerged, especially in the U.S., along with a resurgence of liberal practices. As Eric Hobsbawm tells it, "nobody predicted" this resurgence.[23] And this raises a second point of clarification. I do not mean to assert any teleological claims about the fate of liberal modernity. There was nothing inevitable about the transformation of this moment into a liberal one. Liberal modernity does not have an exclusive hold over the fate of the West, to say nothing of the rest of the world. What emerged in this moment was a fortuitous combination of changing conditions to which surviving elites oriented to liberal modernity could respond and out of which the U.S. could be drawn into the project of liberal order-building.[24]

But my third point is that it was not a liberal moment for everyone. Although the effects and ramifications of the liberal moment were global in scope, the changes were not experienced universally as an opportunity to help reorder the world along liberal lines, certainly not for many people, for instance, in Africa and Asia. (It is unlikely Stalin saw it that way as well.) Decolonization would take decades to unfold. Many peoples were perhaps experiencing other types of moments in the 1940s, or no moments at all. However, the reverberations of the liberal moment would ultimately reach nearly everyone through institutions such as the IMF and the charged political environment of the Cold War.

War-Making as Liberal Order-Making

These points of clarification underscore the extent to which the crucial mix of forces in a historical moment is between rapid and rupturing historical changes and new articulations of political and social agency that can reorder relations. The point of making the liberal moment central to this inquiry is that it allows for analysis that captures the play between changes in historical context and agency. That is, instead of initially framing this inquiry with the question of why the U.S. made a commitment to the postwar hegemonic pursuit of international liberalism—a question that tends to focus too quickly on the level of U.S. state agency[25]—we can ask whether there were conditions in the international realm that helped make such pursuit compelling. The answer to such a question requires that World War II not be viewed only as a contingent historical event that projected U.S. power abroad and opened the way for U.S. intervention in Europe (based, for example, on the high levels of wartime devastation).[26] Rather, we might consider the ways that the social and political outcomes engendered by the war were associated with the rise of liberal conditions in the international realm that facilitated the emergence of a U.S. liberal hegemonic agency. In doing so, it will become clearer why this was a *liberal* moment as opposed to something else.

In the first place, the defeat of fascism led to a resurgence of state sovereignty, self-determination, representative government, and liberal rights in much of Europe. By mid-1947 Kennan had recognized that:

> The broad pattern of our recent foreign policy, including the confidence we have placed in the United Nations, has assumed the continuation in Europe of a considerable number of free states subservient to no great power, and recognizing [sic] their heritage of civil liberties and personal responsibility and determined to maintain this heritage. If this premise were to be invalidated, there would have to be a basic revision of the whole concept of our international position. . . .[27]

Outside of Europe, World War II has been widely acknowledged as also having spurred the emergence of anti-colonial movements, which cast their claims in terms of the principles associated with national self-determination.[28] In the least, the war made the return to prewar European imperialism problematic.

In the second place, the release of Atlantic economies from the pressures of war-making or fascist economic controls cleared a space for the reconstitution of more open national market economies and removed a major barrier to international exchange. Bretton Woods and the 1945 British loan can be understood not only as responses to an opportunity to remake the international economic realm along more liberal lines—in a manner consistent with U.S. interests and ideals—but also as further steps along a trajectory of developments that constituted a loosening of state-based economic controls. It began with the war itself in 1939, when the old imperial systems were disrupted, and continued into the last years of the war when a postwar end to wartime controls in Britain and France were in sight. These changes marked a new point in the history of Europe which the U.S. could both respond to and help shape if it chose to do so at the end of the war.

In thinking about the impact of the war, it would be inaccurate to portray 1944 or 1945 as "year zero" for the commencement of U.S. liberal order-building.[29] Diplomatic historians, of course, like to locate the "origins" of the Cold War at least as early as 1941, at America's entrance into World War II. Consistent with this periodization, it is possible to locate the emergence of international liberal conditions and the rise of U.S. liberal hegemonic agency well before 1945. In effect, the war, as a conflict between liberal and nonliberal forces, can be seen as an international condition itself that helped move the U.S. toward its role as a liberal order-builder. In that role the U.S. contributed significantly to the emergence of liberal conditions; conditions that, in turn, served further to help propel the U.S. to act as a liberal hegemon.

By 1939, the growing power of Germany and Japan had forced the U.S. to choose between isolation and a more extensive commitment overseas. The disruption of the U.S.'s external realm and relations had reached a point where it had either to begin taking action to preserve those relations or abandon them altogether. Even before the U.S. entered the war, aid to Britain and the symbolic commitment of the Atlantic Charter were two manifestations of this action. It became clear by 1941 that the U.S. would not only defend the survival of Britain, but also try to force it to consider more liberal international practices including the abandonment of the imperial preference system. By supporting the survival of a liberal democratic state against aggressive nonliberal forces and evoking principles of a liberal peace, the U.S. administration already reflected a concern with conditions after the war and the possibilities of a liberal postwar settlement. (I am using the term, as distinguished above, to describe what war belligerents might understand to be their task upon defeat or victory.)

It is true that, for any state, winning a war entails making a peace. For the U.S. this could not be just any peace: the global scale of this war forced the U.S. to confront a global peace. Some historians, among them Lynn Davis, place considerable weight on the U.S. endeavor to postpone discussion of the specifics of a postwar settlement until after the end of the war.[30] However, such a view ignores the conditions inherent in the war itself that had important ramifications for a settlement or order-making. The decisions to concentrate on Europe first, to make a second front in Northern Europe, and to forge an anti-fascist alliance are only a few examples.[31] That the U.S. limited its order-making mostly to wartime activities is understandable given that the will to hegemonic agency was being forged in the war itself. In other words, a commitment to the broad principles of an international liberal postwar settlement made political sense for a state whose agency as a hegemon was being formed only within the process of war-making. Only at the end of the war could international conditions compel the U.S. to seek a specific settlement with all the implications the role of liberal order-builder would entail.[32]

The conduct of the war, the concomitant necessity of making a peace, and the conditions associated with a liberal moment, especially in Europe, had placed the U.S. in a position that was open to the assertion of the agency of liberal hegemony. Not only was the historical situation different at the end of World War I, but it is also clear that the U.S. was not able then to locate the political will for hegemonic agency. The question is, how was the U.S. able to organize the political will to continue and even expand its role as a liberal order-builder after World War II?

There is, of course, no simple answer to this important question. It will take much of this chapter to get a handle on it. We can begin answering this question by considering some conditions at the conclusion of the war that helped make the continuation of liberal order-building a compelling course for the U.S. To start, there was a residual extension of the U.S. military in Europe and east Asia as a result of the war effort. This carried with it the political duties of occupation and was applicable, with the aid of the Allies, to the international politics of the pursuit of a war settlement. Also, the allies of the U.S. were unable and reluctant to take on the costs and responsibilities inherent in the leadership of a postwar settlement. France's defeat and occupation by Germany; the wartime drain on resources experienced by Britain; and the concern in both countries with the reestablishment of their colonial empires hardly left these countries in a position to take on the leadership of the postwar settlement. Moreover, in contrast to World War I, the postwar settlement of World War II was not burdened by a host of secret wartime agreements.

An additional factor underlying the U.S. commitment to continue its order-building was formed in a somewhat backhanded fashion. Above all, a multilateral economic system was not just a basic liberal goal in the U.S.'s economic interest, it was the one global economic model that rested on a set of reciprocal multilateral agreements which U.S. policymakers believed might constitute a de facto settlement. State Department historian Harley Notter observed a faith that "the common interests of nations were more generally recognized in the economic than in the political field."[33] Thus, international economic liberalism led not just to peace, but also to conditions that might help minimize the thorny problems of having to construct a peace politically.[34] The U.S. would hardly be able to avoid a politically based peace. However, as we shall see below, U.S. policymakers believed that by promoting state sovereignty, self-determination, democracy, and human rights they could help produce the required independent political strength in the international realm to minimize the necessity of U.S. intervention and ultimately facilitate U.S. withdrawal. Ironically, the effort to achieve such withdrawal and leave in its wake a liberal order became the driving force for a continued U.S. commitment to liberal order-building and intervention. As we shall see, the very pursuit of a settlement by the U.S. that could facilitate a withdrawal from U.S. overseas engagements would necessitate a continuation of those engagements.

Agency and Liberal Order

If one of the distinguishing marks of modernity is the enduring possibility of organizing forms of large-scale human agency, then surely the ordering of relations that occurred in the 1940s counts as a robust modern project. Indeed, one way to understand the stakes of making a peace is to focus not just on the types of relations that are ordered but also on the forms of agency effecting this order. This is one advantage of employing modernity as a category of analysis. It permits us to problematize and historicize the formation of agency and the institutions associated with it.

Along these lines John Ruggie has pointed out that the state as "a particular form of territoriality—disjoint, fixed, and mutually exclusive" represents what came to be "the most distinct feature of modernity in international politics."[35] This mode of modern agency received a considerable boost in the 1940s through a UN Charter that recognized and legitimized the normative and juridical status of the state. The post-World War II period also became home to an extensive web of international institutions associated with liberal practices and a remarkable exercise of international leadership by a preponderant U.S. state in a number of spheres of international life. The U.S. state was at the center of the construction of an extensive global politico-strategic system that bound together, however unequally, the members of what has often been referred to as the "free world." Thus, other types of agency were also being formed besides those associated simply with the territorial state.

In very general terms, agency is a specific status that can be assigned to a subject. In the context of this discussion, agency is an identity we can attribute to those subjects that shape political and social life. (To objectify things, an agent is a force that shapes relations or outcomes.) This way of looking at social actions leads to questions about who will act for whom or be empowered to build or maintain aspects of the social and political order that structure a given social existence. Thus, in a given historical context, the formation of agency can become a serious political problem. The contests and deliberations in the U.S. Congress over the nature of U.S. leadership in the 1940s, which will be discussed below, are pointed examples of this type of problematization. Likewise, the negotiations over the shape and powers of the UN held at Dumbarton Oaks in 1944 are also illustrative. Empowering the Security Council to initiate military operations and ensuring a veto for every permanent member of the Council were controversial issues that shaped the character of the UN as an agent in international relations. And we could make the same point about deliberations, which began in 1946, over the formation of the International Trade Organization, as a body dedicated to the oversight of trade relations housed within the UN. The U.S. Congress, which viewed this form of agency as being, among other things, potentially far too interventionist, ultimately rejected it. These examples show that in the making of international order, weighty contests can emerge over which—or even whether—concentrations of agency and arenas of cooperation will form at a given historical juncture.[36]

Notice that the possibility of contests and deliberations over the scope of agency implies purposefulness and deliberate action. That is, the activities of order-making, construction, and organization share the common implication of willful or intentional design. A great advantage to using a category such as agency is that it forces one to become sensitive to the problem of attributing forms of will to actors. It is one thing to observe from the heights of hindsight that a process of order-building has been unfolding, and quite another to attribute to policymakers a consciously defined and identified project of liberal order-construction. Recall points made about the use of the term "settlement." Were U.S. policymakers, in their minds, settling a war or making a world? At the heart of this problem are the difficulties of specifying the terms and limits of conscious action, intentionality, and even motivation. These issues have long vexed social thinkers struggling to interpret meaningful action.[37] For our purposes we need only focus on the question of whether we should impute to policymakers the existence of an explicit intention to construct liberal order, or—far more grandly—to shape the contours of liberal modernity. There is no simple answer to this question. But answering it matters because it provides a basis for understanding the approach of this study.

Many policymakers in the U.S. understood upon reflection that in the making of the UN, multilateral economic institutions, and even NATO, they were fashioning an international order that they assumed would be liberal in character. But they did not consciously work from an explicit concept of international liberal order, nor did they need to be self-reflexive liberal order-builders. Senator Arthur Vandenberg, an important policymaker and articulator of the Republican Party's perspective on U.S. foreign policy, wrote in 1944 to Secretary of State Hull about the UN and the U.S.'s "quest of permanent peace with ordered justice in a free world."[38] Roughly nine months later Vandenberg wrote to FDR to express his "profound conviction that we must *organize the postwar world* on the basis of effective, collective security [my emphasis]."[39] Thus, Vandenberg, who was initiated into postwar policymaking circles, understood that the stakes of decisions and policies were about making order. It also seems that for him the goals and terms of order were liberty and collective security, concepts well within the currency of the modern liberal tradition. Neither he nor any other policymaker of his time, however, wrote or spoke about liberalism with the same self-reflexiveness we are able to today or with the historical perspective of a Karl Polanyi or John Dewey.[40] Nonetheless, it is clear that the terms Vandenberg used, such as the "free world," were articulations of a contemporary—if not popular—understanding of what I have been calling liberal modernity (democracy, rights, markets, and self-determination). That is, what matters is their deliberate ordering of relations relevant to liberal modernity, not the degree of self-reflexivity about the historical dimensions of their effort.

It is interesting that as one reads through *The Private Papers of Senator Vandenberg*, published in 1952, there is a marked decrease in explicit pronouncements or judgments on the broad project of order-building. Toward the end of the 1940s, Vandenberg's concerns gradually focused more exclusively on the immediate policy issues and perceived crises of the day. No doubt this change reflected the new circumstances and perceived crises surrounding the rise of the Cold War that will be discussed below. But there is an important lesson to draw from his changing tone. Just as Vandenberg, FDR, and even Kennan could advocate and direct policy toward the building of an international order that was liberal without having to be self-reflexive and critical users of the concept, they could also pursue liberal order without having the project of liberal order-building constantly before them as an explicit issue. Vandenberg seemed to understand at least the basic principle behind this point when he wrote at the beginning of 1945: "A global conflict which uproots the earth is not calculated to submit itself to the dominion of any finite mind. . . . Each of us can only speak according to his little lights—and pray for a composite wisdom that shall lead us to high, safe ground."[41]

If we could confront Vandenberg today he would likely agree that there could be no grand, meta-scheme for constructing international order, nor would policymakers need to have it at the front of their minds at all times to be effective order-builders. There was the goal of organization, and specific plans to effect order such as the UN and the IMF. Yes, the immediate post-World War II period was an extraordinary time—a historic moment—which put far more pressure on the question of goals and the making of strategic decisions and designs. But even within the context of those times, policymakers had to face specific issues and problems, which they faced exactly because they had embarked on the project of liberal order-building, whether they were conscious of this project at a given time or not.[42] Anthony Giddens, taking his cue from the phenomenologist Alfred Schutz, has put these points in broader, social-theoretical terms: "A person's cognitive activity can be regarded as involving an interweaving of short-term purposes and longer-term projects. Long-term projects are often 'held in suspense' or lie dormant in the varied contexts of daily life; they nevertheless help give over-all phenomenal 'shape' to the individual's existence."[43]

Another way to think about the status of liberal order-building as a conscious project is to go back to Braudel's sense of different time horizons discussed at the conclusion of the last chapter. While liberal modernity emerges in the *longue durée*, and liberal order is lodged in a particular historical conjuncture, it is on the level of events, Braudel's third horizon, that policymaking is so often trained.[44] One need only read through the State Department archives to see how true this is.

By recognizing the different time horizons in both history (Braudel) and agency (Giddens), we can understand the relationship between liberal modernity, liberal order, and the decisive agency of the U.S. state, embodied, in practical terms, in U.S. foreign policymaking and actions. For example, the U.S. state's construction of a multilateral economic system with institutions such as the IMF and the World Bank helped shape the dimensions of liberal order and the unfolding of the liberal moment. But it also transformed the character of liberal modernity in the domain of international economic exchange, as a new mode of multilateralism emerged.[45]

At the same time that state agencies are shaping liberal order and transforming liberal modernity, this example reveals another process at work.

The substance and possibilities of agency are being formed to a great degree in the shorter term by the dynamics of the liberal moment and the emerging order, and in the longer term by the historical trajectories of liberal modernity. This dialectical process has been described most famously by Giddens as "structuration."[46] Whereas structures—in this case the liberal moment and liberal modernity—shape the action and practices of agents, those agents in turn are able to shape and transform structures. Moreover, structuration helps us see that it is only in and through the action of agents that structures are produced and reproduced through time. A similar play between agency and structure is inherent in Braudel's sense of historical time, as events, conjunctures, and broad historical structures are mutually dependent upon one another.

I therefore need to qualify the assertion made in the last section that the liberal moment facilitated the emergence of U.S. hegemonic agency. My qualification is that U.S. state agency itself was among the decisive forces shaping the course of the liberal moment (other agencies—such as Western European states—were, of course, also important). Some readers may be tempted to level the charge of circularity here. But I believe that they can do so only by overlooking the significance of my broader argument. It is agency, the liberal moment, and liberal modernity more broadly, that together yield the liberal order-building process. Agency and historical context (or in Giddens's terms "structure") in their interaction produce a third term of analysis, the liberal order-building process.[47]

By placing the liberal order-building process at the center of analysis and clearly linking both agency and historical context to it, I have, in effect, cast the U.S. as an agent of liberal order, if not also liberal modernity. It was not the only agent. But it was, by virtue of its material preponderance and its role within the liberal moment able to muster the political will to become an essential agent in the building of liberal order. This is hardly an innocent identification. Although the transformative and dialectical relationship between agency and liberalism that I have established avoids any reification of liberal order or liberal modernity, there are other important issues engendered by this identification. Concepts such as hegemony, interests, configurations of power, and even empire are always close at hand when any pronouncements on the status of the post-World War II U.S. state are offered. They have populated much of the discussion about the politics of the postwar period, and it is to these concepts that I now turn.

Hegemony

The expression, U.S. (liberal) hegemonic agency, has been used rather loosely in this text to denote the extensive and critical role of the U.S. state in the making of post-World War II liberal order. Indeed, the attachment of the label "hegemonic" to the U.S. state, at least as it operated in the early decades of the postwar period, is so prevalent in the field of international relations that it is tantamount to something like an automatic reflex. For decades the most prevalent approach to thinking about U.S. hegemony in the field has been hegemonic stability theory. According to the theory of hegemonic stability, the range of economic, political, and strategic benefits a hegemonic state enjoys in a given international order justifies the costs such a state entails in the establishment and maintenance of that order. In the specific case of the postwar U.S. state, the effort to construct and sustain an international order that was liberal, above all in economic terms, is shown to make sense within the context of the theory based on two factors. An order comprising a liberal economic system, marked by relatively open economic terms, is understood to be highly beneficial to the national economic interests of the U.S. state and society. In addition, such an order would also be consistent with the political and economic organization of the U.S. as a liberal state.[48] Throughout its post-World War II liberal hegemony, so it goes, the U.S. achieved investment, trade, and monetary gains based on an international liberal economic system it protected with a political and security order extended across the globe. Those states with sufficiently developed economies have also benefited from the economic system and international political order established under U.S. hegemony. The character of the order as a public good in turn is rewarded with legitimacy, which limits the necessity of extensive hegemonic intervention and direct control that might otherwise increase the costs and compromise the liberal nature of the hegemonic order.

This logic, while it shows why liberal hegemony makes sense, does not explain how a liberal hegemon is able to organize itself as a hegemon and muster the political will as an international actor to build a liberal order. The structure of hegemonic incentive is, in effect, underdetermining as an explanation of the "agency" of hegemony, even when it is combined with the condition of preponderance in economic and military power. It does not establish the ability of a potential hegemon to exploit preponderance and pursue incentives, which depends on the marshaling of political forces necessary to legitimate and authorize this exploitation and pursuit. Nor does it show that a state can translate this will into effective international political action. In its deliberate focus on the dynamics of order maintenance and hegemonic decline, hegemonic stability theory has generally paid little attention to the dynamics of "hegemonic ascendancy."[49] As I have tried to show in previous sections, it is in the process of order construction that agency becomes especially salient. What we are left with in hegemonic stability theory is a rather thin basis for understanding how states become hegemonic, and how that "becoming" is related to the emergence and shaping of international order.[50]

In contrast to hegemonic stability theory, U.S. diplomatic history has concentrated on America's emergence as the central political agent of the post-World War II international system in the West. Diplomatic historians of all ilks have attempted to identify the specific forces that created and shaped the character of the U.S. postwar overseas commitment. For the most part this effort has yielded a mix of contingent, perceptual, and structural factors that explain specific aspects of the rise of U.S. leadership and its role as a major element in the shaping of the contours of the international system. That is, factors such as World War II, domestic politics, anti-communism, a sense of threat, bureaucratic politics, and the capitalist world economy are called upon to explain particular facets of U.S. state agency located in policies and decisions.[51] I will have more to say about how the arguments in this book differ from some of the relevant traditions of diplomatic history, as well as realist international relations, at the conclusion of this chapter. But for now it is enough to point out that diplomatic history does not really problematize the concept of hegemony, U.S. or otherwise, even though historians such as John Lewis Gaddis, Michael Hogan, and Melvyn Leffler have offered very important insights into the nature of that leadership. Hegemony as a political form remains recessed in diplomatic histories behind the focus on specific aspects of leadership. True enough, at least one diplomatic historian has explicitly adopted the world systems approach associated with Immanuel Wallerstein.[52] Wallerstein stresses—in a way that is consistent with hegemonic stability theory—the benefits of "a maximally free world market" to a hegemon in a world capitalist system based on the competitiveness of its products.[53] But rather than questioning and explore the advantages and stakes in using the concept of hegemony, the adoption of a world systems framework, along with other approaches, only takes the concept for granted as a starting point.

Hegemonic stability and world systems theory have not been the only approaches where the concept of hegemony is applied in the context of international relations. Robert Cox and what is generally understood to be a Gramscian school, because of the inspiration drawn from the writing of Marxist theorist Antonio Gramsci, place the category of hegemony at the center of its analysis of international relations.[54] In general, Cox distinguishes his understanding of hegemony through the notion that it is not a powerful state per se that can be hegemonic but an international or global order itself. Cox describes the former condition as one of "domination," which he sees as the main concern of hegemonic stability theory. Still, for Cox, hegemonic orders rely on the agency of a predominant state to rise to—and remain in—ascendancy.

Cox takes care to point out that it is not just any order that can become hegemonic. We can expect hegemony to emerge for "an order within a world economy with a dominant mode of production which penetrates all countries and links with subordinate models of production. It is also a complex of international social relationships which connect the social classes of the different countries."[55] Bear in mind that hegemony is about more than relations of power and material organization. It also entails "a structure of values and understandings about the nature of order that permeates a whole system of states and non-state entities."[56] In his major work, *Production, Power, and World Order*, Cox identifies a post-World War II international order centered initially in the U.S. as a global hegemonic order that warrants the label *Pax Americana*. In this order, U.S. economic, political, and military power, multilateral corporations, visions for the construction of international institutions, radiated outward and were entwined with an ideology of mutual economic benefit, new models of the state (e.g., neoliberal and welfare-nationalist), and specific patterns of capitalist accumulation, class formation, and relations of production.[57] According to Cox, global hegemonies emerge when a social class ascends to hegemony within a powerful state and a shift in interstate power relations favors the international preponderance of that state and class. With this innovative formulation, Cox offers us a sense of the dynamics of hegemonic ascendance that is missing in the other approaches.

Cox's approach to hegemony and order represents an important advance over hegemonic stability theory. His points about order and hegemony's consensual and ideological dimensions, the unfolding of order within a larger macro-historical context (i.e., capitalism), and the possibility of an order itself being hegemonic are provocative departures from more tradi-tional approaches. Cox has clearly informed my own thinking about order in profound ways. In the liberal order that was described in the previous chap-ter, ideological and consensual forces figure prominently in all the liberal domains. I have also repeatedly stressed the importance of viewing liberal modernity as the wider historical context for the emergence of liberal order.

However, there are some notable differences between Cox's thinking and my own, which were touched on in the last chapter but warrant further clarification. Essentially, these differences revolve around the use of the term *hegemony*. Cox has viewed the same historical juncture and the mak-ing of order in the post-World War II period that I am looking at from the angle of capitalist, rather than liberal, modernity. For him, the starting point is the set of social relations of production, relating to how forms of material life (e.g., work and economic distribution) are organized. From there, Cox goes on to analyze how institutions, perspectives on order, and configurations of power (mostly interstate)—all operating on a global scale—bear on the establishment or maintenance of different "modes of social relations of production." In contrast, I build my understanding of order from the starting point of liberal relations and practices (i.e., liberal modernity). Despite the wide range of social existence comprised by the liberal domains described in chapter 1, liberal modernity is a far more cir-cumscribed macro-historical context than the (capitalist) world economy. Obviously there are lots of overlapping areas regarding, for example, the governance of states and markets. On one level, the difference is one of gaining a perspective on a complex historical juncture that can be viewed from multiple angles, each with their own field of vision.

However, there is another level of difference. I took considerable pains to argue in the last chapter that multiple forms of modernity and even order can coexist in the world, with liberal modernity and order being only one form, however extensive its reach. It therefore makes little sense to attach the term hegemony to a (liberal) order itself. Liberal modernity and order shaped different societies often in very circumscribed ways (e.g., markets in capital cities). In effect, except in the North Atlantic region, the depth of lib-eral order was limited. Cox recognizes that hegemony, which can be "firmly established at the center of the world order, wears thin in its peripheries."[58] It should be noted, an advantage to Cox's labeling of an order as hegemonic is the emphasis it places on the way that a center can lord over peripheries. But if hegemony fundamentally rests on the permeation of values and understandings throughout the global system, then we have to be careful about claims that an order is globally hegemonic when peripheries make up nearly eighty percent of the planet. This issue is to a great extent an empirical one, and it cannot be settled here.[59] But it can be said that it would certainly be wholly inaccurate to make the hegemonic claim in the case of liberal order and modernity. Perhaps ironically, it is exactly because the liberal order pursued in the 1940s was global in scope and, therefore, thinly spread that it makes little sense to speak of it being hegemonic in Cox's sense.

Thus, rather than seeing hegemonic agency as a function of the rise of an order itself to world hegemonic status, I would prefer to explore how hegemony can emerge within an order, or more accurately, in the process of building an order. On its face, this would seem to be a return to the perspective of traditional international relations approaches associated with hegemonic stability theory, where the focus is on the agency of the preponderant state. In these approaches hegemonic states produce order. However, my approach to agency, order, and the relationship between them opens up a different way to understand the status and meaning of hegemony. In that understanding, the problem of the emergence of hegemony, which generally eluded hegemonic stability theory, is a central concern.

To reach that understanding let me begin by noting that for a hegemonic stability theorist like Gilpin, hegemony "refers to the leadership of one state (the hegemon) over other states."[60] Equating hegemony with the leadership of a predominant state is a usage of the term that extends back to nineteenth-century descriptions of the ancient Greek state system.[61] Despite its pedigree, the equation of hegemony with leadership is a tautology. There is no distinction between an agent's status as a hegemon and hegemony per se. If a state is a leader it is a hegemon and hegemony is simply the condition thereof.

While tautology is not a problem in itself, it becomes one if it limits the scope of analysis. The "hegemony equals leadership" notion renders the state/agent in question an agent for itself, i.e., an agent of its own status as a hegemon/leader. This agent can then pursue its interests in making an international order to its liking, as described above. But what if we treated the relationship between agency and hegemony differently and proposed that a hegemon is a state that is an *agent of hegemony*? And by hegemony here I do not mean, as Cox does, the predominance of an order per se, but the formation of a specific category of political activity that can be associated with the making of an international order. The category of activity I have in mind is a "constitutive presence."[62]

A helpful analogy for constitutive presence is the way that walls, floors, and ceilings constitute the space of a house, but may not determine the dwelling's purpose, decoration, or the daily pleasure and pain that occurs inside that space. Within the context of international relations an analogous constitutive presence is inherent in the establishment of a military base, the opening of an administrative office, the transfer of funds, or the formation of a communication network.

Typically one starts with the assumption that hegemony at its core is about power or even domination over others and things based on the capabilities of the hegemon.[63] This formulation, consistent with the hegemon as leader approach, views resources and organization as something internal to the hegemon that can be turned outward to dominate others. But this view, in effect, equates hegemony with the conventional Weberian understanding of power, i.e., the prospect of an agent achieving its goals in a given social environment. Hegemons, in this view, are thus the most powerful actors, and by virtue of that power they are international leaders. But what actually distinguishes a hegemon from other states is not just its deployment and exercise of great power, but the nature of that deployment and its effects. A hegemon must be able to shape practices and ideas in the international realm, which is an ability that is mostly dependent on the effective presence of institutions, norms, and material resources. This shaping presence is hegemony and the agent that effects it is the hegemon. Such presence is essential to the production of consensual and coercive relations that have been associated with hegemony ever since Gramsci emphasized the distinction. For instance, such shaping occurs when coerced actors are prompted—or merely choose— to react or adjust to a given configuration of relations in their international environment, as when a state is compelled to change its policy in reaction to punitive signals from a multilateral institution. Consenting actors, on the other hand, can adapt themselves to and even exploit the ideational and material sinews of a given presence, making these sinews commensurate with their own needs, interests, and identity. The classic example of this is the small state that takes advantage of the order underwritten by other, more powerful, states. In doing so, such states are likely to acquiesce in or internalize norms and practices in their international environment which they come to view as advantageous.[64] In actuality, coercion and consent are part of a continuum of effects of an ideational and material deployment that is constitutive of practices and relations in the international realm. The same constitutive presence can be both coercive and consensual. A military base can socialize states into an alliance system and it can be used to threaten punishment.

One advantage of viewing hegemony in this way is that it allows us to associate a range of actions and relations with the emergence and operation of hegemony. Hedley Bull, for instance, distinguishes between "dominance" (violent disregard of other states' rights), "primacy" (compelling sway over international relations of a group of states), and "hegemony" (midway between dominance and primacy).[65] But we might imagine that all three types of relations can appear in the establishment or maintenance of a constitutive presence. They might for instance exist coterminously in the same hegemony or characterize different periods of hegemony. In the case of the U.S. it is clear that the type of hegemonic interventions in Southeast Asia differed considerably from those in Europe.

With this conception of hegemony we also gain another way to view the relation between hegemony and imperialism. An empire is a special type of constitutive presence which involves either formal incorporation of colonies or informal modes of dominance in the way Bull uses the term. Michael Doyle differentiates imperialism from hegemony by claiming that "[c]ontrol of both foreign and domestic policy characterizes empire; control of only foreign policy, hegemony."[66] This distinction is one way of communicating the point that, as commonly understood, hegemony operates in the context of juristically sovereign polities and that if, even in that context, there is significant control of domestic spheres, this is likely to be a case of (informal) imperialism. Even so, I feel this distinction is too hard. Hegemony and imperialism for me share the common political modality of a constitutive presence. Differences emerge in a constitutive presence's character (e.g., collaborative versus incorporative) and fields of operation (e.g., independent states vs. "territories"). For example, while the U.S. in the first half of the twentieth century established imperial relations with territories in the Caribbean (e.g., Puerto Rico and Cuba), it had something closer to hegemonic relations with South America. Arguments over whether the post-World War II U.S. external presence has been imperial rather than merely benignly hegemonic miss the point. A constitutive presence can take on different forms in different contexts. Even within the same context one set of relations might be imperial while another is not, which may hold for one period of time and not for another.

By distinguishing hegemony from agency through the concept of constitutive presence we can map more clearly the ways that agency, hegemony, the liberal moment, and the liberal order-building process stand in relation to one another. In the previous section, I argued that the intersection of the agencies of especially North Atlantic states with the liberal moment yielded a liberal order-building process in the 1940s. Hegemony can be understood as a product of this same intersection. Consider once again the depiction of the liberal moment offered in the section above. The historical forces associated with the liberal moment (e.g., the war itself) and the agency of the U.S. and other states shaped the contours of a constitutive presence (vis-à-vis the U.S.) emerging in the aftermath of war. This constitutive presence and deployment—ultimately taking form, for example, in organs that would oversee the Marshall Plan—was essential to the making of international order. At the same time, the dynamics of making order helped determine the character of U.S. hegemony. For instance, the specific political and economic dynamics at play in the integration of European economies after the war shaped the institutions of the Marshall Plan. Moreover, the formation of hegemony has a direct impact on the emergence of various dimensions of order described in the last chapter—orchestration, construction, concentrations of agency, and institutional arenas. NATO is perhaps the most pointed example of this intersection. The agency of North Atlantic states constructed a new form of alliance, allowing for an orchestration of security policies in an unique arena structured by a concentration of U.S. agency that formed a long lasting constitutive presence in Europe. These relationships are depicted in figure 2.1.

In the bottom half of the figure, one sees the intersection of agency and the liberal moment described in the previous section. Looking to the top half we can see the same intersection refracted into the formation of hegemony as just argued for above. The line connecting the formation of hegemony and the liberal order-building process is meant to convey the way that these two processes shape one another. Each line has arrows at both ends in order to emphasize that the forces and processes in play were mutually constitutive. For example, the trajectory of hegemonic formation, shaped most of all by the agency of the U.S. in the context of the liberal moment, in turn shaped the nature of U.S. agency as certain types of action became feasible. For instance, once the Economic Cooperation Administration was formed by the U.S. state to execute the Marshall Plan, the U.S. could push for economic outcomes in Europe in ways that would otherwise not have been possible.

This figure and the discussion of it is set at a very abstract level. The relationships it depicts need to be fleshed out in more concrete terms.

FIGURE 2.1   Hegemony & Agency

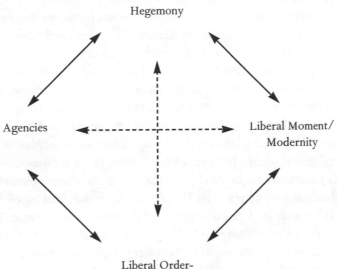

Perhaps the best way to begin doing so is by considering the more specific terms of U.S. hegemony.

The External State

Hegemonic states deploy organizational and material resources beyond their borders that are substantial enough to shape relations and practices relevant to the making of international order. The concept of constitutive presence denotes the effect of this deployment in the international realm. But it does not indicate the actual structure of hegemonic agency itself. In other words, we need to explore the political form hegemonic agency takes and determine how such agency stands in relation to the state that underwrites it.[67] In the more specific terms of the liberal moment, what needs to be considered is the organizational form of the U.S. extension "overseas."

It is tempting to view this extension in simple organizational materialist terms (i.e., with reference solely to the organizational and material resources deployed). Stalin did this when he claimed in an interview: "This war is not as in the past: whoever occupies a territory also imposes on it his social system. Everyone imposes his own system as far as his army can reach."[68] While Stalin may very well have accurately described his intentions in eastern Europe—and his desire to pursue a heavy-handed hegemony of domination or even imperial relations—his statement is hardly an apt description of dynamics of the U.S. presence in Europe. The nature and purpose of the constitutive presence of the U.S. would emerge only as the liberal order-building process unfolded. Indeed, it was hardly clear, as I will show, that the U.S. constitutive presence would be maintained at all. Of course, it is true that in 1945, armies—in the West as well as the East—were the main organs of extension, becoming especially involved in occupation duty in Central Europe, above all in Germany. But it was hardly clear what kind of "social system" would emerge in Central Europe since, as I will discuss, this was a highly contested issue in the U.S. state and in the West more generally. Nor was it clear exactly what role the U.S. should play in the remaking of that system. Of course, the U.S. knew that it did not want Stalin's system. To treat this crude fact as evidence for Stalin's organizational materialist viewpoint on the fate of the postwar world is to ignore the diversity of social and political outcomes that were possible and ultimately realized across the states and societies of Europe. More than this, it ignores the extent to which European populations themselves—especially the middle and upper classes—were choosing and shaping their own social system in the context of a liberal moment and an emerging U.S. hegemony.[69]

Although Stalin's organizational materialist statement misrepresents how things would develop in the West, it does usefully convey that one of the outcomes of World War II was the projection of the U.S. and Soviet states into their respective external realms. One way to think about the set of state organs that are literally situated and deployed in the external realm is as simply the external face of the state. J. P. Nettl made famous the concept of the janus-faced state, a state that was oriented both inward toward its sovereign territory and outward toward its external realm.[70] I believe this conceptualization is far too limited. All states are oriented externally in janus-faced fashion, making foreign policy and deploying diplomats and consuls. Any powerful state can pursue its interests aggressively in the external realm. But what distinguishes postwar West Germany or Canada from the U.S., with regard to their presence in their respective external realms, is that the latter externally deploys an extensive array of state organs. At the end of World War II, only the U.S., Britain, and the Soviet Union were in a position to do so.[71] And while Britain spent much of the

1940s rapidly dismantling its external presence, both the U.S. and the Soviet Union made decisions that would expand theirs to unprecedented heights.

As an alternative to the generality of the concept of there being an external face to the state, I would prefer to think of the organs that are literally situated and deployed in the external realm as forming an "external state." An external state is distinguished from those organs which operate inside state borders—i.e., the internal state—as well as those institutions which command authority over the deployment process itself, the state center. This formulation goes further than others in capturing what is distinct about states that are hegemonic in the way I have defined it. It also provides a unique analytical window on the tensions and dynamics at play in the formation of a liberal hegemonic agency.

In general, the positing of an external state permits us to move beyond the portrayal of U.S. hegemony as simply an outward projection of U.S. power, bureaucracy, and interests. As we saw above, this sense of outward projection is typical of hegemonic stability theory. But it also marks two other relevant formulations. One, which emerges out of a neo-Marxist perspective, is that of the "imperial state" associated with James Petras. He defines the imperial state "as those executive bodies or agencies within the 'government' that are charged with promoting and protecting the expansion of capital across state boundaries by the multinational corporate community headquartered in the imperial center."[72] This formulation fails to distinguish between organs at the center that are oriented externally and organs that are actually deployed externally. We can imagine any state fulfilling the role Petras points to, even if their corporate community does not form an imperial center.[73]

Another relevant, and far more prominent, formulation is that of the "national security state." It is typically viewed as "a state within a state" comprising the "unified pattern of attitudes, policies, and institutions" organizing the U.S. for "perpetual confrontation and for war."[74] The advantages of the external state over the national security state as a formulation of the structure of hegemonic agency in the postwar period are threefold. First, the latter conception is already prejudiced as to the character and purpose of the state: namely, to produce national security. It does not allow for the possibility, explored below, that the predominance of security concerns emerged through time and after a deployment of external state organs. A second and related advantage is that the external state construct allows for a recognition that organs could serve multiple purposes, with some more oriented to economics while others are more oriented to security. Indeed, in the case of the Marshall Plan's Economic Cooperation Administration (ECA) they could serve both.

A third advantage to the external state construct is its specificity regarding the scope of its actions. What constitutes an external state—in contrast to the mere posting of representatives or sending of troops abroad—is the deployment of organs that administer a range of relations in the external realm. Such relations can bear on states, societies, or multilateral institutions. In this capacity, external state organs move across state boundaries and territories. They are transterritorial.

The external state construct does more than identify what is distinct about hegemonic agency. As I mentioned above, it also provides a unique analytical window on the tensions and dynamics at play in the formation of liberal hegemonic agency. Recently Robert Putnam has argued for viewing "central decisionmakers"—or "the state"—at the junction of domestic politics and diplomacy, facing pressures from both the internal and external realms in both foreign and domestic policy decisions.[75] This conceptualization innovatively conveys some of the dynamics of internal and external interests. But it does not offer an Archimedean point from which to discern what might have been at stake in the making of U.S. hegemony. The external state formulation does. The contest within the congressional arena between "nationalists" such as Senator Taft and "internationalists" such as Senator Vandenberg and Dean Acheson pitted one vision of how to organize the U.S. external realm against another.[76] Isolationist-oriented nationalists—whose main interest was in conditions and relations in the internal realm—resisted building a substantive constitutive presence at the war's end. Their approach to the external realm was to project only military power outward in a string of island bases that could depend on the air delivery of nuclear weapons. They had scant interest in the administration of relations in the external realm, and the little interest that remained was focused on the administration of military aid to Asia. This lack of interest was complemented by general public opinion. Public pressures for withdrawal from the external realm, as manifest, for example, in the domestic demand for demobilization, were clearly in tension with U.S. efforts at liberal order-building. The point is that, while forces associated with the liberal moment may have helped create situations such as the occupations of Germany and Japan that lent themselves to the construction of a de facto U.S. external state, there was no guarantee that this presence would not be dismantled. (As implied above, continuity of commitment rather than establishment per se is the issue.)

In general, the construction of an external state is a rare historical occurrence that depends on a particular conjunction of forces that lie inside and outside a given state. Such building will always face resistance from internally directed agents who do not want to expend resources in the external realm. Given the access internal agents have to the state center in a liberal state—especially in legislatures—the pressures against building an external state are particularly acute. On one level, the tension between the nationalists and the internationalists can be understood in economic terms. A liberal state that becomes deeply involved in the domain of international exchange, as had the U.S. through much of the first half of the twentieth century, must still contend politically with the representatives of economic actors whose scope remains limited to the domestic market domain. In other words, policymakers in the center state who endeavor to build or maintain a liberal external state in the context of international economic exchange must still address themselves politically to the interests of their own internal state, just as they must deal with the domestic interests of other states in the external realm. Nonetheless, some form of legitimacy was required in the state center for so weighty a project as building or maintaining an external state. Cold war historians such as Richard Freeland have argued convincingly that internationalist state-center policymakers offered an exaggerated portrait of the Soviet threat to Congress in order to gain domestic support for external state programs such as aid to Greece and Turkey (the Truman Doctrine) and the European Recovery Program, or ERP (the Marshall Plan).[77]

Although I will not focus specifically on the dynamics of the domestic level contest, it remains relevant to the concerns here because it influenced how the contours of the U.S. external state were set. U.S. policymakers faced a basic tension between the call for withdrawal from external commitments and the perceived need for external engagements in the building of liberal order. In the face of this tension, policymakers and Congress chose to shape the character of the U.S. external state as a set of *temporary* organs and programs.[78] The first manifestation of this outcome was the expected withdrawal of U.S. troops in Europe as soon as necessary occupation duty and a basic war settlement was complete. This pattern continued even when the U.S. increased the scope and range of its external engagement with the ERP.[79] What is important to bear in mind is that the property of temporariness does not belie the notion of an external state; rather the very presence of this property is one factor that helped permit the U.S. to begin to act hegemonically while minimizing domestic pressures against such agency. That is, the temporariness helped allay U.S. domestic resistance to order-building.[80]

The external state construct is obviously only a heuristic. Policymakers and legislators did not consciously perceive themselves as engaged in a debate over the formation of an external state. But the same could be said for the political agents who were involved in state-building processes in early modern Europe before the language of the state began to be articulated by thinkers such as Machiavelli.[81] In this light, the main advantage of the external state construct is that it opens up the possibility of considering that what was at stake in U.S. foreign policymaking on one level was the delineation of the contours and character of the U.S. external state. Many of the major policy debates of the period bearing on the nature and extent of a U.S. commitment to Europe, such as those associated with the Truman Doctrine and the Marshall Plan, can be viewed as debates about whether or not—and in what form—the external state should be expanded or ultimately extinguished.

Interests, Strategic Action, and Liberal Order

It is not difficult to imagine that some readers would want to view the external state as simply the organizational projection of U.S. military and economic power and point out that if an order was established, it was a direct function of U.S. political and economic interests, rather than the liberal moment and its bearing on order-building. Hegemonic stability theorists, most often associated with realism, would likely take this type of view. And neo-Marxists, such as James Petras, as well as historical revisionists, such as Gabriel Kolko and Fred Block, might for different reasons do the same, in that they share a common concern with the establishment of a specifically U.S. capitalist system based on a (imperial) global projection of U.S. power.[82] I will explore the differences between realism, revisionism, and my own perspective further below. Here, I would like to confront a skeptical question about the external state, hegemony, and their relation to liberal order-building: Is it not, in the end, economic and security interests that are the real stakes of U.S. hegemonic agency?

This is a somewhat charged, if not problematic, question because it pits interests against other forces shaping agency and political outcomes. Over the last decade, there has been a growing concern in the field of international relations with establishing the impact of ideational factors on political processes and outcomes. Those factors have ranged from sets of ideas and world views to international norms and fields of discourse constituting identities, if not also the very meaning of security.[83] It no longer makes sense to force a choice between interests and norms, culture, or a historical context such as liberal modernity.[84] While it might be tempting for some to take a hard nosed, interest-driven attitude toward international politics, what is far more challenging is the exploration of how interests form a part of a given social context. I will argue in this section that interests are deeply imbricated in the making of liberal order.[85]

To start with, the very posing of the question of underlying interests as the real driving forces of agency and international political outcomes rests on an important assumption: that interests and the ideational dimensions of liberal order and modernity can be separated. This commits us to a certain way of looking at the problem. Partly we have E. H. Carr to blame for this view. He made plain for us that underneath the feel-good language of international order and cosmopolitan idealism we are likely to find the real driving forces of national interests.[86] But Carr was no simpleminded instrumentalist, or vulgar realist. He went on to show that we actually need to "feel good." Orders, while being in the interests of the most powerful, need to be legitimated. Power rests on consent as well as coercion or the fear of coercion.

Carr's argument neatly suggests two basic ways of viewing the intersection of interests and what he calls utopianism, the latter of which refers to the ideas about how to organize international relations based on principles associated with justice and a commitment to the effectiveness of international law and institutions. In the first view, ideas cloak interests. For example, among historians of the Cold War, there is a tendency to consider international liberalism (outside of its manifestation as a type of economic system) as simply an ideological or "moral dimension" of U.S. hegemony and rivalry with the Soviet Union. Liberal principles, such as the right to national self-determination, expressed in universalist terms, are viewed as having served as ideological sheaths justifying more calculated real interests and the expansion of U.S. power more generally.[87] The U.S., in this view, would advocate liberal norms only to build up international political legitimacy for, or to deflect attention from, actions dedicated to material and power interests, such as the creation of favorable economic conditions for U.S. multinationals over other economic interests.

A variant of this first view is that liberal ideas are ultimately subsumed by interests. There are three approaches to this variant. The first is associated with both revisionists and historical traditionalists. The latter wrote especially in the 1950s and tended to justify U.S. hegemony on the basis of the existence of a hostile Soviet Union. Where traditionalists see a slightly naive U.S. effort to put Wilsonian liberal principles into practice being corrupted by Soviet ill-intentions, revisionists posit a corruption of liberal ideas by U.S. economic and power interests, including the military-industrial complex.[88] This corruption thesis is also developed along traditionalist lines in the argument that the naive pursuit of liberalism resulted in its failure because of the rise of Cold War power interests.[89] The second approach to this variant informs us that liberal principles in the Cold War were suspended indefinitely for the sake of pursuing them more directly under more secure future conditions.[90] Finally, there also is the proposition, laid out by the revisionist Lloyd Gardner, that liberal principles were bound up in a "covenant" with the real power interests inherent in the U.S.'s global hegemonic role.[91]

In the variations of this first view, the intersection of interests and ideas takes form either as harmonious cooperation between interests and ideas (e.g., in the legitimation of interests by ideas) or a clash between interests and ideas based on tensions, or even contradictions, which ultimately lead to the ascendancy of interests. There is, however, a second way to view the status of ideas that is suggested by Carr's formulation. International liberal principles do not just pervade the language of policymaking and public statements—and therefore function as legitimizers—they can shape the character and scope of postwar international political outcomes and relations. For instance, liberal principles such as self-determination might be injected into a strategic situation where the politico-economic status of a state and society is contested. In this capacity, universalist discourses such as self-determination can help strategically dispute the politico-geographic boundaries of an international order. It might help empower one set of actors over another. Such an injection may well have been operative in the U.S. assertion, however unsuccessful, of liberal universalist claims regarding self-determination and democratic governance in Eastern Europe in 1945.[92] Understood in this way, universalism can be seen as a component in a more comprehensive effort to construct a liberal international order that embraced political, social, strategic, and economic dimensions.

Both the first and second views on the intersection of ideas and interests share the following: ideas are generally taken to be normative principles that can be used instrumentally to further interests that are exogenous to those principles (e.g., economic ones). The problem with Carr's formulation is that it is a rather limited vision of what the ideational dimensions of order are about. There is simply a lot more going on than moral claims. For example, there are "ideational ensembles" that organize material and political life and that find expression in media such as law, policy papers, international agreements, ideological tracts, intellectual treatises, and simply observable practices. These ensembles are not merely instruments of consent. The stakes for agents can involve decisions about and commitments to "the basic dimensions that shape their way of life."[93] For example, a well-known ensemble relevant to liberal order was what Charles Maier identified as "productionism."[94] An ideational focus on the technologies and logics of economic growth was part of an effort of Americans and Europeans to reduce conflict over economic distribution and the political polarization of the Left and Right in Western Europe. This would make it possible to establish states governed as liberal democracies which could become stable participants in international economic exchange and institutions, an outcome crucial to the building of liberal order.

Thus, in the context of liberal order-building, the notion that exogenous interests lie beneath a veneer of ideas and represent the true stakes of international action misses the point. Economic forces and interests are part of liberal order-building. There are also parallels in the realm of security. A security interest such as the continued survival of a state as a sovereign political unit in a potentially violent world only exists as a *force in and of itself* determining international political outcomes in the abstract space of the minds of international relations theorists.[95] States are much more than simply sovereign units. They are places in which lives are made and lived. Survival means continuing to be able to live, and that means living in a particular way. Being able to live in a sovereign state with longevity is one such way. Mid-twentieth-century realist writers understood the stakes of survival in exactly these terms. Arnold Wolfers saw security as a measure of "the absence of threats to acquired values." Walter Lippmann saw security as the ability to avoid "having to sacrifice core values."[96] Indeed, an interest in securing sheer physical survival is predicated on the notion that continuing such existence will allow actors to go on in the particular forms that their lives take, forms that make it worthwhile facing armed and potentially hostile forces in their environment. Such forms might include the continued enjoyment by state actors of a preeminent position of dominance over a society. Whatever those forms are, the conditions that make survival worthwhile are what will motivate a state to hold its own against external threats and risk physical survival in the first place. If sheer, abstracted physical survival were the final word in the stakes of survival, then the best course might as well be to avoid defending against external threats. Surrender, if not outright demilitarization, would be the best course. At least this is what was argued by the Athenians to the leaders of Melos, an island they chose to subjugate, in the famous Melian dialogue of the Thucydides' *History of the Peloponnesian War*.[97] According to the Athenians, safety should be the highest value for the Melians. Therefore, surrender in the face of overwhelming force would be the most rational course. But states will sometimes avoid surrender and will defend themselves militarily exactly because there is something worth defending, at least for those agents who can determine policy. The Athenians missed the point that the concern with what we may call with Lippmann and Wolfers "values," such as preservation of one's existence and homeland, might also provide the grounds for a will to stand up against overwhelming odds (and, thus, an interest in doing so). As any realist might argue, in a world of states what is worth defending may be independence, sovereignty or, as the Melians put it, "liberty."[98] But on what basis should we stop there in designating the dimensions of social existence (or values) worth defending? The Melians also mention honor and justice, but it could just as easily have been any other of the many dimensions to their form of life. Once we accept sovereignty as one such dimension we have no intellectually honest way to occlude the presence of other dimensions as well. Setting limits to such dimensions can be done only by the agents themselves.

We may approach the same point from the other side of the Melian dialogue. The Athenians themselves are absorbed in the project of empire, which commits them to a form of international life that brings them to the shores of Melos.[99] Their interest, as they see it, is continuing in the capacity as an empire and not something else.[100] (An interest in a particular form of existence emerges only as a function of the social fabric that gives meaning to that form.) Survival is deeply embedded in the character of our social existence. In fact, modern realists understand this all too well. A collectivity's political life as a state is what throws it into certain types of logics of interaction, such as anarchy. Much of the current debate in the field of international relations is over questions about which logics states are thrown into, why,[101] and what other dimensions of social existence beside stateness determine the character of international political life.

These questions are central to the approach here. I am arguing that states and societies drawn up into liberal modernity had, to varying degrees, a number of dimensions through which to view the terms of—and interests in—their survival.[102] Such terms could encompass liberal statehood, a market society, a participant in international economic exchange, or a self-determining and sovereign political entity. The liberal moment made these terms possibilities, to varying degrees, for many states across the globe. But these possibilities were contingent on and vulnerable to the unfolding interaction of states and societies. For it is the very pursuit of these terms that throws states and societies into the interaction that can be a requisite for fear. Making the notion of sheer physical survival abstract misses exactly what usually creates insecurities if not the fear of war itself: the activity of state actors and citizens that forces them into the external realm with engagements, commitments, and challenges to and from other states that must be defended. Indeed, Kenneth Waltz has always insisted that interdependence between states can be a potential source of conflict for the simple reason that the more states interact, the more opportunity exists for states to have disputes.[103] Whether or not there is any validity to this claim,[104] it does underscore that security interests and dynamics can conceivably emerge out of potent international social contexts. In the 1940s, the commitments and engagements that grew out of the liberal moment and drew states in the West into the liberal order-building process generated far more complex political dynamics than interdependence per se ever could. As I will argue in subsequent chapters, these dynamics shaped the strategic relations and interests of these states and ultimately drew them into a Cold War. If anything, the terms and stakes of survival were set by the dynamics of liberal order.

I have argued in this section that liberal modernity and order constitute an ideational context that shapes outcomes, agency, and interests in many ways. In so doing, I have joined a growing community of scholars who are concerned with showing how ideational forces, from norms to discourses, impact international life. However, some of the work in this growing community, exemplified by a recent volume, *Ideas and Foreign Policy*, focuses on ideas as discrete variables (e.g., as road maps, policy solutions, or as institutional norms). These variables are drawn out of broader historical contexts such as liberal modernity or capitalism, which tend to fall into the shadows in analysis. This "micro-ideational" approach reproduces too much of the type of separation between ideational forces and material interests that was an important dimension of Carr's seminal work.[105] It rests on the assumption that ideas are just one more set of factors along with interests and material capabilities determining action. While not denying the existence and relevance of interests, in this study I am emphasizing that we need a "macro-ideational" approach in order to show that interests are part of a given historical context, along with the identity of the agents that assert them (e.g., as liberal states or as self-determining collectivities). Moreover, we need a macro-ideational approach to make sense or interpret the significance of practices, material conditions, and capabilities ranging from economic resource distribution to military power accumulation.

In the end, the decision to adopt a micro- versus a macro-ideational approach will likely correspond to differences in methodological starting points. A micro-ideational approach complements a positivist effort to determine the extent to which ideational variables account for the variance for a given phenomenon. In contrast, building a plausible and comprehensive interpretive framework, especially for the range of history analyzed here, requires a broad macro-ideational context against which to discern the meaning, significance, and force of phenomena ranging from practices and principles to the material "facts on the ground."

Security and Militarization

Today, the notion that survival and security are about more than military defense and war is likely to be far more readily recognized by scholars and policymakers than in the past. Barry Buzan, who was instrumental in articulating this wider view, counts, alongside military security, concerns with political, economic, societal, and environmental security. These other forms bear on the quality of economic life, the integrity of environments, the survival of collectivities, and the stability of our polities.[106]

Security more generally, as Buzan points out in *People, States and Fear*, is an essentially contested concept, open to endless debate over its definition and application, not unlike terms such as "imperialism," "democracy," or "liberalism" for that matter.[107] Consistent with the discussion in the previous section, security revolves around the question of how threats to contending ways of configuring social existence are identified, mitigated, or governed. In other words, the pursuit of security is about the organized effort of a given social form (e.g., a polity) to contend with what it articulates and identifies as forces (e.g., a military faction, another polity, or economic collapse) that threaten its social existence.

Of course, the intersection between military power and forms of social existence has been of longstanding concern in the history of social and political thought. Raymond Aron, for instance, made sure to point out in the 1960s that "[m]ilitary systems and weapons are . . . the expression of political and social systems."[108] More recently, Buzan has argued that the expansion and practices of military defense can create economic burdens and their own forms of risk (e.g., nuclear attack) that might lead to a decrease in a state and society's sense of security.[109] This intersection has been at the heart of the literature, discussed above, that has shown how war-making can be a crucial force in the shaping of states and international orders. But the most prevalent locus of concern over this intersection has been the phenomenon of militarism. It is mostly through this conceptual portal that my own effort to probe the intersection between military power and social existence is made below.

Ever since the seventeenth century, a growing number of thinkers have drawn attention to and problematized the status of the military in states, societies, and the international realm. It was not until the second half of the nineteenth century that the term militarism came into increasingly regular use.[110] Like security, the concept of militarism is essentially contested, as we might expect any term to be which has been subject to so much debate. There is, thus, no consensus over its meaning. For the most part, the chief reference point for militarism over the last two centuries has been the causes and implications of the ascendancy of military organization and ideology across different societies. Writers in the late nineteenth and early twentieth centuries concentrated on Europe, with a special view to Germany and its Prussian tradition. After World War II, attention in U.S. social science turned to the Third World, where the role of the military as a force in modernization was an especially prominent concern. Across the twentieth century the problem of civil-military relations increasingly occupied scholars. Alfred Vagts wrote his seminal text, *A History of Militarism*, in 1937 and distinguished between the mere concern with efficient use of human and material resources in war-making ("the military way") and "every system of thinking and valuing and every complex of feelings which rank military institutions and ways above the ways of civilian life, carrying military mentality and modes of acting and decision into the civilian sphere" (militarism).[111]

For obvious reasons, the study of militarism has not been focused solely on processes unfolding inside given societies. Scholars such as Otto Hintze looked to the international realm and the pressures of war-making for causes of domestic militarism.[112] More recently, in the face of the massive military buildup in the Cold War era, attention was fixed on the global dimensions of military power, the international patterns of which some believe formed a "world military order."[113]

A central category of analysis in this second line of study is militarization. Like militarism, this concept has many meanings but can be generally associated with a process of growth in military power, organization, or values on a domestic or international basis. In a recent well-known attempt to clarify the usages of the terms militarism and militarization, Andrew Ross distinguished between militarization as processes leading to more militarism (behavioral and ideational) and militarization as sheer "military buildup" (force levels, war, and military regimes).[114] Ross's goal was to focus attention on fully measurable categories of militarization as military buildup, including such things as arms imports and production levels. But he conceded that military buildup can contribute to militarism and vise versa. Thus, while Ross may have helped identify some of the measures of militarization by concentrating on the second meaning, he has simply occluded the difficult and perhaps most interesting questions about its causes and entwinement with social and political life that are inherent in the first meaning.[115] It is with these issues that the real challenge of clarification lies.

One lesson that I take from Ross's effort is that when using the term militarization, one should make sure that it refers to the militarization of something. In Ross's case that something is the production, accumulation, and use of military resources within and across societies in the Third World. At the outset of this study, I made clear that the concern here was with the militarization of international relations: more specifically, the process by which military-strategic issues, relations, and institutions come to constitute an increasingly predominant dimension of the overall international political life of a set of states and societies. This definition of militarization falls within the first meaning distinguished by Ross, i.e., that which leads to more militarism. Thus, in my formulation, militarism in international relations exists when the military-strategic becomes predominant. And like so many of the phenomena associated with the first meaning of militarization, predominance is something that is not necessarily subject to the type of quantifiable measurement that Ross advocates for his notion of military buildup. But there are useful qualitative markers for discerning predominance that also allow for a direct connection between militarization and liberal order.

In a noted essay on militarization in international relations Marek Thee was concerned with, among other things, the world military order and relevant hierarchies of military power across states; the influence of military ideology and organization in domestic life and foreign policymaking; and the proclivity to use force in relations with other states and in domestic affairs.[116] I consider all of these factors relevant to the post-World War II militarization with which I am concerned. But what is most relevant here is one specific, albeit highly significant, marker of postwar militarization: the militarization of the U.S. presence in its external realm. By 1958, the U.S. had agreed to train and equip the forces of more than 70 countries, made formal security commitments to 43 of them, and stationed almost 1.5 million troops in hundreds of bases in 35 countries around the globe.[117] What is most important for me about the impact of the U.S.'s militarized global presence on international relations is something that is not easily expressed in military deployment statistics: the degree to which the strategic-military dimension came to dominate the international political relations among states in, or associated with, the West. That is the reason for defining militarization the way I have. I want to explore how, from the end of the Second World War to the outbreak of the Korean War, the process of building liberal order, which was so entwined with U.S. hegemonic agency, was tied to a growing militarism. In other words, in the course of those years the U.S. external state that was constructed in the making of liberal order was increasingly configured along military lines. This means that the constitutive presence associated with U.S. hegemony became more and more military in nature. Increasingly, military organs replaced civilian ones and military-strategic issues overshadowed nonmilitary ones. How this happened and why is the focus of chapters 3 and 4.

Structuring the Argument

I have concentrated in this chapter on the initial phases of the liberal moment and have taken the first steps in the development of a conceptual infrastructure for interpreting the remarkable trajectory of international change emerging out of the Second World War. Besides describing the nature of the liberal moment, I have delineated the sinews of hegemonic agency, identified the implications of the formation of an external state, and defined the terms security and militarization. I have also sought to highlight the basic lines of relation among these elements. Before moving ahead, I want to reflect on how the argument I am developing is structured and how it can be distinguished from the main alternative interpretations of the international political and strategic dynamics of the postwar period.

At the most basic level, the interpretive explanation I am fashioning is functional in structure. For me, the militarization of the West and the rise of the Cold War occurred because of their consequences for the liberal order-construction process. The functional relationships can be expressed as shown in figure 2.2.

While Western militarization and the rise of the Cold War had distinct consequences for the liberal order-construction process, developments associated with each phenomenon fed into the other (as depicted by the solid arrow at the bottom of figure 2.2). As I will argue below, the deepening of the U.S.-Soviet confrontation into a cold war was a result of liberal political dynamics, which in turn helped propel Western militarization. An increasing reliance on military force as a means to build liberal order contributed to the deepening of the rising Cold War confrontation. Distinguishing Western militarization from the Cold War reinforces the idea that the militarization of the West was not simply an outgrowth of the U.S.-Soviet confrontation.

Adopting a functional logic is nothing to be ashamed of. Arthur Stinchcombe, long ago, and G. A. Cohen, more recently, have shown that func-

FIGURE 2.2   Basic Explanatory Scheme

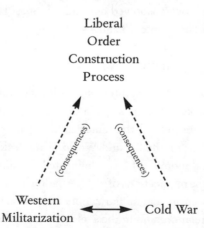

tional explanations can be useful and need not be inherently conservative, teleological, or tautological.[118] Functional explanation, of course, must be distinguished from the various forms of functionalism and neofunctionalism associated with anthropologists such as Bronislaw Malinowski, sociologists such as Talcott Parsons, and political scientists such as Ernst Haas.[119] These approaches make claims about systemic integration that are not made here.

My primary incentive for setting this interpretation in functional terms is that a functionalist schema serves to underscore the interaction between historical contingency, political structures, and agencies. Much of this chapter has been dedicated to showing how contingency (e.g., aspects of the liberal moment), structure (e.g., constitutive presence), and agency (e.g., that of the U.S. state) interact in different processes, such as the process of hegemonic formation. Indeed, in the functionalist schema set out above liberal order-building is not the only process; militarization and the rise of the Cold War are processes as well. Functional explanation, as I want to employ it, is inherently interactive. There is an ongoing interplay between the elements of explanation (i.e., liberal order, militarization, and Cold War) which are mediated through the consequences these elements have for one another.

For agents, such as those of the U.S. state, who were caught up in the liberal order-building process, the consequences of processes of Cold War formation and militarization mattered in places like Germany. Moreover, conditions change, the unexpected happens, and agents react and change their policies. They, in effect, must reformulate their policies in a way that suggests a logic similar to the Darwinistic natural selection process that unfolds in reaction to changes in creatures' environments.[120] As my interpretation moves forward, it will become clear that there were changes in the historical conditions which formed the context of the selection of policies and strategies bearing on liberal order-construction. Sometimes these changes emerged from the very actions and policies that were set in place to deal with previous historical conditions.

As critics of functional explanation have made clear, it is not enough simply to posit agents who can react and formulate action around consequences.[121] In an ideal functional universe, we would see agents self-consciously identifying consequences for liberal order and acting accordingly. But as I made clear in my discussion of agency above, U.S. policymakers were rarely self-reflexive about their role in liberal order-making as they devised policies and made decisions, especially once they had embarked upon the task of order-building. Thus, once inside the project of liberal order-building, policymakers were pushed and pulled by the daily, weekly, and monthly tribulations and travails of making order. Sometimes they responded to what they perceived to be constraints in their policymaking universe, including the interests of other liberal states, the resistance of Congress, and the political instability that they perceived around them. Often times they simply tried to remain consistent with what they understood to be the policy they had established in the past for ordering a particular set of relations in a geographical region. Still other times policymakers arrived at policies on a negative basis, i.e., because of the outcomes a given policy avoided rather than what it provided. The avoidance of outcomes that might challenge existing constraints too severely or were inconsistent with defined goals implies that the degree to which a "blueprint" existed for the construction of a liberal order was limited. There were no pregiven markers or directions regarding how to pursue order or exactly what order should look like. Contradictions and tensions were manifold. This too reinforces the contingent nature of the process.[122]

Altogether, underlying these constraints, resistances, and tensions was the influence of different political structures and logics of operation inside the liberal order-building process. Laying out these structures and logics will take up a large portion of the chapters that follow. We may think of the play between those structures and logics and the agency of U.S. policymaking as the crucial set of mechanisms for turning "consequence into a cause,"[123] given the limits of self-reflexive, consequentialist agency. This means that, on the one hand, we had policymaking and action that shaped the structures and logics of liberal order-making. On the other hand, the same structures and logics in turn shaped policymaking and action.[124]

Neorealism and the Liberal Moment

I can imagine that some readers will be tempted to point out that the whole schema makes a fairly bold claim, since they would prefer to look to the external threat of the Soviet Union as the driving force of militarization and the Cold War rather than liberal order-making. They might then argue that even if there were consequences for liberal order-making that does not mean that those consequences were determinative, relative to external threat. My response to this type of challenge—something a realist might pose—is not a simple one. I will begin by describing another way to view the forces that are encompassed by my interpretation.

Although the functional schema designates the type of explanatory logic generally guiding this interpretation, it does not provide a complete picture of how the relevant forces impinge upon one another. Above all, it fails to show how the liberal moment and the liberal order-building process stand in relation to one another and the other phenomena that are at the center of this interpretation. But consider the structure of forces depicted in figure 2.3.

Here we see the relation and impact of forces on one another mapped out hierarchically. The liberal moment, as described above, represents the decisive historical shift that precipitated the process of liberal order-building. This process engendered a specific set of political dynamics which, in turn, prompted the emergence of a confrontation between the U.S. and Soviet Union. This confrontation ultimately led to the Cold War and the militarization of the West as well. Analyzing those political dynamics will be the main task of subsequent chapters. But it can be pointed out here that the relationships articulated in the functional schema (figure 2.2) map onto the inner three boxes of figure 2.3. Indeed, this is why the arrows in figure 2.3 move in both directions. The rise of the Cold War and the confrontation that preceded it had consequences for liberal order-building. This relationship is part of a wider set of feedback effects that occur across the different dimensions. As we saw, there were feedback effects between liberal order-making and the liberal moment.

FIGURE 2.3   Explanatory Dimensions

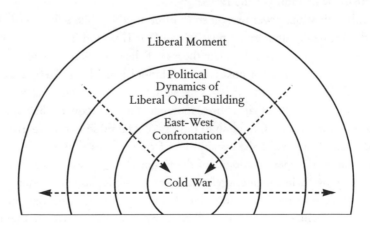

Figure 2.3 lays bare the terms of difference between my approach to the Cold War and that of the most predominant approach to security in the U.S., neorealism. Neorealism distinguishes itself by its emphasis on structures and dynamics operating at the level of the international system as forces shaping security outcomes. This was a departure from its predecessor, realism, which looked mostly to the play of power politics manifest in the foreign policies of states in pursuit of their interests. We have already encountered the neorealist approach in the discussion about survival. One of the distinguishing turns of neorealism is its claim that it is a concern with survival that is a core motive of state action relevant to security rather than the pursuit of power per se, as earlier realists such as Hans Morgenthau would have it.[125] Another key principle is the imperative to self-help. States will rely on themselves to provide for security in an international system that has no ultimate authority to protect them (i.e., one that is anarchical). Moreover, the effort of one state to protect itself does not lead necessarily to a sense of safety but often to increasing levels of insecurity. Others are provoked to increase their security efforts, prompting yet another round of increases. This has become known as the security dilemma.

The wider realist tradition has an extensive literature and set of analytic tools that I cannot hope to adequately address in these pages.[126] My more modest aim is to consider the validity of the neorealist interpretation of the Cold War against the background of my own, so that the challenge posed at the start of this section can be addressed. I will use Kenneth Waltz's *Theory of International Politics* (1979) because, in the words of one realist, it "shaped much of the theoretical debate during the 1980s" and continues to "reverberate in the literature of the 1990s."[127]

Although Waltz never pretended to offer anything like a theory of the Cold War, he did discuss the post-World War II period in a fashion that implied his approach could explain the rise of the Cold War. If Waltz were to construct his own set of boxes they might look something like figure 2.4. He would likely situate the war—as the signal event precipitating change—in the outer box, rather than a liberal moment. The war reduced the number of great powers from five or so to only two. And these two were grossly predominant relative to the capabilities of other states.[128] This structural shift changed the operating logics of the system so that it was in accord with two superpowers in competition for survival. These logics would constitute the second box. Although Waltz discusses a number of logics bearing on the operation of a bipolar world, those that seem to count as relevant to the rise of a Cold War are: (1) the expansion of the arena of security competition to include the entire globe; (2) an increasingly comprehensive concern on the part of each superpower with the other's capacity to produce power (e.g., the application of technological and economic forces within each state); and (3) a tendency to overreact to changing political conditions as crises. The first logic (globalization) flows from the principle that each superpower is so big that the fate of the entire system affects it more than any other state. Thus, the gain of one in that system is a loss for the other. The basis for the second logic (relative power concern) is the notion that since each superpower can hurt the other the way that no other state can, they become fixated on each other's disposition. Finally, the third logic (overreaction) emerges out of the sheer desire of the superpowers to avoid the miscalculation of underestimating the importance of events and developments— overreaction is more prudent.[129]

It is easy to envision the heightened tensions, sense of impending crisis, and obsessive fixation on the other that marked the Cold War emerging from Waltz's logics. (Thus, the inner box appears.) Why would we ever need the extensive ideational and macro-historical baggage that goes along with a liberal moment and order? To answer that question we need to unpack the assumptions of the Waltzian interpretation.

On its face, the way Waltz lays it out seems like an ironclad logic. But it holds only if we are unwilling to enter into an engagement with the history

FIGURE 2.4   Waltzian Explanatory Dimensions

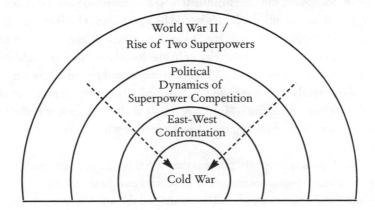

of the period. Even in terms of raw capabilities, by Waltz's own criteria of "superpowerhood" (military, economic, and technological supremacy), the Soviet Union did not qualify with the decimated economy and inferior military it took out of the war.[130] Even its massive manpower permitted the Soviet Union only to maintain its occupation duties, especially given its lack of equipment. The U.S. military clearly recognized these limits.[131]

And yet across the second half of the 1940s, the Soviet Union did come to be viewed increasingly as a threat. However, as I will show below, the basis of that threat stemmed to a great extent from the pressures the Soviets could bring to bear on the political process of building an international liberal order in Western Europe, rather than the physical safety of the U.S. Although U.S. policymakers did not on balance take a Soviet invasion of Western Europe seriously as a prospect that was likely in the near or intermediate term, fear of invasion in Europe had important political ramifications. The Soviet army, deployed very near to Western Europe at the war's end, mattered to the U.S. to the extent that it provided a means to challenge and contest the outcomes of the liberal order-building process.[132]

Waltz in actuality was reading history backward. He assumed that the operating logic of an up-and-running Cold War could explain its emergence.[133] This is the reverse of the genetic fallacy, in which one mistakes the processes involved in the emergence of something for its operation in its extant form. The war did leave two states clearly above the others (however unequal that predominance was). But we have no basis to conclude that the predominance of these states led them into the kind of security competition Waltz describes (precipitating the logics described above). If the Soviet Union in the 1940s or even the early 1950s was recognized as being incapable of destroying the U.S. or threatening its continued survival as a state why should we assume the logics would be operative? The fear that, in an invasion of Western Europe, the Soviet Union would garner a resource-rich region to exploit and thereby enhance its relative power could only emerge once the thinking of U.S. policymakers had become zero-sum.[134] But this is exactly what needs to be explained. To merely assume it makes the theory less interesting. (Moreover, as we shall see below, it is the U.S. investment in order-building that makes the region particularly valuable in this regard.)

What I think is happening here is that Waltz is painting with very broad strokes which cover over the many processes that help move things from one historical point to another. Historians call this the telescopic fallacy to denote "interpretations that reduce an extended trend to a momentary transformation."[135]

As we saw with hegemonic stability, just because something makes sense does not mean it explains why things emerge as they do. The extent to which Waltz commits this and the other fallacies mentioned above can also be appreciated by briefly considering his understanding of the emergence of U.S. hegemony and its bearing on the making of international order. The way Waltz sees it, these forces impinge on one another as follows: The war precipitated the preponderance of the U.S. state based on its capabilities. This made it compelling to be engaged on a global basis (see logic number 2 above). Order, within which the U.S. would be globally hegemonic, was pursued because a functioning, stable system is in the interest of a state that has the most to lose or gain in the system. That the order would be liberal follows from the need of the U.S. to justify its global actions and is anyway consistent with its interests as a liberal state and vision of how the world should work.[136]

This formulation is quite different from my own. For me the forces lined up above affect one another as follows: Coming out of the liberal moment, the project of liberal order-making drew a preponderant U.S. into a global engagement, whereupon it increasingly deployed itself in its effort to build an external state that could effect a constitutive presence or hegemony in the context of that project. The problem with Waltz's approach is that it assumes up front, as a matter of principle, the very agency and global engagement that would emerge only in and through the order-making process. More-over, capabilities would be shaped as military, economic, and political forces were deployed and constructed across the 1940s. I have already shown how tentative the external commitment was. As I will argue below, its character and extent would become known only with time and effort.

What is necessary is some sort of historical process within which hege-mony can form. Interestingly, Waltz hints at such a process in his conceptu-alization of power. He tells us that "[w]hether A, in applying its capabilities, gains the wanted compliance of B depends on A's capabilities and strategy, on B's capabilities and counterstrategy, and on all of these factors as they are affected by the situation at hand."[137] Waltz is emphasizing the interactive nature of power, the play back and forth between agents in a given context or "situation at hand." He is contesting the straightline equation of power with control that was underlying arguments at the time that U.S. hegemony was declining, evidenced by the increasing lack of U.S. control over outcomes. He rightly politicized power by emphasizing the "give and take" inherent in political situations, shaped by capabilities as well as projects or strategies and contexts. But for some reason he did not think through the implications of his conceptualization. Waltz intended to apply his understanding of power to a circumscribed set of events or outcomes. However, there is no reason why we cannot apply it to a wider context of historical time. Specifically, we can think of the whole period of 1945–1950 as exactly the type of emergence of power (in this case U.S. hegemony) based on the interaction of states over the fate of Europe and other relevant regions. The strategies were the play of interests in the making of international liberal order (i.e., the situation at hand).

The extent to which neorealists recognize this gap in their theory is evident in Robert Gilpin's distinction between power defined in materialist terms as "the military, economic, and technological capabilities of states," and "prestige," which he equates with a kind of sense of authority where others will actually take the dictates of a hegemon seriously out of "respect or common interest."[138] Gilpin points out that a lag can emerge between the actual possession of preponderant power by a state and the perception on the part of other states.[139] Gilpin avoids the question of whether power as he understands it can actually be shaped in the process of constructing prestige. This is the way I am arguing U.S. "power" was formed in the 1940s. It involves, as we shall see, far more than prestige. Again, the interesting political historical questions about the formation of hegemony—even in Gilpin's sense of leadership and control based on power plus prestige—are passed over and deposited in the "black hole" identified as a "lag."

The same appeal to lags is made by Stephen Krasner in his attempt to understand why the U.S. did not become a hegemon in the interwar years despite being economically preponderant.[140] He argues that a "catalytic external event" such as World War II was necessary and even then it would not be until the 1950s that a U.S. capacity to manage the international monetary system would emerge. At the time, Krasner was taking on the interdependence school in the field of international relations that emphasized the importance of nonstate actors. He wanted to show the continued centrality of the state in shaping international relations. But the story he did not tell was the centrality of the historical contexts in which both state and nonstate actors played a part, including the war. In Krasner's interpretation the war reorients the U.S. state in a manner that makes hegemony possible. Yet so powerful an affect is treated as a mere intervening variable. We are left to guess as to how central it was, why World War I was not central, and what the full extent of the impact of the war was for shaping the postwar world as well as U.S. hegemony.

I find it odd that neorealists such as Gilpin and Krasner recognize the formative nature of hegemony and yet still insist that the hierarchies of "raw" material power are the ultimate shapers of much of international political life. What is at stake in all of this is the meaning and significance we want to assign to power, war, and other phenomena that help make international political life what it is. That is why I have explicitly adopted the language of interpretation. As a way to understand the rise of the Cold War, neorealist interpretations, unfortunately, end just where they should begin.

Diplomatic History and International Liberal Order

Far more attuned to the value of interpretation is the field of diplomatic history, where, in contrast to international relations, the history of this period has been engaged extensively. Much of what is central to the interpretation I am developing here has been profoundly informed by the work of historians of U.S. foreign relations. For instance, a work such as Gabriel Kolko's *The Politics of War* has illuminated the impact of World War II and how it shaped directions in U.S. policymaking. Specifically, Kolko shows how concerns with potential worldwide social upheaval, the impact of the Soviet Union, and the future of Britain were important elements in the making of U.S. wartime policy that was directed at the possibilities of postwar international order.

What diplomatic historians have to say about the period is extensive. The field has formed into different schools which can be differentiated by the varying social forces that focus their interpretations. Where revisionists have drawn our attention to the ways that the capitalist economic system and the interests and world views of economic actors—many of whom served in key positions in the U.S. state—have shaped foreign policymaking, postrevisionists have stressed the concerns of state actors with national security and the difficulties they faced in making security policy against the background of sometimes hostile domestic and bureaucratic politics. Other scholars, inspired by the revisionist turn, have taken what is termed a corporatist approach to U.S. foreign relations. They stress the effort of capital, the state, and, ultimately, segments of labor to establish liberal capitalist forms of political and economic governance and order across the West. Still others have adopted the world systems approach associated with Immanuel Wallerstein.

I do not wish here to enter into a review of the many strands of this field as they have emerged in the post-World War II period.[141] Since so much of my interpretation builds on the rich empirical and analytical traditon of diplomatic history, the many ways I engage diplomatic history will become clear only as I go along and build my own interpretation. I have already had occasion to do this in the above discussion. At this point, I want only to set out the most basic lines of distinction between my own effort and those that are the most proximate to it in diplomatic history.

To start, my differences with diplomatic historians are not either/or propositions. No one set of forces should be seen as determinative, no one paradigm can be thought to work best to the relative exclusion of others. And no one approach could inform us of the full import of the Cold War and its emergence against the background of questions of interest here about modernity, international order, and liberalism. If we take interpretive knowledge seriously, then we need multiple perspectives so that there can be arguments over rival interpretations.

The connections I am trying to make in this book between hegemony, the state, and the external realm in the context of a particular macro-historical context (i.e., liberal modernity) would not have been possible without the critical efforts of historical revisionists such as Joyce and Gabriel Kolko in making connections others would or could not. Well-known revisionists, among them William Appleman Williams, Walter LaFeber, Fred Block, as well as the Kolkos, have been anything but vulgar economic determinists.[142] They all appreciated the contingent play of forces within and between domestic politics, hegemonic construction, and international political life.

There are, however, important differences between the analysis of this book and revisionism. For much of revisionism, the goal has been "to place the Cold War in the context of the American effort to create a certain type of economy."[143] Revisionists have a tendency to focus on the dynamics of U.S. capitalism establishing an economic order for its benefit as a set of forces shaping policy and outcomes. I have stressed that I want to treat as the primary political and social, as well as economic, context of analysis not capitalism per se, but liberal modernity. Moreover, I have emphasized that such a context was international, not just "American." The centrality of the U.S. in the making and maintaining of order does not necessarily imply such an order was the equivalent of an American lake. To point to liberal order as little more than the "U.S. interest writ large" is to identify the actors caught up in this whirlwind, including not just Europeans, but also colonial peoples struggling for self-determination, to a great extent as objects or victims, rather than witting and unwitting agents themselves in a profound historic moment. Revisionists have rightly been especially sensitive to the fate of these peoples as well as of labor in the West. And the agency of non-Americans has been prominent in their work, ranging from British negotiators at Bretton Woods to Indonesian rebels. But in an endeavor to critique U.S. power and interest they have exaggerated the "Americanness" of international order. Many other interests have operated through the postwar order. It has been their order as well, whether they have liked it or not.

Those who interpret postwar history through the lens of the world capitalist system, while retaining a focus on economic contexts, certainly do not suffer from the same Americanization of contexts. As I have already pointed out, the world-systems approach has been essential for my appreciation of the importance of looking at broad historical modalities. Beyond this, the ramifications of the historical moment described above and the Cold War more generally for the unfolding of the world capitalist system in the twentieth century has been thoughtfully analyzed by Thomas McCormick in *America's Half-Century*. But, as indicated in chapter 1, since much of the ordering that was going on took place more immediately in the context of liberal modernity—however much the making of markets and states was entwined with capitalist outcomes—I prefer to view the period through the lens of that context. It is indeed interesting that McCormick must refer to visions or blueprints for order that are very much about the liberal order-making I am focusing on here (e.g., principles of free trade), in order to discuss what policymakers were actually doing.[144] But by keeping his analytical vision trained on the world system, McCormick fails to provide a framework for analyzing the dynamics and impact that were specific to that liberal order-making.

If anything, the ensuing analysis of the postwar period has its closest affinity with corporatism. This is not the case because of any overarching commitment to corporatist analysis as described above. Rather it stems from the effort of corporatist historians such as Michael Hogan and Charles Maier to place the making of social, political, and economic order, both domestic and international, at the center of their analysis. They have underscored how, in the midst of the outbreak of a Cold War, phenomena such as the construction of markets and the setting of terms for liberal democratic governance were unfolding with strong lines of continuity relative to the earlier decades of the twentieth century. And they have given considerable attention to non-U.S. agencies, both public and private. In general, corporatists have purposively set themselves up as counterpoints to the more traditional focus on international strategic processes that has marked much of diplomatic history. Instead, corporatism "is far more concerned with the globalization of economic, political, and social forces; with the connections between state and society and between national systems and foreign policy; and with the interaction of these systems internationally."[145] As will become apparent below, corporatists such as Hogan have drawn out important links between security and order-making, especially regarding the question of the integration of European states and its ramifications for regional security. What they have not done—and what distinguishes my own effort—is to show how order-making actually precipitated the formation of the main strategic configuration of the postwar world, the militarized Cold War.

The other major school mentioned above is postrevisionism. It emerged— most forcefully in the work of John Gaddis—as an antidote to what was judged to be a too-excessive focus on economic forces on the part of revisionists.[146] Postrevisionists stress the multiplicity of factors explaining the historical developments of the postwar period. They point to the impact of domestic political factors, such as public opinion and congressional and bureaucratic politics. Also, they generally concentrate on policymakers' security concerns and perceptions of threat in a postwar world marked by a new configuration of interstate power.

Like that of other historical schools, the work of postrevisionists has been extremely useful in this study. Gaddis and Robert Pollard, for instance, have explored how dimensions of liberal order-making, both political and economic, became deeply entwined with the pursuit of security. Despite the important links they make, there are notable differences between the postrevisionist approach to the postwar period and my own that turn exactly on the question of security. Consider Leffler's recent monumental historical study of U.S. security policy in the immediate postwar period, which crystallized the security-centric approach of postrevisionism.[147] Leffler argues that immediately after the war a state as powerful as the U.S. could secure on a global basis its physical, social, economic, and political existence and configure relations in its external realm in a fashion that is supportive and consistent with that existence. In the name of security it would exploit its existing power base to gain a preponderance of power in the international system.

In his conceptualization, Leffler does not really use the language of social existence, as I have articulated it in my discussion of security above. Rather, he adopts the traditional language of students of national security policymaking during the Cold War, which "encompasses the decisions and actions deemed important to protect domestic core values from external threats."[148] The operative phrase here is "core values," which allows Leffler to incorporate such things as economic interests in the configuration of national and international markets and commitments to political principles associated with national self-determination. Making an international liberal order or "world environment hospitable to U.S. interests and values" was what preponderance allowed.[149]

There has been much material to mine in Leffler's work over the last decade, most of which has gone into the making of his massive study.[150] However, I have reasons for not viewing the period through the lens of national security, reasons that illuminate my differences with postrevisionism. To start, the overlay between national security and my own definition of security is far from perfect. Security for Leffler is ultimately about the security of the state and the society contained within it. I find this too confining. The reason I defined security in terms of threats to modes of configuring social existence is exactly to leave open the possibility that the entity which is to be secured (i.e., the social existence) can be an international order and the various states, societies, and actors caught up in it. In Leffler's construct, such a configuration is a subject of security only to the extent that it forms a part of the security of U.S. core values. He must, in effect, nationalize it.

Thus, Leffler is put in the odd position of viewing external phenomena such as political economic instability in the U.S.'s external realm only as national security issues (i.e., in terms of the U.S. need to stabilize its environment in a mode that would be to its liking). While this was consistent with the way many U.S. policymakers expressed things in policy papers, it only tells us part of the significance of such developments. The question that I would put to Leffler is why a national security perspective so broadly conceived along social, political, and economic lines, had so much salience for policymakers. While Leffler magisterially shows "how core values emerge in the policymaking process,"[151] and what the elaborate schemes for securing these values were, he does not show why it is these values that are in need of being secured. To say they are simply a reflection of U.S. identity (i.e., it is liberal democratic capitalist) is to only restate the question. In order to get beyond the restatement, we need to step outside the auto-referential paradigm of national security. It is a paradigm where the stakes of U.S. agency can be only what policymakers themselves say they are (i.e., their core values defended by their security systems). These issues hark back to my comments at the beginning of the first chapter on Tony Smith's work, *America's Mission*. The question for me focuses on the position of the U.S. state and its policymakers within historical forces and contexts. Despite the great preponderance of the U.S., it was not a liberal state in and for itself. It was part of the changing fabric of liberal modernity. Illustrating this has been part of the task of my study up till to this point. A central task of the ensuing chapters is to show that the forces associated with that modernity—its order-making and historical moment—generated dynamics and structures that shaped U.S. agency, including its tendency to treat tensions and problems in the external realm as security issues in the first place.[152]

Leffler might remind me that the international system had changed so much through the war that power vacuums appeared and the Soviet Union could, despite weaknesses at the time, in the future come to fill them, rendering "Eurasia" a hostile and threatening landmass to the U.S.[153] The way out would be to secure these regions and put in place systems that were consistent with U.S. core—liberal, democratic, capitalist—values. This formulation is quite consistent with Waltz's. I do not dispute the formidable evidence Leffler marshals to show that its logic came to dominate the way many presidential policymakers came to view the world. But it is not the whole story.[154] That is, the formulation holds only if we keep our view trained on the making of security and power such that the making of order appears to be function of the former. That is why I am so drawn to the corporatists, who train their view on order-making per se. The fate of Eurasia mattered, and has significance and forms part of the fate of the U.S. exactly because there is an engagement in order-making in the first place. This is, as I have argued above, what the Second World War itself became. To see it otherwise puts us in the uncomfortable position of claiming it matters only because policymakers say it matters. That is problematic, as my discussion of agency above shows.

Ultimately, the difference between Leffler's analysis and my own is that he is focusing on the making of power regarding its extent, its purposes, and its ramifications for the character of agency within the U.S. state and outcomes abroad. I, of course, take that focus seriously, and see much to exploit in it for my own interpretation. But, in the end, I am coming at the period from the opposite side. I focus on the making of order and the role of power therein; and on how making liberal order shaped not just power but the international system.

There are other historians, like Bruce Cumings, who do not easily fit into one school or another, but who have influenced my own view considerably. In general, I believe that much of diplomatic history, although it has often been telling other stories, offers crucial insights and knowledge about the story of making liberal order and its relation to the emergence of a militarized Cold War. I have drawn liberally from that body of insights and knowledge in order to help tell that story, a task to which I now return.

This chapter has brought into view the range of concepts and attitudes which together make up the intellectual and historical starting point from which further analysis can proceed. The understandings of the liberal moment, the external state, hegemony, security, and militarization developed in this chapter will enter explicitly or underlie implicitly the discussion of the rise of the Cold War and the militarization of the West that follows. The complexity of this starting point for analysis should make clear to readers that this study does not rest on or advance a single proposition about the impact of liberal order-making. Rather, what is being argued for is the consideration of an analytical perspective that is complex, variegated and, it is hoped, useful for asking questions about postwar international life.

3

✸

An Enemy Is Better Than a Friend

As World War II came to a close in 1945, the major tasks of order-building would still lie ahead. Of course, plenty of order-building had taken place during the war. Besides the crucial agreements and institutions carved out at Bretton Woods, the foundations for the establishment of the United Nations organization were laid in the summer of 1944 at Dumbarton Oaks in Washington, D.C. In the U.S. state center, extensive bureaucratic machinery was set up, under the aegis of the Department of State, for planning postwar political structures, territorial settlements, demilitarization, and "trade and financial relations."[1] This effort was to a great extent stimulated by the activities of the Council on Foreign Relations. The Council, which comprised business leaders, journalists, academics, and top State Department officials, commissioned as early as 1939 a large-scale study on the potential shape, stakes, and issues of the postwar world.[2] It was in the Council and the U.S. state wartime planning committees that many of the details of the plans for the U.N., Bretton Woods, and even the notorious Morgenthau Plan to deindustrialize Germany were worked out.

Planners and political leaders were in no position to anticipate how much order-building needed to be done after the end of the war. Few actually thought that, by constructing a United Nations organization and institutions such as the IMF, their order-building tasks were finished. Under Secretary Joseph C. Grew pointed out, in his contribution to the State Department campaign toward the end of the war to "sell" the idea of the U.N., that: "There is one mistake we must avoid at all costs . . . and that is the mistake of thinking that the machinery itself will solve our problems. . . . The way of international cooperation is hard; the process painful and grueling."[3]

Nonetheless, most policymakers assumed that the UN did provide a basic institutional arena for cooperation among the allies, if not all nations that generally abided by international law, in the tasks of making a postwar order. Its two-tiered structure would allow for the type of concentration of agency in the Security Council that the univeralistic General Assembly, reminiscent of the failed League of Nations, could not. The possibility of the UN engendering both dimensions of order-making—arenas and concentrations of agency—was expressed starkly, for instance, in the differences between chapters six and seven of the UN Charter regarding conflict and aggression. In chapter six, parties to a dispute come to the UN to "seek a solution by negotiation, enquiry, mediation," and so on.[4] In chapter seven, the Security Council takes it upon itself to identify threats to peace and to act accordingly with measures such as blockades or the deployment of military force.

In principle, the UN Charter and the associated organs such as the IMF represented a complex set of mechanisms for addressing the issues of order-making articulated in statements such as the Atlantic Charter that were so clearly the expressions of a liberal moment in history (emphasizing, for example, self-determination and material and social well-being). These efforts were also informed by the security doctrines of the liberal tradition, such as collective security.[5] But U.S. planners and political leaders did not think that there would be no liberal order-building activities going on outside the context of the UN. Indeed, the UN Charter, in chapter eight, made ample room for "regional arrangements" for the provision of security (an allowance exploited in the making of NATO). More generally, as Grew's statement makes clear, leading planners understood that the UN did not in itself accomplish the orchestration and construction of practices and policies, and the articulation and pursuit of interests that are essential to making an order. The charter had no built-in answers for what to do with Germany, Japan, colonies, or the faltering economies of Europe.

We now take it for granted that the tensions generated by these tasks overwhelmed a still fragile UN that might otherwise have served ably as an arena of cooperation or agent of collective security and agreement. Although there were skeptical voices during the war, by 1946 Hans Morgenthau could comfortably declare that "[w]hat was true of the League of Nations has already proved to be true of the United Nations."[6] The UN, Morgenthau believed, could not face the basic "political issues" that led to conflict in places such as Greece. Writing in the same year, E.B. White was even more hyperbolic: "The preparations made at San Francisco for a security league of sovereign nations to prevent aggression now seem like the preparation some little girls might make for a lawn party as a thunderhead gathers beyond the garden gate. The lemonade will be spiked by lightening."[7]

From the perspective of our own time, it should be clear that the UN simply become one of a number of arenas and agencies involved in the making of postwar order. For instance, it is difficult to deny the central role the UN has played as a site for the production of international norms, especially in the domain of self-determination and human rights.

But if we focus on the incapacities of the UN as an arena and an agent we risk missing another related point about its role in the making of an international order. U.S. policymakers intended that the Soviet Union would find its place in that order as a reasonably productive member of the Security Council, as an enforcer of global peace, and as a signee to the necessary postwar political settlements. Even as late as September 1946, presidential counsel Clark Clifford could still write, in a hardline report to the president:

> The primary objective of United States policy toward the Soviet Union is to convince Soviet leaders that it is in their interest to participate in a system of world cooperation, that there are no fundamental causes for war between our two nations, and that the security and prosperity of the Soviet Union, and that of the rest of the world as well, is being jeopardized by the aggressive militaristic imperialism such as that in which the Soviet Union is now engaged.[8]

Whether or not the Soviet Union had any desire to fulfill the various roles engendered for it by the liberal order-making process, it is obvious that they were willing to become an active member of the Security Council, to enter into negotiations, and to sign agreements with the West. The Soviet Union may well have viewed these activities as instrumental to their security and the strengthening of socialism in their country and around the world. But the point is that they were pursuing these interests through an order-building process that was a project of the West. They were hardly engaging the U.S. and Western Europe in a socialist order-building process, however much they might have wanted to.

In this chapter, I intend to show how the effort to make a liberal order (Clifford's "system of world cooperation") inclusive of the Soviet Union generated tensions that led to the confrontation that became the Cold War. Some of those tensions were directly related to the attempt to include the Soviet Union. Others were tied to the general political dynamics of liberal order-making itself.

Constructing a Liberal Order

In my discussions of liberal order so far, I have paid little attention to how liberal order is pursued. Therefore, let us now examine what is entailed in actually building an international liberal order. At its most basic level, the construction process of any type of social order involves defining boundaries regarding: a) what elements of social life will be ordered; b) how those elements will be ordered; and c) who will be involved in the ordering. These tasks can never be completed definitively by order-makers. All they can do is set out provisional parameters and craft policies addressing certain aspects of boundary-making. Moreover, a stasis would have to be assumed to think they could be completed definitively. These tasks are rather the basic problems of order-making. The contests over them are what render order-making political. In effect, order is never finally achieved, it is only pursued. It is never an outcome, it is only a process.

What makes it possible to generalize about constructing social order in this way is the compelling analogy between order in the domestic and international spheres.[9] Like international order, the ordering of a domestic realm is likely to occur in the context of significant change: e.g., postwar, postcolonization, and post-revolution. Where international order is distinguishable as an ordering of relations between different states and societies, domestic order analogously involves the ordering of the different geographical or political elements that populate a given state and society. And while in a domestic order we might expect to see the organization of a far wider range of social and political relations than in an international order, this type of ordering can occur at the international level. The most obvious example of it is the ordering of international economic relations.

Parallels between domestic and international order are possible because underlying both notions is the assumption that there exists a common political and social fabric greater than any of the units it comprises. Such a fabric need not just be a field or system of interaction between units, as Kenneth Waltz understands the international system to be. A social fabric can create—and, in turn, be formed by—common interests, identities, and a web of social, political, and economic relations. The obvious designation for this web is a "society." It, of course, has been the central object of analysis for the mostly domestic-focused field of sociology. In the field of international relations, Hedley Bull became famous for his concern with the societal dimensions of international life. For him "an international society exists when a group of states, conscious of certain common interests and values, form a society in the sense that they conceive themselves to be bound by a common set of rules in their relations with one another, and share in the working of common institutions."[10] "Societizing" our conception of international relations has the attractive advantage of emphasizing the normative and historical dimensions of order between states.

However, for a phenomenon such as international liberal order, as it has been considered here, we ought to be suspicious of the use of the term society to ground our thinking. The term "society" brings with it the implication of an identifiable and extant social fabric that is potentially ready to be ordered and that does not apply to international life. Bull gets around this problem by focusing on the society that forms among states suggesting a limited number of actors and range of (interstate) relations. But as I indicated in chapter 1, liberal order lies somewhere between Bull's notions of international (i.e., between states and societies) and world order (i.e., the totality of human interactions encompassing multiple societies). Liberal order is, therefore, conceptually far messier than Bull's more circumscribed order of a society of states.

This messiness also suggests an important difference between international (liberal) order and the ordering of a society. The central term of that difference is the central term of order-making more generally, the question of boundaries. Of course, geographic boundaries, for instance, are rarely definitively settled for a state and society that is being ordered in the aftermath of war or revolution within its territory. But there are far more discernible limits in comparison to the international realm, which is in part defined exactly by the crossing of boundaries. Boundary markers, such as cultural identities, for determining which and how units are to be brought into the project of order-making are far less automatic in the international realm. Those markers that do exist (e.g. the historic relationship between Europe and the U.S.), are likely to be thinner than domestic markers or more politically problematic (e.g., the historic colonial relationships between Europe and the Third World).

When it comes to the question of which elements of social life are subject to order, boundaries are also far more open in the international than in the domestic sphere. Societies are generally ordered by states, through rather standard repertoires, which have developed over the centuries. From policing and regulating economic activity, to educating and taxing, states create domestic social order usually in predictable ways regarding what is ordered and how it is ordered.[11] In the international realm, there is far less to build on of this sort. In the 1940s, planners could look back on economic orders and international organizations (e.g., the League of Nations), but these models of order-making pale in comparison to the state-society models. Even if there were more models, it is not obvious that they would be able to help answer the crucial questions about which relations are to be ordered, how so, and for whom (across as well as within states and societies). True enough, international order builds on the ordering that occurs in domestic spheres. But the question is which and how much of these spheres are built on and drawn into the making of international order.

Identifying the what, how, and who in the making of a specifically *liberal* international order is an extremely difficult definitional task, given the complexity of liberal modernity. If, as I pointed out in chapter 1, international ordering is the orchestration and construction of political and social relations, then to a large extent the process of defining liberal order will entail three activities. Actors, institutions, and principles common to the states and societies participating in each domain of liberal modernity must be identified. Relations and principles that facilitate interstate and intersocietal transactions within and across the liberal domains must be constructed. Last, the geographic boundaries of liberal relations on a global scale must be considered. These would in the main be the terms of the what, how, and who of liberal order.

By virtue of their active pursuit of a liberal order, U.S. policymakers placed the U.S. state at the center of this definition process. The U.S. seemed to assign itself the role, as one historian put it, of "interpreter and regulator of changes in the status quo anywhere in the world,"[12] for reasons explored in the last chapter.

But even if the mechanism of a U.S. center was available for the definition of liberal relations, the task of defining the contours of the liberal
order remained formidable. Heterogeneous forms of liberal practice
across different states and societies make difficult the identification of
common actors, institutions, practices, and principles. Such identification
however was not impossible. For instance, while the British and U.S. states
differed regarding the extent to which they would intervene to adjust market outcomes in their societies, they both shared a commitment to market
principles, both domestically and internationally.[13] On the other hand,
international liberal traditions provide no map as to which institutions and
relations are most productive in the establishment of a common framework. Nor do they indicate which liberal principles should receive priority
when they clash. As we shall discuss further below, although U.S. policy
toward colonies such as Indonesia initially discounted assertions of self-
determination made by nationalist leaders—among other things because
of the recognized benefits continued colonialism provided to international
economic exchange in Western Europe—the U.S. ultimately did support
Indonesian independence.[14]

Beyond the question of priority, the very extent and nature of U.S.
intervention in other countries in the process of defining relations was
itself open to definition, rather than being an automatic outcome of liberal
order-building. Indeed, as we saw in the last chapter, this role was rather
tenuous as hegemony itself emerged only in the actual process of liberal
order-building.

The Soviet Union and the Making of Order

From the outbreak of the Cold War until its end, the Soviet Union was generally viewed in the West, relative to the United States, as a rival force. The
historian Vojtech Mastny points to a "clash of values" based on "two incom-
patible notions of world order."[15] Such a view assumes that the Soviet
Union was from the start located in some externalized space, outside of the
liberal world, attempting to inject its antithetical values and interests into
that world. In actuality, there is every indication in the very immediate postwar years that the Soviet Union was viewed as a participant in the order
being constructed, an order that in part flowed out of the international relations of the wartime Allied powers. As I pointed out above, facilitating that
participation was one of the purposes of the UN. This vision was echoed in

the sentiments of leaders such as FDR and Truman and policymakers in the State Department. One aspect of this vision was the desire to avoid spheres of influence. The State Department warned in mid-1945 in a briefing paper for the Potsdam conference: "Our primary objective should be to remove the causes which make nations feel that . . . spheres are necessary to build their security, rather than to assist one country to build up strength against another."[16] Even the early effort of hardliners such as W. Averell Harriman, U.S. ambassador to the Soviet Union, to get tough with the Soviets is best understood as an effort to discipline them for challenging the construction of order in which they too were involved.

It was in regard to the difficult tasks of the definition process, i.e., the setting of boundaries of liberal international relations, that the Soviet Union emerged as particularly salient in the building of liberal order. More specifically, the Soviet Union was especially relevant to the demarcation of a geopolitical region in which the liberal order would operate.[17] But it was also crucial for locating, on a nongeographical plane, the scope, range, and character of common relations—be they socialist, laissez-faire, or statist— that would be included inside the domains of the international liberal order.

In this formulation, the Soviet Union is best understood to have been an international force that could alter definitions of liberal relations from a position within the liberal world. True enough, the Soviet Union had a political system that was decidedly nonliberal. It understandably would try to push political and economic outcomes that were consistent with that system. But the point is that the pursuit of many of these outcomes beyond Soviet borders unfolded within the context of negotiations and relations directly bearing on the construction of a liberal order. Many of the contentions between the U.S. and Soviet Union took place in terms of alternative interpretations of agreements such as Yalta, or the potential agreements offered at the Council of Foreign Ministers meetings.[18] Indeed the councils were conceived by Secretary of State James Byrnes as a sort of arena for the avoidance of the spheres of influence referred to above.[19] Such avoidance can be understood, in one respect, as an attempt to keep the Soviets inside of the realm of international relations associated with the West.

For the most part, the nature of the Soviet Union's shaping of the construction of international liberalism was negative. Soviet influence over the construction process bore mostly on the question of which, and to what degree, societies would participate in liberal relations. In this respect, Soviet nonliberal values came very much into play—within the context of international liberalism. George Kennan's 1946 "Long Telegram" captured this negative force by pointing out that—through its illiberal tactics—the Soviets sought "to tear down sources of strength beyond the reach of Soviet control."[20] Communist ideology and political practice were vehicles for altering the scope and boundaries of liberal order exactly because they were perceived as having the power to distance or even cut off societies from the range of application of liberal relations. While this power may have been seen by U.S. policymakers as unstoppable in eastern Europe, it could and was met as a challenge in countries such as Iran, Greece, and Germany.[21] The point is that it was not Communist ideology per se but the Soviet use of such ideology to change relations and political outcomes in a given country that constituted the character of the Soviet challenge to liberal order-construction.[22] It was, for example, the basis for the advancement of an alternative concept of social relations that generated tensions over Germany, at least as early as the 1945 Potsdam conference.[23] Thus, Soviet power mattered exactly because it could impact negatively on liberal order-building.

The notion that the Soviet Union could affect, from 1945 on, the construction process of international liberalism is not in itself a sufficient condition for the rise of the Cold War. After all, France and Britain both deeply affected this process as well.[24] What was different about the Soviet Union was its capacity to affect the definition process to a far greater degree than other leading states based both on its ideology and its sheer power, manifested most clearly in the Red Army's occupation of east and central Europe. This difference was decisive in the context of a set of liberal relations which, as we shall see, could not easily be bent to accommodate the interests of the Soviet Union inside the parameters of the emerging liberal order.

It may seem strange that the West attempted to incorporate a state organized in such an illiberal form into a liberal order. But as global economic relations were being constructed, the Soviet Union found ample room to attempt to advance its economic interests within the domain of international economic exchange. The Soviet Union was often a willing trading partner with the West and sought a substantial loan ($6 billion) from the U.S. at the end of the war. Although it failed to ratify the Bretton Woods agreements, it came to the bargaining table to negotiate over the terms of U.S. Marshall Plan aid.

Perhaps even more relevant was the domain of self-determination. It was universally understood that the Soviet Union had a legitimate fear of a revived Germany which could once again threaten the Soviet Union on its western borders. As far back as the 1941 Atlantic Charter, the link was made between the right of a self-determining people to set the terms of its existence and the security of that people within the given borders of that existence. The charter stated that in a world of self-determining peoples, the signees "hope to see established a peace which will afford all nations the means of dwelling in safety within their own boundaries."[25] The UN Charter reinforced the notion that a state and its people could find security in the emerging international order either through prevention, self-protection, or collective action. Article 51 was clear about the right of a state to protect its people from any aggression against it through "self-defense."[26] The Soviets repeatedly justified their intervention in Poland in terms of their own right to security.[27] The emerging normative discourse allowed the Soviet Union to make claims that could only reinforce the likelihood that the U.S. would take them seriously, no matter how much the U.S. objected to the Soviet intervention in the political life of Poland. In other words, the connection between security and self-determination established in the postwar period gave the Soviets new grounds and legitimacy for their security claims.

These links have generally been overlooked by historians of the period. John Gaddis has rightly pointed to the tension in U.S. policy between its desire to support Polish self-determination and its inclination, often reluctant, to recognize Soviet security needs.[28] What Gaddis does not consider is the way that both the fate of Poland and the security interests of the Soviet Union were instances of the same intersection of self-determination and security. The Polish people were attempting to secure a social existence on their own terms. The Soviet interference was a threat to that process. A few short years back, the Soviet Union itself had been invaded and occupied by Nazi Germany, suffering a fate that, in principle, was not so different from Poland under the Soviets. Whether or not they only sought to dominate Poland, Soviet leaders were able legitimately to claim that securing themselves against a repeat of that outcome was a matter of self-protection.

The choice the U.S. faced in the end was between the security of Poland and the security of the Soviet Union in the context of constructing a liberal order. What seemed in part to be at stake in Poland was a chance to facilitate the establishment of a liberal democracy. However, there was no intrinsic reason why that possibility should have taken precedence over Soviet security claims and their bearing on the wider political dynamics of order-making within which the fate of Germany and other countries deemed more important then Poland was at stake. It was the attempt to accommodate the

Soviet Union in that order that sealed Poland's fate. Soviet leaders would have to give up their efforts to bind Poland politically to them or U.S. policymakers would have to give up on the fight to protect it. The U.S. did exactly that in June 1945, when it settled for a mildly reorganized Polish government that incorporated some politicians sympathetic to the West.

The problem in all of this is that for a liberal order to work, the interests that emerge in the context of order-building and the historical moment more generally must be successfully incorporated into the framework of liberal relations. This must be done without undermining the definition process of order-making itself. Otherwise, the project of liberal order-construction might be severely hampered. If an incorporation is not possible, then such interests must be altered to allow for such an incorporation. In itself, the Soviet domination of eastern Europe did not undermine order-building. But the recognition of Soviet claims regarding its security needs in the eastern Mediterranean or Germany would have upset the U.S. effort to rebuild a liberal international economy, which depended on Western access to resources such as oil and the productive potential of Germany.

The comparison with the accommodation of Britain and France is telling. Although both Britain and France made claims that were perceived by the U.S. as threats to international exchange, especially in their reluctance to surrender imperial preferences, these claims could be accommodated and adjusted through compromises that were based on the dependence of these countries on U.S. economic power. Important agreements such as Bretton Woods rested on this type of accommodation and adjustment. Without this leverage over the Soviet Union the same sort of outcome was unlikely. As a result, the ability of the U.S. and the West in general to accommodate the even more far reaching Soviet pressures on liberal relations through negotiation and compromise was far less elastic than it was for other states.

But one might ask whether the pursuit by the U.S. and the West of something other than a *liberal* order would have made the Soviet Union more incorporable? This is a very complex counterfactual. It is of limited value, however, because a whole chain of commitments, engagements, and conditions are associated with the construction of liberal order (e.g., the long-term fate of Germany, the economic health of Western Europe, and the broad shifts associated with the liberal moment). Indeed, such a counterfactual is rather absurd since the construction of liberal order did not rest on only one or two factors such as liberal democratic regime-type.[29]

Instead, it involved a wide range of factors associated with particular ways of being modern. But we can imagine a far more circumscribed order being established, where outcomes and processes in Europe and elsewhere have far less salience for the U.S. In such an order, the U.S. would chiefly be interested in guaranteeing its territorial security. Indeed, just ten years earlier, the U.S. maintained a rather isolationist posture to do exactly that, despite outcomes in Europe that were unattractive to many of its leaders. In this circumscribed, imaginary order, it would likely be recognized that the Soviet Union could legitimately pursue its own territorial security. Given its economic and military weakness in the aftermath of world war, the Soviet Union would have quite a difficult time dominating all of Europe and Asia. Moreover, such an order might even resemble the nineteenth-century Concert order, where, in the longer term, the U.S. could take on the role of Britain as a balancer on the European continent, helping to prevent any undue dominance of Europe by the Soviet Union. Thus, just as a Russian empire was accommodated in that far more circumscribed nineteenth-century order, the Soviet Union would conceivably have been accommodated in a parallel twentieth-century Concert order. What happened in Germany, Poland, and Southeast Asia would have been far less salient for a U.S. that also had the perceived luxury of being the sole possessor of nuclear weapons.

The Liberal Uniaxis

Post-World War II order was far more complex than any nineteenth-century Concert order-maker in Europe could have ever dreamed.[30] Quite simply, there was a great deal more of political and social life being ordered on an international basis in the twentieth century. The making of order would understandably be a far more complex and intricate enterprise. Whatever the degree of complexity, it is requisite that the units involved develop some kind of common engagement vis-à-vis the project of order-making. In the nineteenth century, the Concert of Europe drew states into a common effort to avoid destabilizing wars through principles such as the balance of power. Although the chief states (or "great powers") involved often had different interests and competing visions of the specific outcomes to be pursued through the Concert, they shared a sense of obligation to one another regarding the mechanisms (e.g., treaties and diplomatic consultation) for the mediation of foreign policies to avoid war. There were remarkably few times this obligation broke down across the century.

The ordering of social and economic relations (e.g., in the area of trade and communications) through different international institutions increased as the nineteenth century came to a close. This ordering of relations grew in the first half of the twentieth century as well. By the 1930s, there were dozens of institutions dedicated to the governance of international quotidian intercourse.[31] Thus, in the making of post-World War II international order, planners could rely on the international organizational reservoir that had been built up across the previous seventy odd years in areas such as international postal service. But they obviously could not rely on the common engagement inherent in this reservoir to settle, in the course of a very compressed moment, the broad range of controversial political, economic, and social issues they faced. That would certainly be a case of the tail wagging the dog. Indeed, the many contentions over order-making that marked the period transcended the inherited hum of international quotidian governance. Something more than the institutional legacy of quotidian governance was necessary to produce a common engagement regarding the controversial issues of the period. At stake was the determination of the boundaries and political and economic character of states, societies, and international organizations ordering large segments of international economic and political life.

Intuition may suggest that the necessary intersubjective fabric was supplied by the existence of community among the policymakers and elites of participating states and societies. As it is typically used, community can refer to a shared existence in a delimited locale or to the more general possibility of a group holding something in common such as identity, interests, or institutions.

In principle, an international community in this latter sense could engender a degree of mutual obligation necessary for a common engagement in liberal order-building.[32] Policymakers especially in the U.S. and Britain did sometimes use the term "world community" to refer to the assemblage of states in the international realm. This was a rather unreflexive understanding of international community. It generally implied an international public sphere of states under obligation to one another to respect the norms and rules of the international system associated with diplomatic relations and peaceful coexistence. This sense of world community is equivalent to Bull's understanding of international society. It refers to the general operation of the state system. Unfortunately, this type of world community, or international society, is insufficient as an intersubjective basis for the construction of liberal order. There are no obligations for generating a common engagement that is specific to the building of liberal order rather than something else.

This understanding, however, does not exhaust the possibilities of international community.[33] Most relevant to the current discussion is the notion of a "pluralistic security community" made famous by Karl Deutsch. In such a community, states as members manage conflict without resorting to war and yet remain sovereign polities. Deutsch points to numerous interrelated factors constituting such a community including: identity "in terms of self-images and interests;" common values; mutual predictability and responsiveness; reiterative communication; the capacity of members to learn about one another; and finally a general sense of community or "we-feeling."[34] It is possible to conceive of some of these same factors applying to a community associated with liberal order-making rather than just "peaceful change." Deutsch, in fact, treated elements of liberal modernity—particularly democratic governance and a commitment to market economies—as core elements of the common values of the North Atlantic community he studied.[35]

But the assumption that a Deutschian community constituted the basis for a common engagement in liberal order-building is deeply problematic for one simple reason. His communities have the benefit of an extended span of time. Predictability, learning, and "we-feelings" are the result of interactive processes that can unfold across many years. More generally, his understanding of political community rests on the existence of mechanisms for enforcement and institutions facilitating interaction, the formation of which in the 1940s is at issue here. Time in the liberal moment was generally very compressed. Compression of this sort stemmed not only from the limited timespan, but also the intensity of change and disruption. Deutsch himself never directly dealt with this problem. His focus was on the emergence of community across the decade from the 1940s to the 1950s. But on his behalf, one might argue that there was the longer term interaction between states especially in the North Atlantic area across the first half of the twentieth century. If we disregard the important point that in the making of liberal order more than this limited—albeit crucial—region of states was involved, there is still an additional problem with treating the pre-World War II period as background to the emergence of postwar community. Many of the states in this region were not even democracies (e.g., Germany, Italy, Austria). And the economic climate of the 1930s hardly lent itself to the generation of "we-feelings," as states imposed beggar-thy-neighbor policies through restrictive tariffs and relatively hostile currency devaluations.

Alternatively, one may argue that the mid- to late-1940s was a period of "nascent community" formation.[36] In this case, the process of community formation itself would engender the common engagement for liberal order building. Developing this concept, Emmanuel Adler and Michael Barnett point to potential "trigger mechanisms"—such as war—that precipitate shifts in material power, the rise of new approaches to order, or great power leadership in making common purpose. The problem with this formulation in the context of the 1940s is that it presupposes as conditions of community emergence the very phenomena that community or its nascent formation might itself be employed to explain (i.e., order-making, hegemony, or responses to shifts in power). Moreover, liberal order-building began with the war itself. A post-bellum community triggered by the war could not generate the common engagement necessary for this wartime order-building.

Looking to community to find the basis for a common engagement is really a matter of putting the cart before the horse. My approach to this issue is different. In principle, I would argue that before any community can exist around the construction of order, agents must confront this construction as a viable *project* through which the possibilities of political and social order in the future would be defined. While agents—who should never be thought of as abstractions—carry a history of identities, roles, and relationships, these can be seen as shaping the terms of engagement with a project such as liberal order-building. That engagement and history might, in turn, constitute the basis for a community.

In practical terms, we saw in the last chapter that, early on in the making of order, there was explicit attention to articulating that a project of liberal order-making per se existed. When policymakers at that initial stage spoke of a "common interest" in a future, they meant that there should exist a common engagement in shaping a future, rather than a common interest in the specific terms of that future since this question was barely on the table. States would share this task or project in a way similar to a group of workers sharing a project. Cordell Hull made that clear when he stated in 1943 that:

At the end of the war, each of the United Nations and each of the nations associated with them will have the same common interest in national security, in world order under law, in peace, in the full promotion of the political, economic, and social welfare of the their respective peoples—in the principles and spirit of the Atlantic Charter and the Declaration by United Nations. The future of these indispensable common interests depends absolutely upon international cooperation. Hence, each nation's own primary interests requires it to cooperate with the others.[37]

Hull was asking policymakers and democratic publics to view their postwar fates in terms of the making of order along the lines he describes. In other words, in contrast to the ruptures and chaos of war and depression, there existed the project of making order, setting the possibilities of an international future. When Dean Acheson was asked in a public interview in 1945 how the Bretton Woods agreements could help the "disorganized and shattered world to function," he answered that the agreements would "point the way out of chaos and economic warfare toward a new system based on cooperative action."[38] That "pointing of the way" was the articulation of common terms for the future opportunities of those participating in—or affected by—the agreements.

In general, states are drawn up into the project of liberal order-building through phenomena such as conferences, treaties, agreements, institution-building, diplomatic relations, economic aid, and even military occupation. Through these phenomena states gain a common orientation toward the range of tasks engendered by order-making. States, in effect, would come into alignment not over the terms of order (a deeply contested set of issues), but over the notion that states were mutually engaged in the setting of those terms (i.e., making order).

Some readers might think that it is wrongheaded to represent states as possessing in common the project of liberal order-construction. They might be tempted to see the project of liberal order-making as something that the U.S. undertook as an "American" project to remake the world. This temptation ought to be resisted. Toward the end of the previous chapter, I argued that it is a mistake to view the making of liberal order per se as a U.S. possession. Likewise, I would argue that, although the existence of the project depended centrally on its articulation by U.S. policymakers, its existence as a project became meaningful only to the extent that the project was recognized and engaged in on an international basis. In the general air of the time, from Bretton Woods to Dumbarton Oaks, few policymakers from Keynes to Nehru could avoid being drawn into the project of liberal order-building. As the *Economist* had put it in 1942, regarding U.S. economic policy: "Let there be no mistake about it. The policy put forward by the American Administration is revolutionary. It is a genuinely new conception of world order."[39]

It may seem somewhat contradictory to claim that the U.S. could be the central articulator of a project that was ultimately held in common. But as the editors of the *Economist* understood, the project presented possibilities that would engage states in the effort to define the terms of international liberal order and their existence within it. In western Europe states were willing to turn to the economic and military power of the U.S. state in order to facilitate the well-being of their own liberal modern existences. In so doing, they retained their own capacity to affect the liberal definition process through foreign policy initiatives and diplomacy. In this respect, "the empire" of U.S. power in Europe that would be made "by invitation"[40] would be decidedly liberal in both its structure and the substance of its relations.

Outside of Europe, states and societies found themselves drawn up in the project of liberal order-building as well. They also tried to facilitate their own welfare in the context of that project. Whereas Europe and especially the U.S. could endeavor to set the terms for the global operation of liberal order, the rest of the world typically struggled over the terms of their existence within the boundaries of their own states and societies or regions, in reaction to the global deployment of order-making.

States forming what can be labeled a core in the making of liberal order might be thought of as being positioned along a single axis, or "uniaxis," representing the common engagement engendered by the project of liberal order-building. The U.S. is at the center and nonliberal states participating in—or simply drawn up into—liberal relations are at the extremes. Along this uniaxis each state and society shapes the making of order to a varying degree, from the local to the global.

In contrast, in a unilateral world, agency emerges from a single point or source. Waltz describes a post-World War II world where relations are essentially unilateral in that the only states that really matter in configuring the structure of the international system are the U.S. and the Soviet Union.[41]

The plurality of the liberal uniaxis was manifested in the significant European contributions to the U.S.-run European Recovery Program (ERP), and in the more exclusively European endeavors within the framework of liberal relations, such as the European Coal and Steel Community.[42] It ultimately was manifested in the European initiatives to form NATO. The U.S. might then be conceived as occupying a "fulcrum" position at, as NSC-

68 expressed it, "the center of power of the free world."[43] Such an image is meant to convey both the leverage the U.S. had in defining and setting the terms of liberal relations, and the fact that its position and the character of the liberal order more generally could be moved by other forces or weights on the axis.

Making an Order Is Making an Other

However much definitions are contested in a pluralistic environment, the definition process and the elements of order-making—its arenas and concentrations of agency—must be taken as legitimate. This closely resembles a rather longstanding requirement of liberal governance: that however much a people may bicker over versions of the good life, they need at the end of the day to accept as authoritative the very constitution that makes this contestation possible. John Rawls has put this question at the center of his recent work by asking: "How is it possible that deeply opposed though reasonable comprehensive doctrines may live together and all affirm the political conception of a constitutional regime?"[44] For Rawls unreasonable persons are those who: "Plan to engage in cooperation schemes but are unwilling to honor, or even to propose, except as a necessary public pretense, any general principles or standards for specifying fair terms of cooperation. They are ready to violate such terms as suits their interests when circumstances allow."[45]

What is missing from Rawls's formulation is the assumption that while anyone may choose to be "unreasonable," the only agents that really count are those with the capability of actually disrupting cooperative schemes. What cannot be accommodated in this type of structure is a force such as the Soviet Union, which could challenge the definition process necessary for making order.[46] Such a challenge would undermine a definitional process that is especially difficult exactly because the order under construction is liberal.

This difficulty does not stem simply from the plurality of agents involved. Any modern international order is likely to face a plurality of independent states. What makes the construction of liberal order especially problematic is the context of that plurality. As argued above, a complex set of political, strategic, economic, and social relations must be defined and established in the same relative time frame. Orders such as the one established formally at Westphalia involved a much more limited range of factors, state sovereignty being for us the most salient. Moreover, in the context of this complexity and range of relations the fact that international liberalism has no automatic definitions of specific relations contributes further to the fragility of order-making. Thus, given the scope of the liberal project, it is vulnerable to challenges to its definitional process such as those presented by the Soviet Union.[47]

Although at the end of the war the Soviet Union may initially have had a place on the uniaxis as a powerful agent among nonliberal participants, as the decade progressed this possibility was increasingly closed off. Indeed, the tensions associated with Soviet participation in liberal relations found ample expression in U.S. foreign policymaking. Even as early as 1945, President Truman had articulated the possibility of a Soviet Union that would become increasingly separated from the liberal world. In his notorious dressing down of Molotov, Truman warned the foreign minister that the Soviets must "either approach closely our express policy in regard to Poland or drop out of the Associated Nations."[48]

As a debate within the U.S. administration was waged over whether or not to cooperate with the Soviet Union in achieving a political settlement of some sort in Europe, the political stakes of incorporating the Soviet Union became increasingly pronounced. More specifically, in a view associated with George Kennan, which received growing support among U.S. policymakers in 1946 and 1947, it was held that a negotiated settlement with the Soviets of key political problems—such as Germany—was not possible. What is important to note is that Kennan's alternative to a negotiated settlement with the Soviets was not simply a "unilateral approach to postwar Germany" as some historians have described it in an attempt to capture the fact that the Soviets would be cut off from Western settlement efforts.[49] Rather, Kennan's alternative was the dovetailing of German economic and political recovery into a revitalized Western Europe, with which the U.S. could "coordinate" its policy.[50] This coordination clearly was realized in one of the pillars of liberal order-construction, the European Recovery Program.[51] Thus, Kennan's approach encapsulated the three key elements of the liberal uniaxis: (i) the plurality of agency in the context of complex relations; (ii) the emergence of a center; and (iii) the existence of forces capable of disrupting the definition process.[52]

Any potential for the Soviet Union to continue participating in liberal order-construction was quickly fading by 1947, when the division of Germany began to take on the appearance of a *fait accompli*. In such a division the Soviets had in effect defined the eastern half of Germany out of the

reach of the international liberal order, and an increasingly tangible boundary was set up between East and West.[53] It would be inaccurate to imply that
the Soviet Union's increasing separation from the liberal uniaxis was based
on any single diplomatic development. The successive failures of the
Council of Foreign Ministers meetings, the suspension of German repara-
tion payments, the Berlin Blockade, and the Soviet rejection of participation
in the Marshall Plan are all part of a growing separation of the Soviet Union
from the realm of liberal relations. Soviet separation would become especially pronounced by mid-1948, with the formal declaration of an independent West German state.[54]

In sum, while we know that nonliberal states such as authoritarian
regimes in Latin America can be incorporated within the liberal order, a
state capable of disrupting the definition process and challenging the broad
contours of liberal relations is unlikely to be housed within that order. Thus,
the increasing distance between the East and the West emerged not just
because the Soviet Union challenged liberal practices in Europe, but also
because this challenge could not be incorporated within the emerging liberal
order itself. As I emphasized earlier, whereas both Britain and France had
the capacity to shape negotiations and affect the course of liberal relations,
only the Soviet Union had the capacity to disrupt the process itself without
being subject to effective discipline. As an occupying force at the end of the
war, it had the power to make claims especially regarding its security, which,
in the negotiations over the fate of Germany for example, threatened to
undermine the very possibility of liberal order-construction.

The Soviet Threat

In the previous chapter I tried to touch on the links between modernity, as
it is conceived of here, and security. As the possibilities of organized
agency are thrown open in modernity, so are the trepidations of profound
insecurity. Organized agency not only can serve one in the development of
projects, but can also make possible the challenges to those projects by the
agency of others. Moreover, in modernity, one's own projects are ever
subject to remaking and revision, to say nothing of the risks of facing historical moments of openness and flux.[55] John Stuart Mill raised the value
of security above all else when he argued: "Our notion, therefore, of the
claim we have on our fellow creatures to join in making safe for us the *very
groundwork of our existence*, gathers feelings around it so much more

intense than those concerned in any of the more common cases of utility.
. . . [italics mine]"[56]

For decades, the term "Soviet threat" was used to depict the perception
among Western policymakers that the USSR was a political and military
menace to the free world. Such perception has typically been understood as
emerging along a single trajectory of development, in which the sense of
threat becomes more intense as the Soviets became more hostile to the West,
ultimately developing into a full-blown fear of potential war and military
attack. The fear for many policymakers was not about physical safety, but
emerging ordered life in the West. Thus, the Soviets could be represented as
the grand "other" of a Western-centric order.[57] Ernest Bevin, British foreign secretary, in a memorandum to the British Cabinet in 1948 entitled
"The Threat to Western Civilization," feared the possible domination of
Eurasia by the Soviet Union, "leading either to the establishment of a World
Dictatorship or (more probably) to the collapse of *organized society over
great stretches of the globe*. [italics mine]"[58] He was not very specific about
what "organized society" meant, but it is likely that the liberal West, the
newly independent states in the Third World friendly to the West, and the
persevering European colonial administrations were central. However, to
take this type of formulation as a summary view of the relationship between
the West and the Soviet Union is to treat Soviet pressures on the states and
societies defined within liberal order in a monolithic fashion, mimicking the
constructions of Secretary of State John Foster Dulles and others in the
1950s. It simply does not go far enough in distinguishing between the different contexts and varying character of pressures at play between 1945 and
1950.[59] The pressures that emerged from a Soviet Union with which cooperation was still possible—despite their capacity to cast a negative influence
on liberal order-building—should be distinguished from the pressures that
emerged from a Soviet Union that had become separated from the liberal
uniaxis. With this distinction, we can fix more clearly what kinds of pressures the Soviet Union exerted on the process of liberal order-construction
and how that state came to be viewed as a threat.

First, despite a growing sense of pressure being placed on the liberal definition process in the very immediate postwar years before the Soviet Union
became separated, it was far from automatic that the Soviet Union was seen
as a threat in either political or military terms. I emphasized this point in the
previous chapter, in my discussion of realism. It is important enough to bear
repeating. It was only in 1946 that the Soviet Union began to emerge more

clearly in military plans as a potential "enemy."[60] The strong impact of Kennan's "Long Telegram" and "Mr. X" article shows that the Soviet Union was hardly taken for granted as a threat by the administration even in 1946. As late as the first half of 1947 there was little evidence of a decidedly anti-Soviet stance in U.S. policy in Germany.[61] In addition, many historians of the period have taken pains to show there was never a serious sense of threat regarding war with the Soviets until the Korean War, a point that Kennan had repeatedly made at the time.[62]

Of course, there was an increasingly U.S. "hard-line" taken regarding Soviet action by as early as 1946. But it is significant that the hard-line was first directed at an international political pressure that could alter liberal relations in undesirable ways. Only by 1947–48 was the hard-line directed at a force coming from outside the liberal world that was potentially destructive to its relations.[63] In wartime negotiations such as those at Yalta, as John Lewis Gaddis shows, FDR appeared to be willing to tolerate Soviet sway over the political fate of eastern Europe as long as it took a minimum of Western influence in the region into consideration and Soviet hegemony was limited to that region alone. But, as Gaddis also notes, given the capacity and sovereign will of the Soviet Union to actually extend its reach and influence beyond that point, the Truman administration faced—perhaps what FDR already began to see before he died—the stark contradiction of integrating the Soviet Union into a liberal order that the Soviets were willing and capable of seriously disrupting.[64] Thus, the hard-line approach to the Soviets grew harder as the machinery of negotiation such as the Council of Foreign Ministers broke down under the weight of that contradiction, and the Soviet Union was increasingly separated from the liberal world. It was in this context that the Soviet Union began to appear to U.S. policymakers by 1947 as a force, located increasingly outside the liberal order, bent on threatening the security of states and societies within that order.

As such a force, the Soviet Union was capable of placing two types of pressure on the liberal order. The first type was internal pressure (often labelled "subversive"), which may be conceived of as forces pulling social and political forces—or even entire societies—toward the Soviet Union. Given the U.S. administration's belief that war with the Soviet Union was unlikely in the near term, an emerging perception of a Soviet threat was more often based on concern with the internal politics of western European states and societies.[65] Influence over the communist parties in France and Italy as well as the attraction of East-West trade to western Europe were but two of a number of internal forces the Soviets were capable of exercising in western Europe even from a position that was increasingly distanced from liberal relations.[66]

The second type of pressure was diplomatic and strategic. Through diplomacy and the political use of military force, the Soviet Union attempted to push states to alter international political and strategic outcomes. These pressures were evident, for example, in the eastern Mediterranean where the Soviet state pushed Turkey regarding access to the Dardenelles and led protests in the UN over the British role in Greece.[67] The Soviets also used military force to pressure countries such as Iran in order to obtain such desired political and economic outcomes as the victory of Azerbaijanian rebels or the securing of Soviet oil rights. The political use of Soviet military force is, of course, typically associated with eastern Europe, where outright political and military dominance over a given state was obtained through occupation.

The push and pull pressures of an increasingly externalized Soviet Union constituted the basis of the U.S. perception of the Soviet Union as a threat to the security of the international liberal order. Although the U.S. had not taken an explicitly anti-Soviet stance in its German policy, by the time the U.S. began planning the European Recovery Program in the spring of 1947, both forms became themselves the basis for a new approach to the Soviet Union that reflected the emerging political dynamics of liberal order-building.[68] That approach was, of course, containment. Although I will have far more to say about containment in the next chapter, a few points are in order in the context of the current discussion.

On a general level, containment can be defined as a strategy "to prevent the Soviet Union from using the power and position it won as a result of . . . [World War II] to reshape the postwar international order."[69] The Truman Doctrine and the Marshall Plan constituted the first publicized programs of containment. But it is easy to see that the efforts of the U.S. and Western Europe to limit Soviet influence on the liberal order-construction process prior to the development of these programs were a form of containment as well.[70] Indeed, what distinguished the formal policy of containment that emerged in the late 1940s from its more informal predecessor was the way that the formal version explicitly addressed what were conceived as push and pull pressures coming from a Soviet Union positioned outside the liberal world. The West should, as Kennan expressed it in his "Mr. X" article, "confront the Russians with unalterable counter-force at every point where they show signs of encroaching upon the interests of a peaceful and stable world." One year later, in mid-1948, NSC 20/1 articulated the emerging logic of containment even more explicitly by advocating not only a reduction of Soviet power but also a transformation into a more liberal fashion of the very way the Soviet Union practiced its international relations.[71] That is, it was argued that the Soviets might be repositioned in the liberal world along its uniaxis if the nature of their foreign policy, if not their regime, could be changed. As we shall see in the following chapter containment as it was actually practiced fell short of achieving this more ambitious possibility, cascading into an increasingly confrontational posture beginning with the Truman Doctrine and moving on—in the period considered here—to NSC-68 and what is commonly referred to as separate spheres of influence in Europe.

Liberal Order and the Rise of the Cold War

So far two sets of forces have been offered to explain the rise of the East-West confrontation. First are the forces associated with the drawing of states into a liberal moment. For instance, that moment and the liberal order-construction process that emerged out of it made possible developments such as the engagement of the U.S. in the fate of Germany and Iran. Second, there are the forces, described in the sections above, associated with the attempt to integrate the Soviet Union inside that order.

Although both sets of forces may account for the rise of the East-West confrontation, they do not explain why this confrontation turned into a Cold War and why that Cold War took the particular shape that it did. Two questions remain to be answered: First, why did relations between East and West take shape as an increasingly acute confrontation that was not simply diplomatic, but also military-strategic? Second, what accounts for the widening gulf in relations between East and West, which ended in the emergence of two separate spheres of influence? To answer these questions, it is necessary to focus more specifically on relations between states along the liberal uniaxis, rather than the confrontation with the Soviet Union per se. So far, I have situated Soviet pressure as a basic force challenging the fundamental process of making order. But this perspective underplays the extent to which Soviet pressure surfaced as a factor in relations between states on the liberal uniaxis, in the tensions that those relations engendered, and in the U.S. policies designed to contend with those tensions. It is these relations, tensions, and policies that not only explain why the Cold War took the shape that it did, but also clarify why the Soviet state could not be accommodated within the liberal order and how it become increasingly separated from it.

I begin by describing some of the tensions the making of order generated. Next, I look more closely at how tensions in liberal order-building prompted policies and processes that led to the heightened confrontation that marked the emergence of a Cold War. Finally, I consider the ramifications of the Cold War for liberal order-making and our understanding of it.

Tensions in the Making of Liberal Order

Looking back across millennia, Adam Watson observes that "[t]here is in states' systems an inevitable tension between the desire for order and the desire for independence." On the one hand, "order promotes peace and prosperity." On the other hand, "order constrains the freedom of action of communities and in particular their rulers."[72] In Watson's view, the all too familiar binary opposition, order and freedom, is, in principle, a zero-sum situation. The more order that is imposed by an empire or hegemony, the less freedom is available to states, by which Watson essentially means either independence or autonomy. This proposition should be familiar to any realist who considers the capacity to be self-helping and autonomous as a basic concern of states in the international system.

Of course, states may pursue a form of order to preserve their freedom. In the nineteenth century, Lord Palmerston argued they could do so through the balance of power principle underlying the operations of the Concert of Europe: " 'Balance of power' means only this—that a number of weaker States may unite to prevent a stronger one from acquiring a power which should be dangerous to them, and which should overthrow their independence, their liberty, and their freedom of action."[73]

Palmerston is pointing to the freedom that states may gain, in concert, by avoiding hegemonic or imperial domination. This closely resembles the classic story told in Western political philosophy (especially by Hobbes and Locke) of how societies can form as individuals move out of the state of nature in order to avoid dangerous threats to their security and form societies where their freedom can be protected—however more circumscribed it is in society relative to the state of nature. Watson recognized that such voluntary systems of order can arise in the making of international societies examined by Hedley Bull, such as the European one, where the hope would be that Palmerston's balance of power would indeed work.

Even though this preservation of freedom through voluntary order moves beyond Watson's initial zero-sum binary opposition, both logics share a common sense of what is at stake in the preservation of freedom. The freedom of states that Palmerston spoke of encompasses what Isaiah Berlin identified as negative liberty, where the issue is: "What is the area within which the subject—a person or group of persons—is or should be left to do or be what he is able to do or be, without interference by other persons?"[74] But it also encompasses Berlin's sense of positive liberty, where the issue is not simply to be left alone in one's own space, but also to be capacitated as an actor that is "self-directed," and master in one's own house.[75] For realists such as Watson, if not also Palmerston, states are left to be states, sovereign externally and internally, setting the terms of their own existences as best possible and with as many degrees of freedom in the interstate system as is feasible.

This view of the relationship between freedom and order is too simplistic. In the order supplied by a Watsonian international society, states are empowered as relatively autonomous and self-directing units within the context of the international system. Although they may operate as such in other contexts (e.g. the capitalist world economy), the concept of international society per se provides no way of knowing what those contexts are, nor of discerning the relationship between them and international society. This is not the case when things are viewed from the perspective of liberal order. A liberal order, in principle, facilitates and empowers states and other agents in contexts ranging from their own societies to the capitalist world economy. In the domains of liberal modernity, the agency of states, as well as corporations, groups, and individuals becomes active in social spaces, domestic and international, that are organized—to varying degrees and in divergent ways—along liberal lines. Liberal order, therefore, helps to organize the mediums that shape social terrains (e.g., markets and democratic governance) within which it should be possible for states and other agents to act. Through liberal order, modes of existence and lines of interaction and movement are constructed. This type of freedom is not simply a matter of self-mastery (however much this is realized, for example, via self-determination or democracy). It is also a matter of constructing the very social spaces within which both negative and positive liberty can be realized.

Thus, ideally, international liberal order can be viewed as a potent way for states to organize the international relations of a complex set of actors which, besides themselves, include peoples, corporations, and international organizations. In the space that it opens up, actors are invested with a greater capacity to determine the character of their social existence and practices than would otherwise be possible without the operation of international liberal principles, practices, and institutions.[76] One need only think, counterfactually, of an epoch marked by closed, protectionist borders, within which rights and democratic practices are subordinated to the dictates of a state in fierce competition with other states for security, resources, and influence over weaker states.

The problem is that, in practice, the basic tension between order and freedom that Watson's international society lays bare gets recast in far more complex terms and contexts across and within liberal domains. Despite the opening up of potentially new terrains of freedom with liberal order, these new terrains also create possibilities for a range of conflicts and tensions that extend beyond the basic terms of state autonomy in the context of the international system. Tensions in liberal order emerge out of the very multiplicity of actors, practices, principles, and institutions which take form unevenly within and across the states and societies drawn up into the emerging liberal order.

Perhaps the tension of liberal order that has been most prominent in the study of international relations in the U.S. has been the one between international exchange and the sovereign state. While this tension, in its basic form, goes back centuries to the mercantilist era, it became particularly robust in the making of liberal order.[77] As pointed out in chapter 1, the norms and principles associated with collective self-determination, enshrined in texts such as the UN Charter, provided a powerful legitimacy, externally and internally, to the claims of states as sovereign polities in the international system that otherwise would not be available in the absence of a liberal moment. This was only reinforced by the salience of the domain of democratic governance, whose institutions and principles were concentrated within the limits of a sovereign state. The making of liberal order, moreover, legitimated the widening scope of the sovereign agency of states that had been developing across the nineteenth and twentieth centuries. The most obvious instance is the intervention of the state in its domestic economy, which, within the context of liberal order, was shaped and legitimated by the individual and group claims of economic rights, the welfare of democratic publics, and the perceived requirements of reinforcing market relations.[78]

But the development of international economic exchange took place based on a very different logic—one resting on an elaborate process of multilateral cooperation and institution-building for its operation. Focusing on such processes and institutions, many liberal economists in the post-World War II period echoed the Cobdens of previous eras in their belief that the sovereign, autonomous state had become relatively anachronistic in the context of international market structures.[79]

The tension between international exchange and state sovereignty emerged, in one instance, in the resistance of Western European states to the perceived encroachment of the Marshall Plan on their control of their political economic destiny. Paradoxically, it was a program that was designed to accommodate and even facilitate the sovereign integrity of European states, especially if such integrity could help resist the pressures of the Soviet Union. And even the Soviet refusal to participate in the Marshall Plan—a program designed among other things to facilitate economic exchange— was cast in terms of an appeal to the principle of state sovereignty, which it believed would have been violated by the procedures of the program.[80]

The resistance of Western European sovereign states to the forces of international exchange that potentially would diminish their sovereignty cannot be dismissed merely as a function of the resistance to the reverbera- tions of U.S. hegemonic power. While Britain's rejection of the establish- ment of any form of supranational authority over transnational economic relations appeared first as a reaction to some of the goals of the European Recovery Program (ERP), the same form of resistance was replayed in reaction to the Schuman Plan which evolved into the European Coal and Steel Community; the latter did not entail any direct U.S. role.[81] In both instances the British reluctance to participate was based in part on its disin- clination to place the emerging socialist elements of the British state under the constraints of an international economic institution that was designed solely to facilitate market outcomes, with little regard to their social ramifi- cations, especially vis-à-vis labor.[82]

Britain's resistance to supranational authority illustrates another fun- damental tension in liberal relations, the tension between the commitment to the viability of national economies and the pursuit of international market exchange.[83] On the level of the individual state, the ramifications of this tension have historically emerged in the politics of foreign policy- making as interests tied to the national economy have vied with those tied to the international economy.[84] On the level of the international system, the tension has taken shape as an effort to arrive at mechanisms that facil- itate international exchange while minimizing the violation of the interests associated with national economies. Of course, such is the logic of "embedded liberalism."

Another complex set of tensions in the construction of liberal order can be observed when the scope is widened to take in the relations of the U.S., Europe, and what came to be called the Third World. In the reestablishment of European colonialism and its ultimate collapse in the face of decolonization movements, competing claims and interests, which often took violent form, clashed within and especially across the domains of collective self-determination and international economic exchange.

Many factors were relevant to post-World War II decolonization, including the specific histories of colonial domination, of decolonization movements, and of wartime occupation and resistance. Without underplaying the impact of these forces, it is possible to consider how the decolonization process was imbricated with liberal order-construction. In part, contests over the reinstitution of European colonialism pivoted around the tension inherent in the clash of the self-determination claims of colonized peoples with the claims of already sovereign European states, and ultimately with the perceived necessities of using colonial resources to aid international exchange demands in Western Europe. It was in Asia where these tensions first became acute in the immediate postwar period. In Southeast Asia, in contrast to the Indian subcontinent, the U.S. played an increasingly important role beginning in the late 1940s between European states and colonial peoples which brought liberal tensions to the fore. This is apparent most of all in the case of Indonesia.[85]

Prior to the U.S.'s role in the "roundtable talks" in mid-1949, which were ostensibly dedicated to negotiating the independence of Indonesia, the U.S. sought to reduce the tension between Indonesian nationalist claims to self-determination and the claims of the Dutch state to colonial rule over the East Indies by pushing for a liberalization of Dutch colonial rule. Such a solution, however, was hopeless because there were no mechanisms to compel the Dutch to follow through on such a policy line. The U.S. and other states, such as the newly independent India, could bring complaints against the Netherlands in the UN Security Council, but ultimately it would be necessary for the Dutch state to live up to any promises it made to move forward with liberalization, if not also decolonization. Efforts were further complicated by the perceived benefits colonial revenues brought to the recovery efforts in Europe. Given the importance of the Netherlands to the

European Recovery Program (ERP), there was a distinct limit to the extent to which the U.S. was willing and able to pressure the Dutch state economically to follow a more liberal line, as was desired by a U.S. Congress that even threatened—if it was not satisfied—to cut off Marshall Plan aid. In effect, the attempt of the Dutch state to set the terms of its own postwar political fate—in particular through the two postwar Dutch military incursions, called "police actions," against Indonesians—could not be balanced with the aspirations of self-determination.

The intransigence of the Dutch forced the U.S. to begin considering increasing support to the Indonesian independence movement or risk—as NSC 48/1 later put it—exposing it as "a fertile field for subversive communist activities."[86] Since the U.S. and U.S. multinational corporations (MNCs) had their own interests in Indonesian resources (i.e., oil), the chief U.S. goal was to keep the East Indies within the borders of the liberal order. Indeed, an independent Indonesia, outside the confines of colonial preference systems, would perhaps be in a better position to assure U.S. access to resources than a colonial East Indies. Once Indonesian nationalist forces showed themselves capable of maintaining their independence from communist forces by executing communist leaders in 1948, the U.S. was willing to support Indonesian independence openly. The old imperialist relations, which frustrated nationalist aspirations, were judged by the U.S. as undermining efforts to avoid communist and potential Soviet pressures. They also limited the possibilities of opening up economic exchange by hindering the access that non-Dutch interests had to local resources.

The positioning of Indonesian independence as a move favorable to the goal of anticommunism dovetailed more generally with the increasing dominance of Soviet containment issues with regard to the Netherlands in Western Europe. Under the single strategic umbrella of containment, even the Dutch post-independence presence and influence in Indonesia (aiding in the fight against communism) could be integrated with the backing of an Indonesian anti-communist nationalist movement under the leadership of Sukarno.

The U.S. concern with the pull of communism ultimately translated into a strong commitment to an Indonesian anti-communist program that was militarily-oriented and dependent on high levels of military aid. This effort did more than maintain the integrity of the Western definition of the boundaries of liberal order in Asia. It also confronted two tensions inherent in the postwar colonial situation. One was the tension between

Dutch independence and Indonesian self-determination. By placing Indonesian independence in the context of anti-communism, the U.S. put both Indonesian self-determination and Dutch sovereign interests within the same strategic dimension. Thus, pressures applied to the Dutch took form less as violations of their sovereign independence, and increasingly as attempts to get them to serve the best interests of global containment in Southeast Asia and Europe.

A second tension associated with the decolonization process emerges in the question of whether, through the exercise of its right to self-determination, a people may in effect define itself out of international liberal order. Albert Hirschman made famous the options available to agents in economic and political contexts of exiting from social relations altogether, of remaining loyal to them, or of protesting (or exercising "voice") in the hope of changing the character or terms of relations themselves.[87] By recognizing the placement of Indonesian self-determination in the context of anticommunism, the U.S. could help set a boundary to the exercise of exit that was consistent with the U.S. effort to define Indonesia within the boundaries of the emerging liberal order. In contrast, in Indochina no comparable effort was undertaken, despite the history of Vietnamese wartime cooperation with the U.S. and the French against Japan and a conscious effort to gain U.S. support for independence after the war. Whatever potential tension regarding self-determination there was in Indochina in the immediate postwar years, it was allayed through French colonialism rather than through a challenge to it.

Although it may be hard to see in the aftermath of the Vietnam War, prior to 1950 Indochina received, relative to Indonesia, little diplomatic attention from the U.S.[88] For one thing, unlike the case in Indonesia the U.S. had no appreciable economic interests in Vietnam. But even the advocacy on behalf of Ho Chi Minh's fight against French colonialism by newly independent states, such as India, was nearly negligible (and these states had far stronger political interests in decolonization than economic ones). In part, Ho's communist credentials—which he tried to soften early on—limited the sympathy his movement could generate especially among U.S. policymakers and Asian governments facing communist opposition in their own countries. Ho had crossed the line laid out in NSC-48/1.

Interestingly, the Soviet Union also provided little support, diplomatically or materially, for Ho's effort until the end of the decade, deferring instead to the decolonization efforts of the French Left, which it hoped would ultimately triumph.[89] Indeed, the relative position of the French in the emerging postwar order might have been the key to the different outcomes between Indonesia and Indochina. The French state was a far more powerful and important agent in the new order, especially as a member of the UN Security Council, than the Dutch state. France was more engaged in and essential to the liberal order definition process inside and outside of Europe, a fact recognized by the U.S. and states such as India. Indeed, for a Waltzian structural realist, the French state in the 1940s could be viewed only as weak to inconsequential relative to the new superpowers. But at the core of the liberal uniaxis, with capacity to help set the terms of liberal order, the French state had considerable power, although it was far less than the Soviet state. Relative to the Dutch, for instance, the French state had a greater capacity to deploy material organizational power, especially for colonial administration. Thus, there was little protest to the French state's dealing with Indochina as it saw fit, and Vietnam, in the context of the emerging liberal order, became for U.S. policymakers and others in the international community an appendage of the French state.

In the end, Ho had little choice but to pursue the option of exit from the liberal order in order to work toward independence for all of Vietnam. His moves toward exit permitted the U.S. conveniently to reconcile backing the French sovereign claims to empire with failing to support self-determination in Vietnam. The sense among U.S. policymakers of what the stakes in Vietnam were would change only when a state of far greater salience in liberal order-making—China—exited abruptly from the liberal order under far different circumstances in 1949. But that is another quite familiar and bloody story.

These tensions are related to another tension that was inherent in the making of liberal order inside and outside the West. We have seen how, in principle, the freedom opened by an international liberal order is universal to the extent that agents can pursue diverse interests and forms of social existence. Yet the cases of Indonesia and Vietnam show how, in practice, U.S. policymakers felt compelled to set limits on the exercise of self-determination. Of course, the effort of a collectivity to define itself out of liberal order is an extreme instance of the exercise of self-determination. Far less extreme is the setting of limits to the political wills of national and democratic actors in a Western Europe that was in the process of building and rebuilding liberal democratic states. The tension between the universal liberty promised, in principle, by liberal order and the tendency to posit boundaries to what and who shall be included in that order has recently been observed even within the doctrinal history of liberalism itself. Uday Mehta shows "how Locke presumes on a complex constellation of social structures and social conventions to delimit, stabilize, and legitimize without explicitly restricting the universal referent of his foundational commitments."[90] Political participation for Locke, which at first glance appears to be based on a universal, open, and natural equality, turns out to depend on exclusionary elements such as "breeding," "discretion," and the "capacity to reason" that restrict political life.

In practice, the actual genesis of this tension in the making of international liberal order begins with a simple notion on the part of U.S. policymakers. In constructing a liberal order, it was understood that political relations and outcomes based on the principles of self-determination and liberal democracy are more viable and, therefore, better anchor international liberal relations than those that are not. Assistant Secretary of State Willard Thorpe claimed, in a memorandum illustrative of this type of thinking at the time, that to end instability in Europe and the appeal of communism required two things:

> One is an economic and political system that works well enough to satisfy the legitimate needs and aspirations of the great majority of the population in each country. The second is a burning faith in and enthusiasm for democratic institutions that are consistent with, although not necessarily identical with, our own democratic institutions.[91]

This formula rested on two interwoven propositions. The first is that institutions and relations based on a popular political will are stronger and better anchored than those dictated solely from above. The second is that international forces that promote political developments along the lines of the first proposition are more likely to be supported or accepted in a given national political arena than those that do not. Under the logic of the first principle, the U.S. was willing to support democratic leftist forces in western Europe knowing that their popular mandate made the states in question better able to resist the pull of the Soviet Union. Thorpe's revealing memo went on to say that "we should give support to political parties that offer Europeans a positive program suited to Europe's political needs and development . . . [and] this may mean support of the moderate Socialist parties of Europe."[92] The operation of the second principle would make the U.S. a more popular superpower than the Soviet Union.[93] Again Thorpe, capturing the essence of both propositions, called on his fellow policymakers to build "an aggressive ideological campaign whose goal should be the raising of a flag of human freedom that all European parties except the authoritative minded could rally around."[94]

Taken at face value, these two propositions can be understood as a basis for undergirding liberal relations in Atlantic states with layers of political strength at the national and local levels. But the operation of self-determination and liberal democracy as generators of political strength meant that they would be serving strategically as instruments of liberal order-construction. As such they would help make more viable other facets of international liberalism, especially the sovereign state, the system of international exchange, and the predominance of market economies. However, it is here that the tension regarding the setting of limits to liberal practices emerges. Because the operation of these domains in this respect would be strategic, it would be necessary to set definite bounds to the terms and conditions of the exercise of self-determination and democratic will. Thus, while the U.S. may have accepted democratic left governments within the liberal uniaxis, this was done only because, and if, their policies were consistent with significant liberal political dynamics. These dynamics included: (a) resistance to Soviet efforts at shaping the emerging order; and (b) participation in the emerging institutions and relations associated with the domain of international economic exchange. French communists, for instance, argued strongly in public that French self-determination and sovereignty was threatened by U.S. plans "to take over the country" through the Marshall Plan.[95] Boundaries to democratic wills were clearly illustrated in Italy in 1947–48 when the U.S. intervened covertly to avoid a communist election victory.[96] Even early on the U.S.'s rather mixed record in eastern Europe regarding support for the results of democratic elections in 1945–46 was a function of whether or not the given country was viewed as being under Soviet control or simply electing too many communists.[97]

Despite the tension in, if not contradiction of, liberal principles inherent in the setting of limits to the operation of self-determination and liberal democracy, they did not pose an obstacle to liberal order-construction exactly because such limits appeared within the context of the strategic needs of the liberal order. That is, it was not capricious hegemonic will but the viability and participation of Western European states and societies in liberal order that imposed limiting conditions on their national and democratic wills. Moreover, by being subsumed under a strategy of building strength to withstand the push and pull of the Soviet Union, the self-determination and democratic will of a people faced limits established in other domains as to how far it could challenge liberal relations and order-building. Understood in this light, the notion that the ERP would be based on the initiative of a Europe that included democratic left governments was not a threat to liberal order exactly because the administration and aims of the program were designed to strengthen international exchanges, the sovereign, self-determining state, and market economies. This was of course one of the key elements to the strategy of containment that emerged by 1947.[98] In general, international liberal principles and institutions emerged in a tension-filled web of strategic needs, interests, and contingencies. Thus, while there might be plurality and diversity in the liberal order, it is plurality and diversity along a single axis or uniaxis. By making self-determination and liberal democracy strategic elements that can undergird the strength of Atlantic states, the U.S. was able to help set and maintain that uniaxis in place. As we shall see in the next chapter, the cost of that effort was an overemphasis on strength that became detached from its democratic origins.

The Strategic Reduction

The tensions outlined above posed formidable challenges to the making of liberal order. U.S. hegemonic agency was caught in the uncomfortable position of building an order based on plurality and difference, the unfolding of which threatened the very effort of construction. Hence, there was a need for boundaries and limits; in order, in effect, to move beyond the free operation of a liberal order of fully autonomous agents as delineated, in principle, in the UN Charter. This basic tension in the making of order was articulated in the 1947 report that set out the rationale for the Marshall Plan:

> National security can be maintained most effectively through the rebuilding of a stable peaceful world, in which each nation respects the sovereignty, integrity and way of life of the others in a friendly manner. This situation can best be attained through effective implementation of the charter of the United Nations, coupled with early satisfactory settlement of certain major world problems, which may be settled partially or wholly outside the structure of the UN, such as the peace treaties with Germany and Japan. However, the UN

charter has yet to be implemented with full effectiveness. A realistic appraisal of the world situation shows that there exist many problems which adversely affect the security interests of the U.S. and which may, particularly at their inception, be outside the purview of the UN.[99]

Moving "outside the purview of the UN" meant combating the political challenge posed by the Soviet Union by strengthening states in Europe and making sure they were "oriented" toward the U.S. Policymakers in the U.S. and Britain came to treat the Soviet Union as an opponent that not only could challenge the process of defining liberal order, but also could destroy—above all, in political and social terms—the states and societies within that order. We already have seen this in the above discussion of the Soviet threat. In order to understand more fully how the Soviet Union was transformed from its status as a threatening state into a full-fledged strategic opponent, wholly externalized from the liberal order, it is necessary to consider more closely the dynamics of U.S. agency and uniaxial politics vis-à-vis the Soviet Union.

First off, my understanding of this transformation contests the argument of some diplomatic historians that the emergence of East-West tensions was facilitated by the increasingly confrontational character of the beliefs and assumptions of Western policymakers themselves. It has been held that, despite the initial efforts at accommodation with the Soviet Union, an increasingly strong confrontational emphasis began to emerge as early as 1944 among such Western policymakers as Averell Harriman and Winston Churchill.[100] Underlying the contrast by historians of this emergent competitive strain with the initially dominant cooperative one is an assumption that conflict did not simply stem from an inherently conflictual distribution of power. Rather, it has been argued that policymakers' belief systems and willingness to adopt hardnosed, *Realpolitik*, approaches to foreign relations need to be factored in as determinants. For Daniel Yergin, the Cold War took its strategically charged form ultimately as a result of the triumph of a paradigm in the making of U.S. foreign policy he called the Riga axioms. At its "heart" is "an image of the Soviet Union as a world revolutionary state, denying the possibilities of coexistence, committed to unrelenting ideological warfare, powered by a messianic drive for world mastery." This paradigm competed with the Yalta axioms, which "downplayed the role of ideology and the foreign policy consequences of authoritarian domestic practices, and instead saw the Soviet Union behaving like a traditional Great Power within the international system, rather than trying to overthrow it."[101]

Other historians point to the sometimes hollow commitment to liberal principles based on such evidence as FDR's willingness to tacitly tolerate Soviet violations of such principles in eastern Europe as long as liberal appearances were maintained.[102] The notion that there resides a realist nut within the shell of FDR's and Truman's wartime and early postwar commitment to international liberal principles is meant in part to show that policymakers were willing to deal with the Soviet Union in straight power terms. Thus, the adoption later on of a hard line was consistent with the realistic approach underlying U.S. and British foreign policy and negotiation. Both appeals to underlying hard-line policy approaches, however, fail to explain why the West was in a position within which some policymakers found it compelling to view the Soviet Union as a competitor.

Gaddis offers an alternative approach that goes further in explaining the rising superpower confrontation. He argues that it was not foreign policymakers themselves but domestic political reaction to international trends that drove the Truman administration to take hard-line positions. Most notably, the public despair over Soviet violations of liberal principles led the administration to abandon the Yalta accords as the basis of relations with the Soviet Union.[103]

In effect, what is in play here is the domestic politics of a liberal state. U.S. policymakers as well as public opinion had become frustrated with what appeared to be Soviet violations of liberal principles in eastern Europe and Asia.[104] That is, the political forces inherent in a liberal democratic regime, including a democratic public and an effective legislature, helped compel Truman ultimately to abandon the policy of accommodation he had inherited from FDR. A hard line could help mobilize support for the survival of his own political career and justify the burgeoning U.S. commitment to Europe against lingering isolationist forces.[105] The construction of U.S. liberal hegemony clearly required support at home.

It is true that the increasing abandonment of Yalta as a frame of reference for the structure of the postwar settlement was an important aspect of the growing confrontation between the West and the Soviet Union. The Yalta accords had shown the ability of the U.S. and Britain to reach broad-based agreements about multiple regions across the globe through negotiations with the Soviet Union. In the least, the agreements broadcasted the commitment of the Big Three to liberal principles such as national self-determination, however much the specifics of the accords allowed the Soviet Union to compromise such principles in practice in places such as Poland.

But domestic political pressure for a reconsideration of Yalta represents a force that made its abandonment and a hard line tenable and desirable for U.S. policymakers only in the domestic arena. By considering its implications for the politics of liberal order-making, we can show why such abandonment matter internationally. At its most basic level, abandonment freed up the U.S. from the constraints that the accords placed on foreign policy, and allowed the U.S. to pursue new policies it had formed after the Yalta agreement had been made.[106] Abandonment, however, was not simply a means for facilitating U.S. hegemonic agency: it also undermined the Soviet Union's capacity to influence the liberal definitional process through negotiation. If so basic an agreement as Yalta could be abandoned, then the Soviet Union's connection to the liberal order through negotiation would be unhinged because its agreements would not be viewed as lasting and binding. Indeed, the emergence of what came to be known as America's "get tough" policy in 1946, especially in regard to policy in Iran and Turkey, represented an unwillingness to negotiate and implied the use of force in the face of Soviet intransigence; it was a first step in the externalization of the Soviet Union from the liberal order. Wiping away the trace of a Soviet negotiated presence in that order in the form of the Yalta and ultimately the Potsdam accords limited the Soviet capacity to participate in that order on such grounds.

By constricting the negotiation conduits of Soviet pressure on the liberal definitional process, U.S. policymakers had raised the salience of Soviet strategic pressures, and thereby created a strong basis for viewing the Soviet Union as a threat. Of course, the possibility of accommodation was left open through 1946, and the logic of building a liberal order strong enough to tolerate diplomatic Soviet challenges would surface often in policy papers.[107] But the U.S. was increasingly willing to rely on strategic power as a mode of resisting Soviet definitional pressures. It was in that year, for instance, that Byrnes made his famous Stuttgart speech announcing the decision to leave U.S. troops in Germany for an indefinite period. In effect, the U.S. "determination to compromise no more" by default left the Soviet Union only the strategic realm in which to affect the liberal definition process.[108] Increasingly, it was the very existence of the subjects of definition themselves, states and societies in Western Europe, rather than relations per se that would constitute the object of the Soviet challenge. States in Western Europe were increasingly viewed by U.S. policymakers as being vulnerable to intimidation by Soviet diplomatic-strategic challenges from without and destabilizing political threats from within the borders of the liberal order by social forces such as communist parties which appeared to owe political allegiance to the Soviet Union.

As the channels of negotiation dwindled, the U.S. external state began to be transformed from being a means to effect a postwar settlement into being an organizational force in the confrontation with the increasingly salient Soviet strategic challenge. The Truman Doctrine signaled the emergence of a U.S. commitment to confront a strategic challenge in the Mediterranean by building and employing the U.S. external state in the form of the American Mission to Aid Greece (AMAG). This type of shift was also sharply reflected in the German occupation: not only would troops remain indefinitely, but a commitment was made by 1947 to build with the external state organs of the occupation a separate West German political unit that could serve as an aid in Western Europe's effort to resist Soviet challenges on the politico-strategic plane.

Finally, the tensions associated with the making of liberal order suggest that the process was a fragile one. Consolidating the fragile political relations between states along the liberal uniaxis could aid the process of order-making. In mid-1946, Kennan had called for "the cultivation of solidarity with other like-minded nations on every given issue of our foreign policy." To achieve this at that time he was "very much impressed with the usefulness of the UN."[109] By the time of the 1947 report quoted above, policymakers questioned that usefulness. They were thinking by then clearly in terms of tactics, strategies, and forces, "all of which are difficult and sometimes impossible to combat under the United Nations Charter," and of "orienting other foreign nations toward the U.S. and the UN."[110] In this context, the U.S. was often fearful of independent lines of negotiation emerging between Western Europe and the Soviet Union. By constricting Soviet pressures to the strategic realm, the U.S. reduced the possibility of multilateral political relations between these states and the Soviet Union. Indeed, the authors of NSC-68 understood that there were great advantages to showing that the Soviets were not honoring state sovereignty in negotiations:

> In the process of building up strength, it may be desirable for the free
> nations, *without the Soviet Union*, to conclude separate arrangements

with Japan, Western Germany, and Austria which would enlist the energies and resources of these countries in support of the free world. This will be difficult *unless it has been demonstrated by attempted negotiation* with the Soviet Union that the Soviet Union is not prepared to accept treaties of peace which would leave these countries free, under adequate safeguards, to participate in the United Nations and in regional or broader associations of states. . . . [italics mine][111]

In addition, the substance of negotiations and relations among liberal uniaxial states themselves became increasingly concentrated and unified by the terms of a Soviet strategic threat. In the negotiations over the future of political and economic development in Germany, for instance, the location of a solution to the conflicting definitions offered by Western European states and the U.S. was facilitated by the identification of the Soviet Union as a disrupting force that sought to exploit German development for its own politico-strategic goals.[112] As Kennan had put it, an enemy was better than a friend.[113]

What we are witnessing in these dynamics of constriction is a reduction of various political dimensions of interaction to strategic concerns. I am using the term strategy in this context to denote plans of action against a clearly defined adversary, whose identity as such is based on its will to harm the interests or existence of its adversary in order to advance its own interests and well-being. This is the significance of the label "enemy." My understanding of the term straddles: a) the more benign understanding of strategy elucidated by Thomas Schelling that emphasizes the way that "players" can be interdependent on each other's "course of action"; and b) the strictly militaristic sense of interest to a Liddell Hart, who focuses on the modes or art of deploying and applying military force to achieve goals.[114] This straddling makes sense because U.S. policymakers such as Kennan sought to clearly define in the containment doctrine a realm of strategy that could rely on economic and political tactics without automatic recourse to military ones. The operative phrase was "means short of war."[115] These issues will be discussed in greater detail in the next chapter, where it will become clear that strategic reductions were not simply moves away from the political—for instance, from the substantial politics of negotiation over a wide range of social and political (rather than simply military-strategic) differences—but a move toward a different type of political agency. Indeed, the recourse to strategic reduction was eminently *politico*-strategic.

Spheres of Influence

As the liberal core consolidated and the confrontation between it and the externalized Soviet Union became increasingly focused on the military-strategic realm, two separate spheres of influence came into view. Spheres of influence in this context may be understood to denote relatively separate realms of relations centered around the U.S. and the Soviet Union. They are taken here to be the defining feature marking the transformation of East-West confrontation into the Cold War. Their emergence was a function of the continued progression of Soviet externalization and liberal consolidation.

The historiography of the early Cold War to a large extent portrays the East and the West on an unintended trajectory leading toward separate spheres of influence.[116] At the global level, however, the record is clearly very mixed regarding the trend toward separate spheres. While it is clear that in Latin America, sub-Saharan Africa, and the occupations of ex-enemies Japan and Italy the West endeavored to minimize Soviet influence and relations, in the Near East there was an effort to avoid the formation of separate spheres. In Europe, the fear that an exclusive Soviet sphere would pull eastern Germany permanently out of Western reach was incentive enough to endeavor to avoid European spheres.[117] At negotiations such as the Council of Foreign Ministers in Paris in 1946, ambivalence and unevenness were manifested in bouts of both contestation and resignation over the prospect of forming strategic areas of influence. Even much earlier, the Yalta conference exhibited the same ambiguity as FDR secretly accepted Soviet strategic interests in eastern Europe at the same time as the Yalta accords appeared to define eastern Europe inside the bounds of the liberal order.[118]

Within the Truman administration itself there were arguments both for and against an increasing exclusivity of relations between the West and the Soviet Union.[119] The seemingly contradictory pattern at work in the immediate postwar years reflected more generally the endeavor explored above to integrate the Soviet Union and its sovereign security claims into a liberal order that had security claims of its own. At the Potsdam Conference, for instance, Stalin and Truman attempted to place a limit on each other's extension of power beyond their positions in eastern and western Europe respectively. And at the Moscow Conference at the end of 1945 the U.S. was willing to trade off recognition of the Bulgarian and Romanian governments, despite their nonliberal nature, in return for Soviet acquiescence on a limited Soviet role in Japan.[120] As the U.S. efforts to influence relations in eastern Europe and the Soviet effort to determine outcomes in Japan show, this type of trade-off hardly constituted separate spheres.

However, as tensions grew, these trade-offs became increasingly less likely. As one British official put it, early on, in 1946: "If we cannot have a world community with the Russians as a constructive member . . . it seems clear that the next best hope for peace and stability is that the rest of the world, including the vital North American arsenal, should be united in defense of whatever degree of stability we can attain."[121] Indeed, by the end of 1947 a central arena through which trade-offs were worked out, the Council of Foreign Ministers, had collapsed altogether. On one level, the externalization of the Soviet Union, which the British official was presciently pointing to, reduced tensions in the liberal world (in his words, "stabilized" it) by minimizing Soviet capacity to influence and directly define liberal relations from within the liberal world. This opened up the way for Western states to consolidate their uniaxis centered on the U.S. state. (This, of course, is part of the strategic reduction.) Such consolidation perhaps found its first strong manifestation in the Marshall Plan which would either bring the Soviets within the liberal uniaxial structure or permit its consolidation without them, and those states which paid allegiance to them, if they rejected participation.[122] The use of the Soviet Union as a means to consolidate the liberal core emerged even before Soviet externalization became clear. This means, Western policymakers could exploit the *emerging* Soviet threat itself as a means of consolidation. The State Department more than once blamed the Soviets for the lack of progress in negotiations regarding Germany instead of the sometimes more guilty French and British.[123]

But consolidation, as many U.S. policymakers then realized, would not be a one-sided affair in that externalization from the liberal world permitted the Soviets to consolidate their own sphere along economic, political, and strategic lines.[124] The Soviets offered their own version of a Marshall Plan for the East soon after their rejection of the West's, and in late 1947 mutual security treaties were signed by Eastern European countries. It is at this point that one may identify the formation of separate spheres of influence marked by the realization among Western policymakers that there was no longer any prospect of incorporating the Soviets inside the liberal world.

As the Soviet Union became increasingly separated, there was a deepening of the strategic dimensions of the East-West confrontation. Despite the emerging contours of separation, the Soviet Union was able to exert push and pull pressures on a West that by then possessed few and rather ineffective institutional means (i.e, the UN) with which to confront them. That is, as the Soviets became increasingly separated, they were less susceptible to the discipline of conferences and negotiations. As a result, the separation of East and West opened the way toward an increasingly militarized confrontation with the Soviets because of the lack of any other effective channels and arenas for managing rivalry. Such a lack conditioned the very character of Europe's response to the Soviet threat. While we will never know whether developing institutional channels of negotiation would have forestalled the deepening of the Cold War, it can be argued counterfactually that, in the least, their continued operation would have left open a more viable alternative to an increased militarization of relations. It is perhaps ironic that the very endeavor to incorporate the Soviet Union into the liberal order through negotiation was an important factor leading to the increased separation that undermined institutional channels of negotiation.

Cold War Alternatives

The Third Force

Although the adoption of a hard line and the move to spheres of influence became the dominant means to contend with the Soviet challenge, alternatives were articulated.[125] The most powerful alternative in U.S. foreign policy was the possibility of following through on the development of Western Europe as a "Third Force" between the U.S. and the Soviet Union.[126] One of the attractions to the Third Force idea was that when strong challenges emerged inside of European states the U.S. would have to worry less about intervention if sufficient "local forces of resistance" existed.[127] However insufficient such forces would have been relative to the Red Army in central and eastern Europe, their development could only have constituted a welcome addition to U.S. power. The prospect of a European Third Force would have supplemented the U.S. as a second—albeit far less formidable—center of power along the liberal uniaxis capable of helping offset Soviet pressures. According to Kennan, it was a matter of "strengthening local forces of independence" and "getting them to assume part of our burden."[128]

A more decentered liberal uniaxis along these lines was not possible because of two conditions—ironically, both of them had made this alternative possible in the first place. First, the plurality of a liberal uniaxis meant any construction of an independent Western European alliance would take place in a complex web of state agencies. Even with the prodding of the

U.S., these states were not able to resolve their differences to an extent that would allow for the formation of the independent political bonds necessary for the development of a Third Force.[129]

A second condition that paradoxically opened as well as closed off the Third Force alternative was the presence of the U.S. external state in Europe. Its continued presence in Germany and expansion via the formation of the Economic Cooperation Administration (ECA) could just as easily undermine independence as foster it. The development of an independent Europe seemed to rest on aid from an organizational force whose very presence implied dependence. And while the U.S. external state, especially in Germany, provided Western Europe with security, it heightened the strategic tensions in Europe by standing face to face with the Soviet external state. It made available a real alternative to the necessity of building a Third Force—i.e., the commitment of U.S. power, however as yet limited and provisional—and highlighted the potential inadequacy of a European Third Force.[130] (The implications of both conditions for the salience of U.S. hegemony in Europe vis-à-vis the making of the Western European community will be considered in chapter 4.)

Program A

By mid-1948, despite his original distrust of negotiation with the Soviets early on—a view for which he was criticized by Walter Lippmann in *The Cold War*—Kennan would offer another alternative that relied on this diplomatic tool and which came to be known as "Program A."[131] It called for a negotiated disengagement of U.S. and Soviet forces from much of Europe that would leave in its wake a unified, "independent"—albeit pro-Western—Germany that could thereupon be absorbed by an integrated and independent Western Europe. Program A in essence constituted a plea for the rollback of both the U.S. and Soviet external states. This alternative, on the one hand, was rejected by U.S. center and external state actors such as the State Department and General Lucius D. Clay—who headed the German occupation—on the grounds that occupation troops were necessary to keep West Germany in the liberal order and counter Soviet strategic pressures so close to Western Europe. On the other hand, it was rejected by France, which understood that international liberal order offered too few controls for a unified Germany that could itself, or under Soviet influence, challenge Western Europe.[132]

Ultimately, the sort of rollback that Kennan suggested was doomed because it called for an undermining of the strategic dimension of the U.S. external state in Europe. The reliance in Progam A on negotiation as a prerequisite overlooked the ways that it had been increasingly displaced in the context of a compelling strategic reduction.

Conclusion: The Trope of Failure

It is tempting to turn to the historical trope of failure in liberal order-building to explain both emerging spheres of influence and increasing U.S. involvement in Europe. After all, the failure of liberal states to accommodate the Soviet Union had serious implications for international politics. The Truman administration was willing to blame the Soviets for economic failures in Europe, for increased tensions there, and for stalemate in German negotiations. Historians and political scientists since then have turned to the "failure thesis" to explain the necessity of the Marshall Plan, NATO, and ultimately the militarization of the Cold War.[133] Failure is a term we have become deeply familiar with in the post-Cold War period, especially through the numerous commentaries on the unfortunate record of the UN in Bosnia.[134] But it should be used with caution. The notion that a policy has failed implies that if one or another condition had been different that policy would have succeeded: that is, that success was a real possibility. But things typically are more complex than that.[135]

This complexity relates to a second point. The recourse to failure to explain historical outcomes tends to submerge the wider contextual point that what makes failure relevant in the first place is the fact that liberal order-construction is subject to all sorts of historical conditions and outcomes. It is the U.S.'s—and in general the West's—deep, and with time increasing, implication in the process of order-building that should be viewed as the basic explanatory force, of which failure is a function, rather than the reverse. That is, the character of that involvement and the nature of liberal order-construction is what opened the way to historical outcomes, including failure. The fear and occurrence of failure was continuously present even as the U.S. increased its involvement in liberal order-construction: it marked 1950 as well as 1947.[136]

I have argued that the forces at play in failure were the very tensions characterized the liberal construction process. Understood as such, failure is best viewed as a starting point for explanation rather than an explanatory factor itself. In the case of the initially planned multilateral economy based on Bretton Woods and the British loan, the combination of devastated European economies together with an inadequate U.S. effort to undergird the international economy are held to be responsible for a failure that required new programs and modes of intervention.[137] The question is, why was the U.S. effort inadequate? On its face the effort appeared to be shaped by the mistaken hopes of U.S. planners that the economic needs of states and societies would be addressed simply by freeing up international exchange. While such optimism flowed from liberal tenets, more than intellectual fashion was involved. Policymakers were, one should recall, also contending with the difficulties of locating the political will to make the extensive external commitments that would become essential to a developing U.S. liberal hegemony. As we shall see, after wising up to the costs of simple market solutions, policymakers continued to pursue a minimizing course, even as U.S. commitments in Western Europe and elsewhere increased. This course not only shaped the character of U.S. involvement, but also played an important role in the militarization of liberal relations. It will become clearer that minimalization stemmed from far more than policymakers' efforts to overcome resistance to commitments among U.S. state-center legislators. It grew out of the tensions faced and strategies applied by policymakers internationally in the building of liberal order.

4

❋

"The Requirements of Freedom"
Containment, Integration, and Western Militarization

In the spring of 1950, the authors of the famed U.S. policy document, NSC-68, argued for a substantial military build-up in the West and claimed:

> A comprehensive and decisive program to win the peace. . . . would probably involve . . . [a] substantial increase in expenditures for military purposes. . . . [a] substantial increase in military assistance programs, designed to foster cooperative efforts. . . . [d]evelopment of programs designed to build and maintain confidence among other peoples in our strength and resolution, and to wage overt psychological warfare. . . . [i]ntensification of affirmative and timely measures and operations by covert means. . . . [d]evelopment of internal security and civilian defense programs. . . . [and r]eduction of Federal expenditures for purposes other than defense and foreign assistance.[1]

As the decade wore on, the U.S. and its European allies assembled the most formidable array of "peacetime" military power and constructed the most extensive system of strategic-military relations in history. The international relations of the Atlantic states—and the "free world" more generally—were successfully militarized along the lines described in NSC-68.

The task of this chapter is to trace the uneven path leading toward this militarization and to identify the ways that the liberal order-construction process shaped and propelled it. It is a path that was simultaneously distinct from, yet related to, that which led to the Cold War, traced in the previous chapter. At its heart is the strategy of containment. Its qualities of flexibility, openness, and universality, I will argue, made it an international *liberal* political form *par excellence*. As it turned out, these qualities undermined rather than facilitated the application of less militarized approaches to order-building and security. But that outcome cannot be understood without also recognizing the other element lying at the heart of that path: the same play between failure and liberal order-building highlighted at the conclusion of the last chapter. Policymakers looked to military solutions to overcome perceived or anticipated failures, especially in pursuit of order and strength in an international environment where there was relatively little. Military solutions were applied to two problems: building institutions whose political and social scope and presence would be minimal and temporary, and transcending the West's own fear of failure.

Economic Security as the Liberal Strategic Weapon of Choice

Despite its association with the increasing salience of strategic concerns, the hard line that was emerging in the Truman administration in 1946 did not represent a militarization of American foreign policy or of relations with Western Europe. Rather, the growing confrontation between the U.S. and the Soviet Union, described in chapter 3, reflected the dynamics associated with the process of Soviet externalization. Although externalization may have been marked by the narrowing of relations to strategic dimensions associated with a "Cold War," it was not initially accompanied by the militarization of U.S. foreign policy or of the international relations of states engaged in the making of liberal order. Such militarization would emerge only at the end of the 1940s.

A strong indicator of the nonmilitarized dimensions of American foreign policy is the conscious commitment held until 1949 to employ economic means as the basis of containment.[2] Even as late as April 1949 most policymakers still agreed that "economic recovery must not be sacrificed to rearmament and must continue to be given a clear priority." In what has come to be known as "economic security," the U.S. was able to use economic aid as diplomatic leverage while simultaneously aiding recovery on the national and international economic levels. Both functions, in turn, dovetailed with the containment goal of helping European states and societies resist the internal and external push and pull of the Soviet Union.[3] Economic security, for the most part, was based on the notion that economic recovery could generate political stability and undermine internal communist challenges and external Soviet pressures. This, of course, is the positive version of economic security, and its application was most notably associated with the European Recovery Program (ERP). The negative (or punitive) version of economic security stressed sanctions and was applied notably in Eastern Europe.[4]

Of course, the association of economics and security in the context of order-making is longstanding. Nineteenth-century Cobdenite propositions to the effect that "trade leads to peace" shaped the views of important U.S. policymakers, including wartime Secretary of State Cordell Hull, who had decided as a congressman—as early as World War I—that "unhampered trade dovetailed with peace; high tariffs, trade barriers, and unfair competition, with war."[5] Wartime planners such as Hull and others expected to exploit this "law" in the post–World War II world. As one 1944 State Department memo put it:

> The development of sound international economic relations is closely related to the problem of security. The establishment of a system of international trade which would make it possible for each country to have greater access to world markets and resources would reduce incentives to military aggression and provide a firm basis for political cooperation.[6]

Before relations with the Soviets became confrontational, it was expected that those "sound relations" would compel the Soviet Union to be at peace along with the other united nations. As relations became increasingly confrontational, this inclusive logic to the application of economic security began to fade away. The exclusive logic associated with containment became prominent. Economic means could be emphasized over military ones in order to secure states along the liberal uniaxis.[7] The strategic power of U.S. economic predominance could be applied to contend with the Soviet challenge to order-making in a manner that appeared to be consistent with the liberal order-building project *par excellence*. Since policymakers had determined there was no immediate threat of war with the Soviet Union this was a feasible course. Indeed, the whole logic of economic security was predicated on the notion that the investment was sound—one does not furnish a house about to be bulldozed.

A further advantage to this formula for containment was that it was more likely to appeal to members of Congress who advocated a pro-business approach to external affairs. In effect, by joining security and economy in efforts such as the ERP, the Truman administration was able to gain support for both the politico-strategic and economic dimensions of liberal order-building.[8]

As this last point suggests, economic security did double duty by both containing Soviet pressures and building stable liberal economic conditions and relations at the national and international levels. In doing so, economic security reinforced the importance of Western European states and societies in the domains of national market relations and international economic exchange.[9]

Economic security facilitated the operation of principles associated with other liberal domains as well. The resources made available to Western European states under economic security programs were designed to achieve political stability and allow states to work out their own social and economic agendas (within limits, of course). While this outcome enhanced collective self-determination, it also supported representative democratic practices by creating space for the demands of the democratic left. In Western Europe economic security was also viewed by U.S. policymakers as a way to enhance "personal freedom and social equality."[10] In other words, creating a stable environment of economic growth would open up room for individuals and groups not only to survive, but also to pursue their interests in the political as well as the economic spheres. It was thought that it would equally undermine those interests—such as European communist parties—which sought to destroy such liberty-enhancing conditions. All in all, policymakers began the postwar period with a far broader understanding of security than the narrower strategic emphasis we have come to associate with the Cold War.

That there was great conceptual consistency between the strategy of economic security and the liberal order-building project does not mean that tensions associated with the implementation of economic security failed to arise. Western European states, as mentioned above, clearly objected to the potential for intervention inherent in economic security programs. Such objections plagued much of the history of the ERP. While Western European states may have wanted access to U.S. economic resources deployed in their region, they did not necessarily want the political intervention that accompanied dependence on a preponderant U.S. state.

U.S. policymakers discovered that the way to minimize such tensions, was to limit the political dimension of the program. During the war, planners believed that the conjunction of political and economic concerns could be minimized in the classic liberal sense of separation: techno-market logics and expertise would triumph over sectarian, power interests. In a Senate hearing on Bretton Woods, Secretary of the Treasury Henry Morgenthau, Jr. claimed that "[t]hese are to be financial institutions run by financial people, financial experts, and the needs in a financial way of a country are to be taken care of wholly independent of the political connection."[11]

The application of economic security was increasingly focused on the technologies of ostensibly apolitical economic growth, which constituted a "productionist" approach.[12] Constricting economic security this way served triple duty. First, states that were protective of their autonomy were willing to tolerate an increase in U.S. intervention along minimal, productionist lines. Second, the productionist approach made it easier for Congress to accept a new U.S. interventionist role because it at least would be expressly limited. Third, in a fashion that mirrored the effects of the strategic reduction discussed in chapter 3, the productionist approach provided a degree of closure for the fragile and vulnerable intra-liberal political relations emerging in the immediate postwar years. Production increases were emphasized over the political challenges of redistribution. Such productionist closure, as Charles Maier points out, not only headed off political challenges by groups associated with the democratic left such as unions, but also ensured that such groups would not be able to abuse easily the opportunities economic growth opened up for them.[13]

Despite Morgenthau's claims, U.S. postwar policymakers never did separate politics from economics. They used economic power to delimit and ultimately shape political outcomes in Europe. If anything, policymakers were supremely political. Through programs such as the ERP, economic relations were politicized in subtle ways relative to the generally strong-arm, neomercantilism of bilateral trade agreements employed by the Nazis.[14]

The politics of liberal order-building took shape as a sort of meta-politics in that it was applied across societies and territories, not unlike the politics of empires.[15] After all, at stake was an international order and an external state. Kennan conveyed this sense of politics when he told a National

War College audience at the end of 1947 that the "days have passed" when foreign policy could be made on the basis of mere principles. "[W]hen we use the word 'policy' today we often mean. . . . *politics* on a world scale [Kennan's italics]."[16]

The substance of the politics of liberal order-building revolved primarily around the setting of limits. It is not unfamiliar in the history of liberalism. The question of limits or boundaries was central to the nineteenth-century tension between democracy and liberalism described in chapter 1 and the tension between international economic exchange and democratic governance described in chapter 3. Productionism, exclusionist logic, and minimalization were all potent mechanisms for the establishment of boundaries to claims, contestations, and demands in the making of states and societies in Europe and elsewhere—practices that we more typically think of as "political." Containment itself was the politics of boundary-making *par excellence*. Perhaps ironically, as I shall discuss further below, the politics of liberal order also entailed containing the character and extent of U.S. hegemonic agency itself.

The sense that there was an imperative to delimit the range of allowable practices in liberal order (e.g. left, but not too left) was most strikingly conveyed by Kennan in a mid-1946 lecture at the National War College on "Measures Short of War": "On the strictly political measures short of war, I only mention one category because it, in my opinion, is our major political weapon short of war. That measure is *the cultivation of solidarity* with other like-minded nations on every given issue of our foreign policy."[17]

This ostensibly innocent plea for consensus is really a plea for limits to dissent, contention, and contest. A plea for containment turned inward, toward the "self" of the West. We now know, thankfully, that the success of such an effort had very distinct limits. Liberal order, of course, has been far more diverse and empowering than the order constructed by the Soviet Union in Eastern Europe, where the setting not simply of boundaries, but also the specific substance and character of social existence was far more prevalent.[18]

The alternative to the closure and boundary-making that was so pervasive in the construction of liberal order is suggested by the possibility, explored in the previous chapter, of agents determining the character and boundaries of their social existence in far more diverse—and less limited—ways than, it turned out, was possible in the postwar period.[19] Of course, such an order would still be marked by limits. Order-making is always, I have emphasized, about boundary-making. But we might imagine in such an order that limits would emerge out of the mutual obligations agents would have to respect or even aid the setting of one another's terms of social existence, rather than the attempt to "cultivate solidarity," as Kennan had put it.[20] We should not however underestimate the institutional inventiveness that would be necessary in such an order to overcome the types of tensions postwar policymakers faced in the actual order that did emerge, and that compelled their recourse to containment.[21]

Economic Security and the Emergence of an American Military-Strategic System

Relying on economic security measures allowed U.S. policymakers to confront the increasing sense of threat posed by the Soviet Union without militarizing the relations among Atlantic states. Despite the reliance on economic security, the U.S. was intent on building a postwar military-strategic system and was willing, when it was deemed necessary, to take militaristic turns in its foreign policy in pursuit of containment. The question is, what was the relationship between economic security and the strategic dimensions of U.S. policy in the immediate postwar years?

In the pursuit of a postwar settlement, the U.S. had committed itself to the establishment of an external state that would be built for the most part on the military organizational extension inherited from its war effort. Between 1945 and 1946 many of the forward bases established in the war would be made permanent in the Pacific and the Atlantic, troops would be committed indefinitely in occupation duty, in both Europe and Asia, the A-bomb would become a part of U.S. strategic calculations, and the U.S. military establishment would set itself the task of keeping the postwar peace.[22] By 1947 the U.S. had begun foreign military assistance to countries such as Iran and Turkey, sent military advisers to Greece, and committed itself to a Latin American regional alliance known as the Rio Pact.[23]

These developments, however, do not establish that U.S. foreign policy or, more broadly, U.S.-European relations, had become militarized. For instance, even as late as 1948 there had not yet emerged a national policy on military assistance.[24] Despite the initially predominant deployment of military organs in the U.S. external state, the character and scope of the duties of these organs shifted rather quickly from activities associated with the cessation of war to political and economic organization (especially in occupied territories). With time, civil organs such as the ERP increasingly populated the U.S. external state. What the strategic developments described above represent is the construction of a military-strategic system that was an important dimension of a U.S. external state that was employed in the settlement of World War II and, more broadly, in the making of liberal order. In this respect, an external state does not differ from state-making in general. It always has its strategic side.

We have already seen that the presence of the U.S. and Soviet external states raised the salience of strategic factors in Western Europe. This understanding of the strategic dynamics of the time is consistent with the view of historian Melvyn Leffler that what unsettled the U.S. about the Soviets was their challenge to the military and economic systems the U.S. was constructing in Europe and Asia.[25] However, Leffler's strategic emphasis should be balanced with the observation, explored above, that it was only because there was a liberal order-building process that Soviet military power mattered so much. And it was the increasing externalization of the Soviet Union from the liberal order that gave grounds, in the first place, to a sense that the Soviets constituted a threat, military or otherwise. Externalization created the position from which the Soviet Union could constitute a threat not just for military planners concerned with the strategic dimensions of the external state, but also for Western European and American political leaders and policymakers.[26]

Indeed, we ought not overemphasize the military dimensions of the Soviet threat at the time. As the Soviets became externalized, it was the political dimension of Soviet military power in Eastern Europe that was thought by U.S. policymakers to constitute the major threat. Soviet military power was seen especially by Kennan as a symbol of power in Europe that might bolster, attract, and create forces that could change the political configuration of Western Europe either through elections, expanded international relations, subversion, or social instability. This view was demonstrated by the very embrace of economic security, which was designed to meet the (political) Soviet threat on an economic plane that was separate from the military one. At least this appeared to be the hope of planners like Kennan. Indeed, in congressional hearings on the ERP the Truman administration repeatedly denied the military dimensions of the program, not because of some secret plan to build up a militarized security system from a stable economic base, but because there was a conscious effort to pursue security in Europe through economic means for all the reasons outlined above.[27]

In addition, the placing of security on an economic plane helped avoid confronting the international politics of military security at a stage when such politics might entail an exercise of leadership the U.S. Congress would not tolerate. That is, it would have required the U.S. to take the lead in 1947 in constructing an alliance system from scratch based, for the most part, on an American effort to recruit, commit, and organize allies. Such a task would have been quite daunting and, indeed, hardly even occurred to American policymakers at the time. As we know it would be up to the Europeans to start the process that ended in NATO. Even the impetus—albeit not the character—of the Rio Pact came mostly from Latin American states seeking a regional alliance.[28]

Containment as an International Liberal Political Form

One conclusion to be drawn from the above observations is that containment—the overarching strategy of U.S. foreign policy—was first conceived as a multidimensional strategy comprising economic, military, and political elements (this holds even though there was a deliberate effort to employ primarily economic security wherever it was judged to be feasible). When the State-War-Navy Coordinating Committee considered some of the basic strategy behind a European aid program that become the ERP, it considered military and economic aid, as well as "political support . . . and vigorous programs of information."[29] However, by 1950 military aid and assistance became predominant in the U.S. approach to containment. What I would like to examine are the forces in play in the rising predominance of military over nonmilitary containment and evaluate the relation between containment and liberal order-building. It was, as I will show, ironically the very commitment to economic security that actually helped open the way at the end of the 1940s toward the militarization of international liberal political relations.

One window on the dynamics of this transformation is found in the application of containment to the Greek civil war. Prior to receiving word from British policymakers in early 1947 that they no longer could seriously aid the Greek state in its civil war, the U.S. extended mostly economic aid to Greece. The Truman Doctrine was the response to the British abdication. It redefined U.S. policy in Greece and represented the first overt application of the containment policy. It also precipitated an increasing emphasis on military over economic assistance to Greece, which by 1950 would mark the containment strategy as applied to Europe as a whole. While there is no reason to believe *prima facie* that a parallel set of dynamics was in play across the Continent, U.S. assistance to Greece under the Truman Doctrine can at least be understood to represent an important instance of the general transformation of economic into military aid in Europe. The difference is that the transformation in the Greek case occurred earlier and within a more compressed time frame.[30] It thus had special significance as a precedent for policymakers to consider as they fashioned policy in other parts of Europe.

In the sections that follow, I will trace the conditions and paths of this particular transformation in general terms and then with reference to the Greek case, keeping in view the goal of showing how containment constituted an international political form that was specifically liberal. In succeeding sections, I will place the main themes of this transformation in the context of changes undergone by Europe as a whole.

Partiality and Nodal Points of Strength

Grasping how containment operated in the context of liberal order-building requires that we understand the terms upon which states were incorporated into the emerging liberal order. Any type of containment keeps things in as well as out. I have argued that liberal order linked a diversity of states and societies, especially because of the way that many *nonliberal* ones were drawn into the liberal moment and order-making. Not only can states and societies be liberal moderns in varying ways, but also a given state and society might only be shaped, *partially*, by one or two dimensions of liberal modernity. This means that regime type is not a sufficient basis for determining involvement in liberal order. For example, numerous nondemocratic states have participated in postwar international economic exchange and developed liberalistic market relations in places such as southern Europe, Asia, and Latin America. The logic of this type of partial participation was most forcefully expressed by Jeane Kirkpatrick, in her controversial 1979 article, "Dictatorships and Double Standards." Kirkpatrick argued for the value of engagement with right-wing authoritarian regimes which, in comparison to left wing totalitarian ones, at least "leave in place existing allocations of wealth, power, [and] status."[31]

Partial incorporation in liberal order occurs because states serve as the primary mechanism for ordering relations across societies and territories. The involvement of states, as centralized political forms, in liberal relations (e.g., the signing of trade agreements, the making of markets, or the assertion of self-determination claims) does not necessarily draw along with it an entire society and territory under its jurisdiction into liberal modernity. Yet this involvement does allow the nonliberal state, its society, and territory, to be subject to the ordering, agency, and interests of other states in a liberal order. This subjection can range from an engagement with elites in a capital city to the establishment of market relations in a resource-rich periphery.

Partial inclusion, I would argue, is what underlies what Robert Jackson has observed about weak, Third-World states (which he labels "quasi-states") in the post-World War II period.[32] States with limited capacity to govern the societies and territories within their formal boundaries are nonetheless legitimized on an international basis through what Jackson describes as a "liberal sovereignty regime." This regime is embodied in the institutions and norms of the U.N. that reinforce the integrity and autonomy of any recognized state based on principles of collective self-determination.

There are two dimensions to liberal modernity that make this regime and, more generally, partiality possible. First, the differentiated, domain structure of liberal modernity precludes it from being totalizing. Varying forms of liberal practices and institutions are possible, as are varying degrees: hence, the salience of the term liberalization (and the general lack thereof for "communization"). (Remember that in the context of the uneven forms of liberalization shaping most of the states and societies of nineteenth-century Europe described in chapter 1, there was a great deal of partiality.) The nontotalizing character of liberalism means that a nonliberal state can participate in sovereignty and international economic regimes that are liberal.

Second, of all the actors entailed in the operation of liberal domains, none is more central than the state. Its centrality is readily apparent in the domains of self-determination, liberal democracy, and market economies. But the same holds for the domains of individual and group rights and international liberal economic exchange. It is the state that legislates, implements, and enforces rules and rights. Despite the presence and struggle of a multitude of actors, the existence of liberal modernity as it has emerged in the nineteenth and twentieth centuries has not depended on an international community of shared values. Rather, it has depended on the embodiment of liberal practices and principles at the level of the state and its society.[33] That is, when it comes to other types of actors, their endeavors are best understood as being directed mostly at changing the practices and policies of states. Liberal order is no exception as a modern order in that the state—liberal or not—is privileged as the primary agent of order. Within the liberal tradition, the pursuit of justice and freedom has chiefly taken form as a project of shaping states. Even the international and cosmopolitan exchange of goods and ideas has chiefly been understood by Cobden and others as forces that ultimately are meant to contribute to that project.[34] That the Westphalian state system predates the rise of liberal modernity and order makes the state and its sovereignty no less an element of liberal order than the market, which has a pedigree that is more ancient than the Westphalian state.

It was therefore to be expected that in the making of liberal order U.S. policymakers would rely extensively upon the state. The state in liberal order could not only establish liberal relations in the context of a given society and territory, it could also keep a society and territory inside liberal boundaries, serving the perceived economic and strategic requirements of liberal order-making. In lieu of a working state, the U.S. external state would have to assume these order-making responsibilities itself, as it did in Germany and Japan. Since extensive external state commitments of this nature were problematic, this was a very ugly prospect. This point was not lost on Kennan, who wrote in October, 1947:

> Basically the stability of international relations must rest on a natural balance of national and regional forces. . . . I would not hesitate to say that the first and primary element of "containment" . . . would be the encouragement and development of other forces resistant to communism. The peculiar difficulty of the immediate post-hostilities period has rested in the fact that . . . Russia was surrounded only by power vacuums. At the outset, these could be filled . . . only by direct action on the part of this Government. This is admittedly an undesirable situation; and it should be a cardinal point of our policy to see to it that other elements of independent power are developed on the Eurasian land mass as rapidly as possible, in order to take off our shoulders some of the burden of "bipolarity." To my mind the chief beauty of the Marshall plan was that it had outstandingly this effect.[35]

The trick would be to locate what I would call *the nodal points of strength* that could generate this "independent power" throughout the states, societies, and territories defined inside the boundaries of liberal order. We saw in the last chapter that the legitimacy afforded by democratic governance was viewed—at least for Western Europe—as a crucial basis for the independent strength and vitality necessary to keep states and societies inside the emerging liberal order. The "beauty" of this form of strength (or state) building was that it also reinforced the internal organization of societies and states along liberal lines. Above, we saw how the recourse to economic security was premised on the notion that building sound economies led to political stability and capacity to resist communist pressures. It might then pose a problem that there were so many states or emerging states drawn into liberal order that were not liberal, and that at least, in principle, governed territories and societies within which liberal modernity was at best only lightly inscribed. Ironically, partial incorporation was exactly what diffused this problem. Because the societies and territories of nonliberal states were only partially drawn into liberal order-making, it would not be necessary to build up their strength across all five domains of liberal modernity in order to assure their continued incorporation and resistance to Soviet pressures. Rather, at a minimum, it would be necessary to locate strength in the state per se, to at least make sure that a society and territory remained inside of the emerging boundaries of liberal order. Joseph Jones, State Department staff member involved in the drafting of both the Truman Doctrine and the Marshall Plan, grasped this logic when he wrote:

> The survival of nations themselves rather than the survival of liberal trading practices became the central issue. The dollar gap, reconstruction, economic integration, United States aid to help create economic conditions in which human freedom could survive—these matters suddenly pushed normal commercial policies into the background, there to remain for several years.[36]

On one level, Jones is simply restating the logic of economic security, especially as it was applied in Western Europe. But Jones evokes these phrases in reference to the Truman Doctrine. In the case of Greece and Turkey, the issue was, as Truman put it in his famous Truman Doctrine speech, "the very existence of the Greek state. . . . as an independent state," which meant, in effect, a state incorporated within the boundaries of liberal order.[37] Indeed, Jones's "human freedom" in this case was equivalent to freedom from Soviet pressures. The movement of liberal (economic) policies, as Jones put it, "into the background," implied that what counted was the sheer capacity of a state to keep its society and territory inside liberal boundaries, rather than to organize them along liberal lines. If a state was not liberal (and Greece and Turkey were not), then economic aid (or security) measures could still be employed to support the state's existence, suspending concern with its liberalization. As we shall see, U.S. policymakers were precipitously close to moving toward the type of economic and military aid to authoritarian regimes that, thirty years later, Kirkpatrick would feel compelled to defend. To claim that policymakers were just being "realistic" is to miss the point. They were confronting the strategic dynamics of building a liberal order that involved partial inclusion and depended heavily on nodal points of strength. These were dynamics of which the challenge of the Soviet Union was only a part.

Containment's Virtues: Flexibility and Universality

Containment was a universal policy that put in place a standard strategic principle for the countering of Soviet-related internal and external pressures across the spectrum of states and societies within the liberal order. The express aim of the containment policy, as discussed in chapter 3, was to stem the push and pull of the Soviet Union. Partial inclusion was essential to the containment of pressures associated with the Soviet Union at specific points along the borders of the liberal world. States and societies whose involvement in the emerging order of liberal relations was relatively tenuous were incorporated in that order, preventing them from being pulled into the Soviet orbit. As early as mid-1947, Kennan had understood this logic regarding fascist Spain. If the West would normalize relations with the Franco regime, then the communist threat in that region could be reduced. Spain could be defined into the liberal world in order to prevent it from being defined out. In a somewhat similar fashion, the extension of ex-enemy Italy's participation in liberal relations to the strategic realm was advanced by its inclusion in 1949 in the North Atlantic Treaty; in part because such an extension of alliance relations would constitute an insurance against any effort of the Communist party to push Italy toward the Soviet Union.[38]

In 1947 Walter Lippmann condemned the Truman Doctrine as a "vague global policy," underspecified as to where, when, and how it would be applied, unless it was intended to be applied everywhere. What he failed to observe at that time was that the loose, unspecified, and universalistic nature of the Truman Doctrine was actually quite consistent with the multidimensionality of containment.[39] Where and how to apply containment would be specified only in each particular case of its application. Indeed, Acheson used the flexibility theme to defend the Truman Doctrine against congressional critics who attacked it for implying a *global* U.S. commitment to aid countries in distress. He told the Senate Foreign Relations Committee in the spring of 1947:

> Any requests of foreign countries for aid will have to be considered according to the circumstances in each individual case. . . . It cannot be assumed, therefore, that this government would necessarily undertake measures in any other country identical or even closely similar to those proposed for Greece and Turkey.[40]

In terms of domestic politics, the nonspecifity of containment avoided the necessity of having to confront the political task of constructing a detailed policy vis-à-vis U.S. allies and Congress. In the international realm the flexible strategy of containment complemented the political dynamics of liberal order-building: in a world of partial inclusion and uneven points of strength, it permitted U.S. policymakers to fit the architecture of its application to the varied character of states and societies involved.[41] What containment opened up for U.S. policymakers was the possibility of working out specific policies as the need for them arose at each point where "counterforce" would be applied. The advantage of such a globalized, albeit unspecified, policy was that it could build on the available nodal points of strength throughout the liberal order. In this sense containment, although it was conceived in universalistic terms, had the advantage of a particularistic approach. In principle it opened up opportunity for actors at the nation-state level to apply containment as they saw fit with the aid and consent of the United States. Kennan had thought it best to fashion a U.S. foreign policy so that universal principles would flow out of initial attention to the particularities of a given situation. But his own containment doctrine called for a broad response to Soviet pressures, which could only lend itself to the universalistic character of the Truman Doctrine. What he did not note was how such initial universalism opened up the way for particularistic solutions at the local level.[42]

The relative lack of pre-given conditions under the containment doctrine, in effect, expanded the "freedom of action" available to policymakers, mirroring the space made available to states, groups, and individuals that is generally a hallmark of international liberal relations.[43] Just as embedded liberalism, as John Ruggie has shown, allowed for specific social and economic solutions at the level of the nation-state in the context of open international economic exchange, containment allowed for the realization of specific solutions in the context of the general application of counter-force to Soviet pressures.

The Backhand of Containment

The problem with the fluid character of containment was that in many circumstances the range of elements that could be relied on as a basis for counter-force—economic, military, or even political—was limited. Containment could depend only those elements that were available as nodal points of strength. In the case of Greece, the application of economic security was untenable. U.S. policymakers decided that Greece lacked an economic base that could respond in the near term to economic aid and development. The domination of Greek politics by a right wing under challenge by leftist guerrillas limited the possibility of a political solution that would incorporate a democratic left in a liberal democratic regime.

Originally, the possibility of a politically negotiated settlement to the Greek civil war held out the promise of a coalition government of left and center parties. However, because of the weakness of the Greek state and economy, U.S. policymakers judged that a risky prospect. Thus, while it is true that in mid-1946 the State Department expressed concern that the rightist government was not representative of the full range of noncommunist parties, that concern slowly disappeared with the rise of a guerrilla movement by 1947. Walter Lippmann warned in *The Cold War* that containment strategy could lead to the support of authoritarianism—a warning echoed by Kennan at the end of 1947. Indeed, by 1948, as historian Lawrence Wittner points out, the U.S. had clearly decided that because democratic politics was not strong enough to counter the rebellion, increasingly stern, authoritarian measures were necessary. The U.S. and the British no longer pretended to believe in a Greek political settlement; instead they came to believe in the "efficacy of violence."[44]

In general terms, what was in operation here is the backhand of a containment that relied on limited nodal points of strength. With that backhand, the possibilities of local solutions on the economic, political, or military planes were constricted to tenable solutions that did not place the survival of the states and societies within the liberal order at too much risk of susceptibility to Soviet-related forces. The obvious contrast is to Western Europe, where strength, as pointed out above, generally could be pursued through political and economic forms of legitimization (e.g., democratic governance or union rights). Such forms were viewed as too risky for states such as Greece, whose inclusion in international liberal relations was predicated for the most part on sheer continued survival. This was survival not in physical terms, but as a specific political entity, which would remain aligned with the liberal uniaxis and defined within the boundaries of liberal order (even if, in the case of Greece, important reasons for such inclusion were access to Middle East oil and the repercussions of a rebel victory for the continued inclusion of other states in the region). Although the Soviets had distanced themselves from any direct connection with the guerrilla movement, such states as Yugoslavia, considered at that time to be within the Soviet orbit, had not. In the view of U.S. policymakers, a guerrilla military victory would have placed Greece in that same orbit.

Partial inclusion thus implies that the hold of the core—and the U.S. in particular—on countries such as Greece was tenuous. Indeed, one of the negative aspects of partiality is that a limited basis of inclusion implies that those states and societies in question are more susceptible to Soviet-related pressures. So, although the recourse to partial inclusion and limited nodal points of strength appeared to be a workable application of containment and an alternative to the costs and risks entailed in liberalization, this recourse had serious drawbacks from the standpoint of building a liberal order. On the one hand, we have seen that it was necessary to close off the possibility of political negotiation with forces that challenged the Greek state, or risk swamping the Greek state with pressures that could not be resisted. This certainly limited perceived policy options and containment tactics. On the other hand, a tenuous basis of inclusion prompted direct involvement by the U.S. external state, which in Greece took shape in numerous organs such as the American Mission to Aid Greece (AMAG).[45]

The very incapacities of a state such as Greece in managing an economy and providing for the collective welfare meant the chances of avoiding intervention would be severely limited. In addition, it would be necessary to intervene rather deeply, once a commitment to the political survival of a state was made. Truman was able to justify in his "Truman Doctrine" speech that U.S. intervention in Greece was based on an explicit invitation by the Greek state. But he failed to note that the (secret) U.S. orchestration of the invitation—illustrating the tenuousness of Greek state sovereignty—

should worry all congressmen seeking to contain the growth of the U.S. external state.[46] However, the very willingness to go, flexibly, with whatever nodal point of strength was available to minimize detailed global programs of political and economic development—in the Greek case the state's "efficacy of violence"—made the kind of growing involvement of AMAG not just more likely (since what policymakers had to work with was so weak), but of a nature more palatable to congressional critics—militaristic and minimizing planned global economic and political programs.

How ironic that the continued inclusion of a society and its territory in the liberal world, based on the survival of the state *as sovereign*, should be so closely linked to intervention by outsiders in it. This is the very outcome that sovereignty is generally meant to prevent. But this linkage was consistent with the way U.N. intervention, especially via peacekeeping forces, began taking form during the Cold War. Beginning as early as 1947, observer missions in Kashmir and Jerusalem were deployed in order to prevent violations of external sovereignty.[47] Future research will have to determine the connection between the dynamics of liberal order-building, the sovereignty regime described by Jackson, and the history of U.N. intervention in the Third World. What happened in places like Greece indicate that we may not want to assume that the notable emphasis since World War II on protecting sovereignty was simply a change in norms, but rather that it had a lot do to with the strategic dynamics of building a liberal order.

In sum, the backhand of containment shows that it is not as open a strategic doctrine as it might first appear. Its degree of flexibility is a function of the existing reservoirs of strength. Where those reservoirs are limited, political closure is likely in the form of an avoidance of negotiation and a restriction on the advancement of democratic political processes, including the open and even sometimes legal participation of the full range of leftist parties and unions. If available points of strength are limited to the state, then few options are left besides military force as a means to fend off pressures and challenges such as strikes and insurgencies. Furthermore, what Lippmann had so cogently observed in his *Cold War* critique of containment was that the very flexibility of the containment strategy meant any given site of challenge among the states and societies that were included in the liberal order on a limited and, therefore, weakened basis was susceptible to the application of containment.[48] That they were weak implied that direct U.S. involvement likely would be necessary. Thus, containment provided a strategic logic to the increasingly globalized engagement of the U.S. external state in 1947–48 which included not simply the Truman Doctrine as applied in Greece, but also information programs and general clandestine activities in Eastern Europe and Western Europe. It also included military missions in Latin America, the eastern Mediterranean, and Asia.[49]

If the strategic dimensions of international exchange meant, as discussed in the case of Indonesia, that the U.S. and other liberal core countries would have an incentive to keep countries such as Greece inside the liberal order, then there indeed was no pre-given limit to the boundaries of that order. One thing the endeavor to establish an international liberal order meant was that all societies would be candidates for inclusion in the liberal order—if not on economic, then on strategic grounds, if not through economic, then through military containment, and if not as democracies, then as dictatorships.[50]

In their famous article, "The Imperialism of Free Trade," John Gallagher and Ronald Robinson offered us the dictum: "trade with informal control if possible, trade with rule when necessary."[51] Only where the political and social conditions made quasi-independent governments feasible could formal annexation be avoided when a given territory and society was judged essential for securing the nexus of global British economic interests. The twentieth-century version of this dictum might read: inclusion in liberal order with democracy if possible, inclusion with authoritarian rule when necessary. Although across a century, very different historical forces and moments separate these two logics, they both express what happens when, in the development of projects that are global in scale, the main agents are inclined (whether out of their liberalism or sheer pursuit of efficiency) to seek out local strength and stability, only to confront in the end themselves and their project, reflected in a distorted mirror, situated in a far-off land. Liberal order-builders might have locked themselves into an undesirable circle, where the type of political and social closures described above limited the basis or means of engagement and compelled them to become far more interventionary. But by doing so, they very likely helped to limit the very liberalization (except in narrow economic terms) that might have otherwise stemmed that intervention. Accepting the arguments of policymakers that there were great risks involved in doing it any other way is not unlike accepting the arguments of nineteenth-century liberals that democratization would lead to the collapse of European society. Tragically, it may be that both international and domestic liberal order-makers adopted these views because of a sense that so much is at stake in the order that they build (especially stability, freedom, and economic prosperity). These stakes compel liberal order-builders to fashion exceptional terms and means of inclusion and exclusion for groups and societies that have no comfortable place within liberal orders.[52]

The reliance on local power is an ancient imperial strategy, facilitating the extraction of resources for the center without having to construct political mechanisms for direct administrative control.[53] What is significant about the twentieth-century embodiment of this legacy is that the strategy could be applied outside the context of formal empire in ways that appeared to make sense to thoroughly liberal moderns.

Evaluating the Ramifications of Containment

The logics and tensions in the doctrine and practice of containment that led to an expansion of U.S. intervention should not blind us to the forces and agents that set limits to the scope of the U.S. external state. States and groups in Western Europe, although they welcomed U.S. intervention in the region, sought to limit the extent to which such intervention curtailed their own relative autonomy to set the terms for their own social existence (this will be explored further below). In addition, we have seen how U.S. policymakers such as Kennan realized there were material and normative limits to the construction of the U.S. external state as a constitutive presence setting the terms for liberal order around the globe. And, as we have seen all along, limits were set by congressional representatives of U.S. internal state interests. Out of all this emerged a tendency toward what I would call a "liberal-minimalization" in U.S. foreign policy and external state-building.[54] It emerged in the attempt to limit the construction of permanent political institutions in the external realm, whether they were explicitly part of the U.S. external state or not (e.g., the UN). Such construction could either be prevented altogether or, if that was not possible, limits could be set to the authority and scope of an institution.[55]

Liberal minimalization, of course, was already apparent in the pursuit of containment, as we saw in the Greek case. Clearly, the principle of flexibility and openness to specific local solutions in the containment doctrine was based on available strengths and, in effect, avoided the construction of a complex strategic program up front. Indeed, given the congressional resistance to such construction that surfaced during the hearings on the Truman Doctrine, the U.S. administration was left with little choice.

The advantage of the approach taken in countries such as Greece was that the ideological manifestation of containment as anti-communism incorporated countries in international liberalism at the global level, while nonliberal outcomes at the local level could be effected. And by initiating a globalized campaign of anti-communism the U.S. created a common ideological resource for states and groups at the local level to "feed from" in their struggle against Soviet-related internal pressures. While in Western Europe the political fate of communist members of government became precarious by mid-1947,[56] in Greece and the eastern Mediterranean their very lives became precarious. Supplemented by the ideological program of anti-communism, containment did not require the construction of a politico-ideological program for each specific country tied in to the doctrinal and ideological dimensions of international liberalism, which might otherwise have necessitated a more direct political role for the U.S. In any case, such a campaign was hardly feasible given the reality of nonliberal practices in places such as Greece and Indonesia. Because they avoided what would clearly have been a much more extensive political and ideological role for the U.S., containment and anti-communism remained consistent with the imperative of liberal-minimalization.

As a strategic doctrine that assumed the necessity of countering Soviet-related forces and pressures, containment also made the intentions of the "enemy" a moot point and served to focus the attention of the West on its capabilities.[57] This became very apparent in NSC-68. Kennan criticized the document for its tendency to freeze Soviet intentions into a permanently hostile and global dominating mold and to emphasize a fear of Soviet capabilities rather than to consider more carefully whether Stalin actually was out to conquer the world.[58] Bradley Klein has recently argued that Kennan very much misread the issue of intentions, in that NSC-68 repeatedly constructed the Soviet Union as an aggressive totalitarian state bent on global domination. The document, thereby, quite aggressively attributed intentions to the Soviet Union (to say nothing of the grossly specious claims about Soviet capabilities).[59] But Klein misses the point: what NSC-68 did was reduce intentions to strategic factors. That is, it insisted that a totalitarian state was strategically capable of challenging the West. Being totalitarian and having the option of pursuing expansive and aggressive projects of conquest were turned into capabilities. What Kennan perceived in NSC-68 was a retreat from the kind of informed political analysis of intentions that he and Charles Bohlen believed they had offered throughout the 1940s.

(Vietnam-era Secretary of Defense Robert McNamara recently lamented the absence of this type of analysis regarding Southeast Asia.[60])

More specifically, in NSC-68, the authors observed that totalitarian systems can change policy and tactics with little regard for the preferences of the citizenry. The West, by implication, does not share this advantage or, rather, capability.[61] Thus, as we saw in the more general reduction of the Soviet challenge to the strategic realm, given the fragility of international liberal politics, the reduction of Soviet intentions to capabilities could help avoid having to reset and redefine political relations and strategy every time there was a perceived shift in communist intentions. In such a context, building a strategy that was sensitive to the uncertain changes in intentions would have been particularly cumbersome. This type of strategic reduction has been observed by Friedrich Kratochwil to constitute a "double reduction of politics," where, on the one hand, there is "the reduction of the game of politics to structures of capability" and, on the other hand, there "is the further illicit assumption that military capabilities trump other forms of power and influence."[62]

Besides overcoming one of the perceived disadvantages of a pluralized order whose core is composed of liberal democracies, the stress on Soviet capabilities reinforced Soviet externalization. It provided a strategic basis for discounting any signs of Soviet desire to re-enter the liberal order while the Soviet Union still could put pressure on relations in that order. Containment in this regard constituted a sort of strategic version of productionism, wherein international political rivalry was reduced to the techno-military capacity of both sides to produce force.[63]

The dynamics of liberal-minimalization, universalism, and political closure in U.S. foreign policy played themselves out in a parallel fashion in the UN, which shared responsibility with the U.S. for the universal promotion of liberal norms. As British policymakers observed, the UN appeared in the immediate postwar years to "relieve" the U.S. of some of the responsibilities of world leadership. And the UN, by facilitating endless deliberations, could help the U.S. avoid the necessity of having to "negotiate real trade-offs with Moscow."[64]

But the UN's role in liberal order-building was limited. For the most part it had became clear by 1946–47 that the UN was an insufficient political arena for ordering Soviet-U.S. relations. One recalls the UN, as it was constructed, certainly could not concentrate enough agency to contend with the problems of building a liberal order.[65] While it might serve the ends of partial inclusion by providing a normative legitimation for survival and inclusion of externally sovereign states, the deliberative nature of and Soviet presence in the UN prevented it from being used in any meaningful way in places such as Greece, once the externalization of the Soviet Union was becoming clear. The U.S. external state had to be relied upon. Indeed, even Senator Vandenberg, who was famous for his attachment to the fate of the UN, claimed during the so-called Greek crisis that "Greece could collapse fifty times before the UN itself could ever hope to handle a situation of this nature."[66]

As confrontation with the Soviet Union expanded, it became more and more clear that the increasingly global scope of this confrontation exceeded the political confines of the UN. This meant that policies directly bearing on important international political outcomes would be made directly by the liberal core and the Soviet Union outside of the UN. Such an outcome, in any event, was consistent with the dynamics of Soviet externalization, in that the Soviet ability to affect liberal definitions through the U.N would be contained.[67] Although the UN came to play a useful role in liberal order— through, for example, its good offices, peacekeeping forces, and development efforts—it remained far weaker and less authoritative than some had hoped for in 1945. In the end, a weak UN was consistent with the more general U.S. unease with authoritative and broad-scoped international institutions.

Containment, Intervention, and the Boundaries of International Liberal Practices

I would like to conclude this discussion of containment by considering further the cross pressures that on the one hand expanded and on the other set limits to U.S. intervention. In the case of Greece, as we saw, the U.S. increasingly took control of the Greek state during the civil war, even though the reliance on the Right and a military solution was originally viewed as the quickest, most efficient, and, therefore, most minimal route to stability. That is, despite this growing involvement of the U.S. in Greece, the U.S. attempted to set definite limits to U.S. intervention. This effort had two faces. First, while the scope of intervention would be extensive, policymakers endeavored to limit the character of the external state organs operating in Greece to an advisory status, thereby rendering them temporary in nature. And second, in order to evade public charges of imperialism from the Soviet Union, the U.S. made sure to avoid sending troops to Greece.[68]

(The transformation of advisers into troops was not avoided years later in Vietnam, for reasons that are too complex to do justice to here.)

To understand how these cross pressures operated beyond the Greek case we need to consider how the application of containment mapped out globally. To start, the Middle East and especially Eastern Europe were both recognized as regions where the U.S. possessed limited organizational reach, particularly in the military sphere.[69] Policymakers were also reluctant to build external state organs in China or India. They were generally happy to defer to the operation of the British external state in its traditional spheres of influence from the Mediterranean to the Pacific. Even within Western Europe the Joint Chiefs of Staff sought a minimum U.S. troop commitment into 1950, in the hope that European states themselves would supply the necessary forces.[70]

Nonetheless, policymakers strategically concentrated resources on "Europe first," privileging it as an important region of the liberal core. But concentration there also made sense because it was the one region where it was believed that an intensive—albeit expensive—investment of resources would pay off in a rapid success, given the scope of the nodal points of strength present there.[71] Acheson let the public know in mid-1947 that it was necessary "to concentrate our emergency assistance in areas where it will be most effective in building world political and economic stability."[72] In this respect the strategy reflected a recognition that there were limits to the range of external state operations.

This strategy closely resembled one of Walter Lippmann's main arguments in *The Cold War*. U.S. policy should stress building the strength of the Atlantic states because they would be the U.S.'s most effective allies.[73] In a fashion reminiscent of Walter Lippmann, historians such as the Kolkos believe there was a contradiction in a U.S. foreign policy with "universal objectives, but finite power."[74] However, as we saw, it was exactly this gap that the doctrine of containment was designed to bridge. The universalism in a doctrine like containment allowed for very uneven forms of involvement. Economic security was applied in Western Europe, while in southern Europe, Latin America, and Asia there was a tendency to stress military security.[75] More generally, under containment, U.S. policymakers were able to rely on particular configurations of available forces, or nodal points of strength, strong enough to contain communism, including repressive state mechanisms. Entire dimensions of social and political life in a given state and society not deemed relevant to the location of strength could be ignored even if these dimensions had some bearing on liberal doctrine and practice. Kennan warned in early 1948 that in contrast to Western Europe "[w]e should not talk about vague and—for the Far East—unreal objectives such as human rights, the raising of living standards, and democratization."[76] The very ability to define out-of-focus categories of social practice such as the exercise of civil rights meant that where links to liberalism were tenuous, the application of liberal principles could be avoided. Indeed, this was very much an advantage of the doctrine of containment: it was not necessary to become involved with or intervene in societies on an even basis. Thus, yet one more bridge between the particular and the universal could be relied upon. Partial integration ensured that significant aspects of the social and political life of a nonliberal state and society could lie outside the operation of liberal domains.

The process of defining out aspects of social and political life in the application of containment led to increased intervention, as we saw, because of the inherent weakness of societies such as Greece. Such an observation would seem to imply that it was only in the weaker, partial participants of the liberal order that the application of containment led to increased intervention, especially in the security realm. But this is incorrect. Even in Western Europe the application of containment, which at first served to minimize intervention, in the end increased it.

This happened, in part, as follows. We have already seen how the universality of the doctrine of containment, despite covert intervention to stem unwanted political outcomes, was designed to open the way for the states in Western Europe to define their own particular terms for the generation of counterforce in the region. Unlike the unstable Greek state, Western European states were strong enough to determine on their own how much sovereign control they would retain over their own security. They were able, to a great extent through their own choosing, to gain the benefits of cooperation with the U.S. in establishing a military security system in the region (i.e., NATO). Because of the universal and nonspecific character of containment, Western European states could define their own sense of what mix of forces would be necessary to contain communism there. Ultimately included in that mix was military security. While the reasons for this turn to military security will be explored below, it can be noted here that the cost to European states of this security was an increase in U.S. intervention. Where economic security entailed a minimum of U.S. intervention in European states, the demand for a system of military security opened the way for further intervention, and ultimately, as we shall see, the transformation of containment from a predominantly economic to a predominantly military program.[77] Although partial members such as Turkey were much more susceptible to encroachment, Western European states often had to resist the U.S. desire for base rights and military advisers in their capitals.[78] The problem was that there was no clear balance between the requisites of security and the boundaries of state sovereignty. Once European states were willing to surrender significant aspects of their control over military security to the U.S., they would have to be vigilant in regard to the encroachment of security demands on those aspects of security not yet surrendered (e.g., specific force configurations). Thus, the very capacity to apply economic security in Western Europe based on the political and economic strengths of the states in the region had made possible the "invitation" to the U.S. to become more deeply involved in Europe's security, and more interventionist. In effect, through their own election, Western European policymakers curtailed what has been historically counted as an important prerogative of sovereign states: direct and self-reliant responsibility for determining and providing for the defense of the realm. It would take a de Gaulle in the 1960s to make a contentious political issue of this curtailment.[79]

Economic Security, Integration, and the Liberal State

The need to apply economic security in Europe makes one thing evident. Despite the relative strength of Western European states, they were far from stable in both economic and political terms. Policymakers in the U.S. and Europe viewed the recovery of economies at the national level as a necessity. But the economic weakness of states and national economies in general belied for U.S. policymakers and legislators any effort to rely only on European state power to generate a recovery. On its own, the nation-state was judged to be "too small a unit to solve the economic and political problems with which the Western world was confronted."[80] This judgment mirrored the more modest nineteenth-century liberal belief that legitimate claims to statehood could be made only by those national collectivities that were, in the words of J.S. Mill, "sufficiently numerous to be capable of constituting a respectable nationality."[81] Respectibility entailed, among other things, viability as an economic unit. The way out of the puzzle of having to build state strength where only relatively limited strength was currently available—without necessitating heavy U.S. intervention—was to pin hopes on the prospect of regional economic and political integration.

The logic behind the U.S. support for European integration can be viewed as an effort to build nodal points of strength in Western Europe directly through relations of international economic exchange. A "coordinated European economy," as Acheson put it,[82] was thought to be able simultenously to increase political, economic, and, ultimately, military strength in Europe and to minimize the necessity of the U.S. external state having to directly administer international economic processes in Western Europe. It would also limit some of the historic excesses of European nationalism and mediate the differences among European sovereign states over issues such as the incorporation of Germany into the West.[83] This, after all, was the significance of linking economic integration with political community, as Ernst Haas discussed in a seminal 1961 article on integration. For him, shifting loyalties and expectations to new common institutions could yield a political community where "there is likelihood of internal peaceful change in a setting of contending groups with mutually antagonistic claims."[84]

In its deliberations on the ERP, Congress had generally expressed a strong interest in seeing the program tied to a European commitment to integration. But Congress was only willing to offer encouragement for integration in the text of ERP legislation. It refused to make integration an outright requisite for extending aid, which might have required it to construct authoritative and broad-scoped external state organs for this purpose.[85] Legislators such as Taft, whose interests revolved around the internal state, and were thereby suspicious of any external state-building, resisted approving an ERP that would imply a permanent U.S. organizational commitment to Western Europe.[86] This resistance led policymakers to construct an external state program that can be described as *auto-extinguishing*. That is, by fostering "self-help" and "mutual aid" for an integrating Europe, the necessity of externally deployed organs and aid would disappear, along with the program itself. Its very success would mean its demise. Thus, if liberal minimalization was an important strategic logic of liberal order-building, then auto-extinguishment was an important tactic. It differed from the earlier faith in an order-generating, self-regulating international economic system in that the necessity of significant deployment and regulation was acknowledged by most leaders—albeit to achieve conditions that ultimately were expected to obviate that necessity.

The reasonableness of auto-extinguishment was reinforced by the judgment of policymakers such as Kennan that the economic, and political, problems in Europe were temporary, and perhaps even only a matter of "bottlenecks."[87] Despite reservations in Congress regarding some European state planning projects, the program was designed to work through individual European governments, and thus remained consistent with the preservation of their relative autonomy. By sharing authority over functions such as the distribution of resources (e.g., counterpart funds) with European states, the U.S. had located a formula that appeared to integrate its hegemonic center with the liberal uniaxis in Europe in a manner that would fulfill the imperatives of auto-extinguishment (since European states were expected to become productive economic agents less dependent on U.S. external state discipline).

Another dimension of auto-extinguishment—and minimalization more generally—was the reliance on private interests in the operation of the ERP, rather than just state organs (especially U.S. ones).[88] At its most simple, this meant that the ERP would rely on private channels rather than governments for the procurement of resources.[89] Far more complex was the participation of business representatives, especially of multinational corporations (MNCs), in "a host of private advisory committees," which had important policymaking functions.[90] They were also engaged in explicit campaigns to strengthen national economies and international exchange through efforts such as the Anglo-American Council on Productivity, composed of industry and labor representatives from both the U.S. and Britain.[91] Most important of all, the Economic Cooperation Administration (ECA), the administrative organ of the ERP, was set up as a temporary independent agency, rather than as a part of the State Department, which, Congress feared, would have made a far more institutionalized addition to the external state. To top it off, the president of the Studebaker Corporation, Paul G. Hoffman, was called on to head the agency, instead of Under Secretary of State William Clayton or even Dean Acheson, who at that time had temporarily left public service.

Senator Vandenberg, who was a key player in the design and passage of Marshall Plan legislation, understood exactly what was at stake in building an ERP that was severely limited as an organ for coordinating and administering economic relations—if not also for achieving other political ends— on a more longstanding and broad-scoped basis. He boasted to a constituent that, in the ECA, Congress succeeded in finding "the most non-political organization which has ever been put together on a government project."[92]

The point was to avoid an "international WPA," and the key to doing so was the program's administrative character.[93] As Vandenberg had put it at the beginning of 1948:

> The question of finding a satisfactory administrative formula is perhaps the biggest single conundrum which the Senate Foreign Relations Committee confronts. We all pretty well agree as to our general objective—namely, that the *business* side of this essentially *business* enterprise shall be under the effective control of adequate business brains which shall be specially recruited for the purpose. At the same time we all must agree that ERP virtually becomes the "foreign policy" of the Government in Western Europe for the next four years. Therefore, our "business administration" of ERP has got to be in successful liaison with the Secretary of State and the President wherever foreign policy decisions are involved. We cannot have "two Secretaries of State" [author's italics].[94]

As it turned out, the ERP did not become the "foreign policy" of the U.S. in Western Europe—the militarization of NSC-68 eclipsed it by 1950. What Vandenberg and other policymakers failed to grasp in 1948 was that by constricting the formation of external state organs they were limiting their options in responding to future tensions and weaknesses in Western Europe. The intractability of states regarding the issues of integration, for example, meant there was little chance of any real headway being made through the ERP. In effect, the minimal character of the ERP and its ECA could not contend with the political and economic issues in Europe which included, besides the demanding question of Germany, the control of exchange rates. In addition, European states not only resisted the U.S. model of integration that was being pushed, but also each state had its own approach to integration. The reliance on private power left a limited range of political and economic institutional instruments directly in the hands of the U.S state.

Turning to private power in the international realm in order to help set the terms of liberal relations, however, was consistent with the general effort to construct a liberal order in the context of a plurality of (Western European) states and other actors such as MNCs. The space left for states and corporations in the ERP accorded with the principles of the domains of self-determination, liberal rights, and economic exchange. But it left a provisional ERP little leverage and room for maneuver.[95] As we shall see, the limited character of the institutional repertoire increased the salience of strategic-military relations as an available—and as it turned out propitious—basis for continuing the liberal order-construction process.

Strategy and the Making of the European Recovery Program

The containment of the ERP along the lines described above should not blind us to the very strategic aims to which the program was applied. These aims were quite consistent, from a congressional perspective, with the Marshall Plan's institutional constriction in that its purposes would thereby also be limited to the requirements of stability and security, rather than remain open to any political aims U.S. planners and Western European participants might themselves define. Indeed, as the Truman administration's effort to get congressional approval for the ERP discussed above shows, it was necessary to emphasize the strategic dimensions of the ERP, rather than the benefits ERP would be able to offer the U.S. economy once the program helped Europe to achieve economic recovery.[96]

The strategic ramifications of the ERP cut across a number of dimensions: orienting Western European governments and electorates toward the U.S. and the West in general (in part by avoiding the pull of markets in the East); removing the presence of communists in the Italian and French governments; aiding the British ability to maintain their external state commitments;[97] and increasing the incentive of, above all, the French to accept the integration of Germany into the fabric of Western European economic recovery.[98] These things, as discussed in chapter 3, helped to consolidate the liberal uniaxis. Although neither integration nor a solution to the incorporation of Germany on a political level would be achieved, the Marshall Plan did force the Soviet Union to a clearly externalized position by virtue of its refusal to participate. In addition, the consolidation to be achieved through the Marshall Plan made the continuation of East-West trade more palatable to U.S. policymakers by reducing the threat of a drift toward the East. And while the externalization of the Soviet Union, as a result of the Marshall Plan, contributed to a stronger Soviet grip on Eastern Europe, as some policymakers had anticipated, the immediate formation of fixed blocs was avoided. With the continuation and even encouragement under the Marshall Plan of East-West trade, the possibility—however dim it was—of eventually bringing Eastern Europe into the liberal order was at least not completely ruled out.[99] As an initial (August 1948) draft of the most comprehensive statement of U.S. policy prior to NSC-68 put it:

> By forcing the Russians either to permit the [Soviet] satellite countries to enter into a relationship of economic collaboration with the west of Europe which would inevitably have strengthened east-west bonds and weakened the exclusive orientation of these countries toward Russia or to force them to remain outside this structure of collaboration at heavy economic sacrifice to themselves, we placed a severe strain on the relations between Moscow and the satellite countries and undoubtedly made more awkward and difficult maintenance by Moscow of its exclusive authority in the satellite capitals. . . . The disaffection of Tito, to which the strain caused by the ERP problem undoubtedly contributed in some measure, has clearly demonstrated that it is possible for stresses in the Soviet-satellite relations to lead to a real weakening and disruption of the Russian domination.[100]

But the economic security pursued in the Marshall Plan embodied strategic considerations that extended beyond political-economic tactics.[101] Even if, as Milward puts it, the goals of the Marshall Plan were mostly political while the means were economic,[102] there were military dimensions embodied in the Marshall Plan as well. Even in its earliest conceptualization within the Truman administration, policymakers tied military-industrial capacity, strategic materials, and human capital concerns into the politico-strategic goals of a recovery program in Europe. The "Special 'Ad Hoc' Coordinating Committee" claimed that:

> It is important to maintain in friendly hands areas which contain or protect sources of metals, oil and other national resources, which contain strategic objectives, or areas strategically located, which contain a substantial industrial potential, which possess manpower and organized military forces in important quantities, or which for political or psychological reasons enable the U.S. to exert a greater influence for world stability, security and peace.[103]

The final claim about enabling the U.S. was, of course, an expression of the logic of nodal points of strength, *par excellence*.

Provisions for the control of strategic resources were ultimately incorporated in Marshall Plan legislation. During the deliberations over the Marshall Plan in Congress, legislators as well as critical commentators, such as Henry Wallace and Bernard Baruch, observed that the commitment to economic security implied a commitment to military security. It was understood that once the U.S. was involved in the former, it had somehow taken responsibility for the region in all its strategic dimensions.[104]

The military aspects of the Marshall Plan, in practice, never formally extended beyond the provisions for strategic materials. But the introduction of military-strategic considerations into early policy formation, as well as congressional deliberations, reveals that the endeavor to limit the specific application of containment to the economic realm was, in the least, questionable. There was no specified limit to the containment doctrine itself. Military ramifications were not ruled out by the specifics of the doctrine itself, which, as I have argued above, remained universalistic. Moreover, the minimal character of the ECA as an external state organ meant that there would be little difficulty in shifting the emphasis in containment from the economic to the military. That is, the minimum invested institutionally via the ECA, could only facilitate its transformation into the Mutual Security Agency. The ECA and the ERP in general mirrored the doctrine of containment well: it was flexible. As such it could respond to the local demands in the external realm, including above all those for military security, to which we may now turn.

The Transformation of Containment in Western Europe and the Militarization of U.S.-European Relations

The Economic Recovery Program and Military Security

In 1949 the perceived need to move substantially beyond economic measures took shape as the U.S. commitment to the North Atlantic Treaty (NAT) and the Mutual Defense Assistance Program (MDAP) providing 1.5 billion dollars in military aid to Western Europe. The latter has been described by historian Timothy Smith as " a significant step in the shift from an economic to a military emphasis in postwar United States foreign policy."[105] By 1950, military security would become the predominant form of containment in Western Europe. NAT evolved in January of that year into a formal military organization as the North Atlantic Treaty Organization (NATO). In general, European relations would be significantly militarized along the lines suggested in NSC-68. The remainder of this chapter will be dedicated to tracing the forces propelling this transformation.

We can begin by noting that Henry Wallace and Bernard Baruch were correct about economic commitments leading to military ones. By 1948–49 it was becoming clear to leading U.S. policymakers such as Acheson that "economic measures alone . . . [were] not enough" to achieve the recovery program associated with economic containment. Under Secretary of State Lovett agreed in 1948 that support "in the security and military field" was necessary in order not to undermine the ERP. What Lovett saw as being at stake in such aid was "the psychological effect rather than the intrinsic military value."[106] In other words, Western European states and societies needed to obtain a higher level of strategic-military security in order to supplement the effort in the economic security program, to bolster politico-strategic security, and to achieve a confident environment for investment. This view was reinforced by a CIA report in early 1949 that argued that the benefit of military assistance "would be primarily psychological," in that "the will to resist is unlikely to outrun the visible means of resistance."[107]

When he learned of the intention to construct a formal North Atlantic alliance at the start of 1949, Vandenberg, in response to a constituent, had to grapple with the tensions in the move from economic to military security:

> There is no doubt about the fact that it is a "calculated risk" for us to even partially arm the countries of Western Europe. It is also very much a "calculated risk" if we do not. One risk will have to be weighed against the other. You suggest that it will be a safe thing to do "when the economic stability of these countries shall have improved." The basic question we have to settle is whether "economic stability" can precede the creation of a greater sense of physical security. I am inclined to think that "physical security" is a prerequisite to the kind of long-range economic planning which Western Europe requires. The fact remains that the problem is fraught with many hazardous imponderables.[108]

What is being questioned is not whether the effort to achieve "economic stability" must precede or be preceded by military security, but whether the end-point of stabilization per se must be reached. Vandenberg assumes an initial commitment to economic stabilization. Indeed, for him it is the very problem of economic stabilization that raises the issue of military security.

In Western Europe the development of a military containment program was situated within the context of economic security. The NSC had insisted in mid-1948 that military assistance should be "properly integrated with the ECA."[109] While this may not have come to full fruition, by the first half of 1949 the U.S. did begin to coordinate economic and military policy. And the link between economic and military containment was not manifest only in the military assistance program and the NAT commitment. The very unity the Marshall Plan was designed to generate was supposed to increase productivity to a level sufficient for a Western European rearmament that would not sacrifice economic recovery.[110]

At first glance, the emergence of military security within the context of economic containment merely appears to fit well within the logic of nodal points of strength as applied in Western Europe. It was one more dimension—albeit a supplementary one—in which to construct positions of strength in the liberal order. In another respect, however, the economic security program itself can be viewed as the very force that made military security appear to be necessary. The priority given to the economic security program made a U.S. commitment to underwrite military security for Western Europe appear compelling. U.S. policymakers believed that Western European states themselves would not be willing to compromise their economic recovery efforts by diverting resources to defense. Paul Nitze, the main author of NSC-68, and Kennan's replacement as head of the Policy Planning Staff, was convinced in 1949 that Western Europe feared that a compromise of economic recovery would decrease the popularity of existing governments.[111] (His fears appeared to be well grounded in that the government of French Prime Minister Robert Schuman fell in mid-1948 over the issue of increasing the military budget.) Given the minimal nature of the ERP program, there was little that could be done within the institutional frame of economic security to overcome this compromise. The inevitable conclusion from the perspective of Nitze is the kind of "substantial increase in military assistance programs" called for in NSC-68.

Thus, rather than viewing the ERP as having failed to provide security through economic containment, it might be more accurate to recognize that the very commitment to economic security was never far from—and even opened the way up for—a growing commitment to the application of military security in Europe, as Vandenberg had realized. This was why Vandenberg felt he was confronted with "many hazardous imponderables." Indeed, given that the underlying logic of security in Europe was the containment doctrine, there was no specified institutional frame for keeping it limited to economic means. A U.S. commitment to contain communism in Europe could not in practice be circumscribed to the economic sphere. This was very clearly articulated by the State Department just prior to the signing of the NAT:

> The North Atlantic Pact is a necessary complement to the broad economic coordination now proceeding under the European Recovery Program. . . . The Pact and the ERP are both essential to the attainment of a peaceful, prosperous, and stable world. The economic recovery of Europe, the goal of the ERP, will be aided by the sense of increased security which the Pact will promote among these countries. . . . On the other hand, a successful ERP is the essential foundation upon which the Pact, and the increased security to be expected from it, must rest.[112]

NATO and the Politics of International Liberal Relations

Prior to the Korean War there were few effective measures taken by the liberal core to build an Atlantic military organization. This was true despite the emergence of a NAT and Mutual Defence Assistance Program. Military assistance only trickled in and French policymakers were hypersensitive about potential German rearmament and ambivalent about the alliance overall. In addition, given the explicit U.S. commitment to militarily aid and defend Western Europe that a NAT represented, Western European states were reluctant to commit their own budgets to defense. The U.S. commitment to provide military aid and a nuclear deterrent helped reduce differences over the formation of the alliance, such as those associated with French reservations. But it had exactly the opposite affect regarding the goal of building an Atlantic military organization: the incentive for Western European states to do so was diminished.[113]

The lack of any real military organization-building indicates that the priority Lovett assigned to the psychological over the military effects of a U.S. military commitment was on target. NAT's import at the point of formation was above all political. Indeed, Kennan had observed at the time that a commitment to nuclear deterrence in Europe could have been made without a formal defense treaty like the NAT. Especially since U.S. troops were already in Germany there was "an adequate guarantee that the U.S. will be at war if they are attacked."[114] In any event, the nuclear deterrent, according to Kennan, could do little to stop a Soviet troop advance. The better strategy was to use military aid as a leverage to get Western Europe to plan collectively and organize for its own defense.[115]

While Charles Bohlen, Department of State Counselor, initially agreed with Kennan that a NAT was not necessary, since the likelihood of a Soviet attack at the time seemed very remote, he did come around to point out that it had decidedly political advantages, particularly in its ability to instill confidence among European policymakers in the U.S. commitment to defend Western Europe.[116] Kennan in the end went along with the NAT, but did so only reluctantly, and pointed out through a Policy Planning Staff paper that:

> . . . the need for military alliances and rearmament on the part of the western Europeans is a *subjective* one, arising in their own minds as a result of their failure to understand correctly their own position. Their best and most hopeful course of action, if they are to save themselves from communist pressures, remains the struggle for economic recovery and for internal stability. . . . Compared to this, intensive rearmament constitutes an uneconomic and regrettable diversion of effort. A certain amount of rearmament can be subjectively beneficial to western Europe. But if rearmament proceeds at any appreciable cost to European recovery, it can do more harm than good.[117]

A subjective sense of confidence was only, for Kennan, a component of the wider interest in building stable nodal points of strength in Europe that began with economic security. But what Kennan did not see at the time was that by legitimating the need for confidence, the U.S. was moving down a slippery slope, since—as a subjective phenomenon—its boundaries were dependent on the very European policymakers and opinion leaders who were demanding to be confidently secure. European confidence in a U.S. deterrent was a problem that would continually plague U.S. policymakers throughout the Cold War. But in the late 1940s this problem was especially acute, given the possibility of resistance to external state commitments by isolationist internal state interests represented by Senator Taft. A formal commitment would instill confidence in Western Europe that a U.S. resolve to defend the region would not be undermined by U.S. domestic resistance. Western Europeans had only to look at the temporary status of the ERP and the struggle over that program to see how elusive such commitments could be.

Interestingly, Kennan's initial views about deterrence paralleled on one level Taft's alternative to a NAT: a "unilateral commitment to Western Europe" through the nuclear air power umbrella.[118] Although the administration achieved a congressional commitment to both a NAT and military aid—the latter of which Taft, unlike Kennan, was decidedly against—its reliance on deterrence as the chief element of U.S. strategic posture in Europe resembled isolationist military strategy. Deterrence, which became such a cornerstone of Western policy, did double duty in the context of liberal hegemony and the external state. It satisfied Western European policymakers who wanted to minimize the pressures on their states to provide for Western Europe's defense, at the same time that it was at least palatable to internal state critics like Taft who sought to keep budgets low and avoid an extensive construction of European military organization.[119]

More central to the concerns here is the overcoming of divisions that had become apparent in the ERP. The program was unable to provide the political context for the consolidation—or "solidarity," as one recalls Kennan had called for—that policymakers in general had taken to be a *sine qua non* of order-building.[120] Britain opposed economic integration; France was reluctant to accept a West German state integrated into Western Europe; and continued economic difficulties coupled with the Czech coup—when in early 1948 a Stalinist leadership grabbed control from a more moderate government—had eroded European confidence among Western European governments that sufficient security institutions were in place to resist Soviet pressures.[121]

As implied in the above discussion, the issue of West German integration was central to the role of the NAT regarding liberal order-construction. It was, above all, the U.S. desire to reestablish a nodal point of strength in West Germany—which could help relieve the U.S. of much of its economic and military responsibilities in Europe—that had led to the problem of how to integrate this newly emerging state into Western Europe in the first place. Acheson was willing to rely on a NAT to assuage French fears regarding a revitalized Germany. The liberal uniaxis could add an important member, West Germany, without having to risk the exit of another important member, France. The acceptance of Germany was made tolerable within the institutional frame of a NAT, which assuaged fears of an independent West Germany threatening France.[122] European representatives themselves had lobbied Senator Vandenberg in the fall of 1948 for a U.S. commitment to the North Atlantic alliance to "protect economic recovery and integrate a restored Germany."[123]

What is at stake here is the endeavor to locate a common institutional arena that could serve as a forum for collaboration for states along the liberal uniaxis. If this could not be accomplished through the ERP, then with the emergence of a NAT the common cooperative framework of the liberal core could be shifted onto the military plane. Ambassador Harriman said it best in 1949 in a meeting of U.S. ambassadors and other leading U.S. policymakers:

> We should have a fresh look at the whole problem of cooperation with our European partners. The mutual security commitments of the Atlantic Pact seem to offer the best basis on which to undertake a concerting of action. Much had already been done through ECA channels but this method would become less effective without concerted multilateral action, although the ECA approach will continue to be pushed vigorously until an alternative is agreed upon. The Atlantic pact machinery would provide *room* for three important aspects of controls which were necessarily absent from the ECA approach. These were: adequate emphasis on security and political factors and the tackling of control of industrial know-how.[124]

The formation of a NAT meant that Britain's resistance to pursuing economic integration—in part because of its Commonwealth interests—did not necessarily have to lead to the absence of a collaborative institutional frame which was inclusive of all the major liberal states in Europe. It is easy to forget—especially in the 1990s—that in the immediate postwar years cooperation in Europe was hardly guaranteed. As Harriman so clearly pointed out, the militarization of liberal relations that took place in Western Europe at the end of the 1940s opened up the possibility of basing political-economic cooperation on military-strategic collaboration.

The Soviet Threat and the Militarization of the West

So far I have concentrated on the forces associated with liberal order-building that helped make the militarization of the West a compelling course of action for policymakers. These forces—and the others I will consider below—are notably complex.[125] Conspicuously missing from the discussion is the simple proposition that militarization occurred because of a growing sense in the West that the Soviet threat was becoming more menacing and militaristic. By 1948 the Soviet threat was, very much, on the minds of U.S. policymakers. Indeed the general explanatory scheme guiding this study implies that by 1948 we are smack in the middle of the inner boxes of figure 4.1, representing confrontation and Cold War.

In one respect, posing the Soviet threat as a counter-explanation sets up a false dichotomy, since its rise has been attributed here to forces associated with liberal order-construction, especially Soviet externalization and strategic reduction. I have, moreover, argued that the Soviet threat can be identified as a function of liberal order-building more justifiably than as a function of bipolarity. Even so, it is still necessary to sort out how liberal order-construction shaped militarization in a policymaking context where concern with the Soviet threat was pervasive.

From the perspective of Waltzian neorealism and the liberal order-building process, one should recall, the (immediate) stakes of the Soviet threat are the same: the fate of Western Europe. For Waltz, a Soviet-dominated Western Europe threatens to throw the distribution or balance of power toward the Soviet Union, whose thereby enhanced capabilities would increase the physical insecurity of the United States. U.S. fear over the fate of Western Europe was a function of a more direct concern with the Soviet Union. For me it is exactly the opposite. Fear of the Soviet Union in the 1940s was primarily a function of concern about the fate of Western Europe and ultimately liberal order-building.

To some, fear of the Soviets and fear for Western Europe may appear to have melded into one overall constellation of threat. But this reduction is

FIGURE 4.1   Explanatory Dimensions

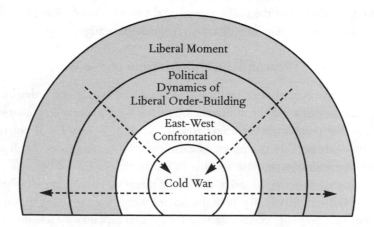

carried out at the risk not only of failing to distinguish among different explanatory forces leading to this point, but also of missing the ways that the interplay between threat and order-building in Europe developed in the Cold War, which were explored especially in chapter 3.

This does not mean that in the late 1940s there was a lack of concern with the possibility of war with the Soviet Union and the damage a Soviet state, made more powerful by garnering Western European resources, could unleash against the U.S. Rather it means concern with that damage—and thus the possibility of war—emerged because the deployment of a U.S. external state for liberal order-building brought the U.S. in confrontation with what came to be seen as a challenging and hostile Soviet state, which might generate "incidents" or "miscalculations" leading to war.

This logic emerged clearly in NSC-20/4, the leading U.S. policy document on the Soviet Union until NSC-68.[126] It was composed and approved in the second half of 1948 and it also points to other connections between liberal order-building and threat. The document begins by portraying a Soviet state bent on long-term global domination and more immediate term "political conquest of western Europe" through the usual subversive means short of war. While it is argued that the Soviet state was attempting to build its military strength—for what the Soviets believe is an "inevitable" war with the West down the road—the possibility that the Soviets could invade the U.S. even after years of build-up was dismissed. And while Soviet capacity to overrun Western Europe was expected to continue for years, the "probability" of the Soviets doing so via "planned Soviet armed actions" could at best not be "ruled out" (that is, because of the possibility of "miscalculations" and "incidents").[127] Moreover, even if the Soviets were to undertake such an action the document points out that they would have difficulty holding—and therefore exploiting—the territory because it would strain their economy, rendering them vulnerable to total Soviet disintegration. Thus, the Soviet threat remained for the most part a political one: political domination mostly through political means. (Interestingly, policymakers were reading in the need of the Soviet Union to rely on nodal points of strength for a Soviet external state to function well.)

But even this political domination was seen as having little chance of success in Western Europe, leading the Soviet state to take more of a defensive posture than anything else.[128] What was halting their march to global conquest was the "resistance of the United States," which was "recognized by the USSR as a major obstacle to the obtainment of" their goals.[129] This resistance was nothing other than the economic and increasingly military security measures undertaken to strengthen Western European states and societies that I have discussed up till this point and all of which were part of the liberal order-building process. Thus, by building a liberal order in the form it had undertaken, the U.S. had thrown itself in the way of the Soviet Union, which might then use its military power in a war that could break out exactly because this liberal order effort increased the risk of miscalculations and incidents. In effect, liberal order-building was a threat to the U.S. Even so, the proscribed policy course was to expand the pressure on the Soviet state. Why this policy made sense will become clear immediately below. It should be noted here that the aim of pressure was not only to reduce Soviet power but to turn the Soviet state into a good member of the constructed international order so that it would "conform with the purposes and principles in the UN charter [sic]."[130]

One of the most vivid instances of how liberal order-building had thrown the U.S. and Western Europe more generally into a threatening position was the Berlin crisis in mid-1948. In response to a Soviet road and rail blockade of West Berlin, the U.S. airlifted supplies. Although this event has been seen as the first direct military confrontation in Europe between the U.S. and Soviet states, it took an Army Chief of Staff, General Omar Bradley, to point out at that time that "the whole Berlin crisis has arisen as a result of two actions on the part of the Western Powers. These actions are (1) implementation of the decisions agreed in the London Talks on Germany and (2) institution of currency reform."[131] In other words (as briefly discussed in chapter 3) the West had taken upon itself a number of crucial policy turns, in a series of meetings in London in the spring of 1948—from which the Soviet Union, a fellow occupier and former negotiator over Germany, was excluded. These turns led to the consolidation of Western zones (laying the groundwork for a separate west German state) and their intended integration into Western economic reconstruction efforts, especially through (Western) control of Germany's industrial center (the Ruhr). However justified Western policymakers believed these actions to be, they generally held that it was Soviet "resistance" to Western policies that made "miscalculations" and "incidents" more likely. French policymakers in 1948 were thinking about the possibilities of a Soviet invasion not so much because of any direct and increasing tension between the French and Soviet states. The main problem for French policymakers was a sense that growing tensions between the U.S. and the Soviet Union over issues such as Germany could lead to violent collateral aggression against France.[132] Similarly, a memorandum summarizing the result of talks between Western policymakers in Washington in the summer of 1948 reasoned that immediate aid should be forthcoming from the U.S. if a country was attacked, "[i]nasmuch as the conclusion of such a treaty [NAT] might increase the existing tension with the Soviet Government."[133] In his memoirs Kennan puzzled about the fears of Western European policymakers:

> Why did they wish to divert attention from a thoroughly justified and promising program of economic recovery by emphasizing a danger which did not actually exist but which might indeed be brought into existence by too much discussion of the military balance and by the ostentatious stimulation of a military rivalry?[134]

He seems to have ignored the security ramifications of the very political and economic measures taken by the U.S. that he was so much in favor of—measures that could generate, as in Germany, this type of danger as well.

A real shift in the way security was being articulated vis-à-vis liberal order-making is noticeable. In the spring of 1947 the special ad hoc committee report that thought through the strategy of the Marshall Plan resolutely declared that U.S. "[n]ational security can be maintained most effectively through the rebuilding of a stable peaceful world."[135] NSC-20/4 shows that by late 1948 it is exactly the pursuit of security (e.g., resisting Soviet pressures), through the building of a peaceful and stable liberal order, that is putting the U.S.—and Western Europe for that matter—at risk. Walter Lippmann captured a dimension of this calculus when he argued in a long 1948 memo to John Foster Dulles that the formation of a NAT would effectively guarantee that the Soviet Union would remain in central Europe,[136] thereby crystalizing the dread it was in part designed to relieve.[137] This calculus was pushed to near absurd limits by those policymakers who, like U.S. military planners and the French foreign ministry, believed "the augmentation" of Western European material life "achieved by the ERP" heightened the risks and costs of their capture.[138] In other words, the very success of liberal order-building efforts in Western Europe increases the threat to the U.S. in that the enhancement of resources that flows from those efforts could be used against the U.S. The "loss" of

Western Europe, thereby, matters to the degree that the social and economic dimensions of order-building by Europeans with U.S. aid can continue, ensuring that there is something worth losing.

Waltz may argue that all of this is merely a reflection of the global reach and power of the U.S. butting up against that of the Soviet Union. But to make such an argument Waltz would have to turn his theory on its head. Threat or fear of the powerful other would be emerging from the friction caused by global projects (such as liberal order-building), which powerful states can pursue, rather than the reverse (the powerful state's fear of the powerful other leads to projects and friction), as Waltz would have it. It certainly will not do to retreat as a realist to a Morgenthauian position and claim that the pursuit of power is what generates projects and thereby threat-producing friction. This only begs the question of what the drive for power could mean as a pure motive for a state, outside of the context that a project could constitute.

But we are still nowhere near the deeper links between the Soviet threat and Western militarization. To get there we can begin by noting that the strategic reduction of the Soviet Union to a control-seeking, hostile opponent in U.S. thinking, reflected in statements such as NSC-20/4, severely constricted the possibilities of agency for the Soviet state. As the Soviets enhanced their power in the eyes of U.S. policymakers—most notably by exploding their own atomic bomb in August 1949—their status as an strategic opponent was reinforced.[139] The reduction made it easy for U.S. policymakers to reject as a mere ploy a Soviet effort to negotiate over Germany after the Berlin crisis.[140] (Recall that what was so threatening about negotiation was the possibility of the Soviet Union influencing and shaping the construction of liberal order.) If the Soviet state's agency was so constricted, then it was only the West that had any serious range of agency. However, rather than being a blessing, this was seen as a sort of curse for the West. The problem was that Western policymakers feared that they would not be up to the task of resistance, especially since liberal order—specifically in the liberal core—opened the way for contest, autonomy, and democratic culture. Perhaps the most recognizable Western "self-fear" was the doubt Western European states had about the U.S. commitment to defend the region, given the recalcitrance of Congress about external commitments so often referred to above.

In NSC-20/4 this Western self-fear emerges in an almost bizarre fashion. Domestic and international conditions in the West are literally treated as

Soviet threat-capabilities (not just as factors that enhance the Soviet threat). These include vulnerability to subversion, military intimidation, or even psychological warfare that would "prevent or retard the recovery of and cooperation among western European countries"; a relatively tolerant society that allows for the political operation of communists;[141] and the potential for vacillation, appeasement, "wasteful usage of . . . resources in time of peace," and "political and social disunity."[142] The U.S. feared that Europe would not be strong enough, unified enough, and willful enough to withstand the pressures and temptations of the Soviet Union. Dean Acheson, for instance, argued regarding the integration of Italy into the NAT that "from a political point of view an unattached Italy was a source of danger."[143] A relatively autonomous state, even one as intervened in as Italy, could through democratic forces choose a neutral or "Eastern" course, unless constraints were in place, such as a NAT alliance.

There was another dimension to self-fear—the fear that democratic publics would not fear enough. To achieve U.S. aims, NSC-20/4 required that the state "[k]eep the U.S. public fully informed and cognizant of the threats to . . . national security so that it will be prepared to support the measures we must accordingly adopt."[144] This type of concern had a more far-reaching relevance to Western militarization. That was the perceived necessity of putting the West, and most particularly the U.S., on a permanent war-like footing during peacetime. NSC-20/4 boldly asserted that it was "essential that this government formulate general objectives which are capable of sustained pursuit both in time of peace and in the event of war."[145] The rationale that stands behind this assertion was expressed in the first draft of NSC-20 emerging from the Kennan-led Policy Planning Staff. There it was argued that "a democracy cannot effect, as the totalitarian state sometimes does, a complete identification of its peacetime and wartime objectives."[146] Democracies generally separate these two "times" and maintain an "aversion to war as a method of foreign policy." Nonetheless, a democratic public could be emotionalist during war, preventing balanced long-term planning. The trick would be "to reduce as far as possible the gap between" wartime and peacetime policymaking, rendering war and the methods short of war as more of a continuum of security tactics. Thus, the memorandum referred to Clausewitz's famous dictum about war being a "continuation of policy, intermingled with other means."[147] What was necessary was that the U.S.—and the West by implication—be kept "in a state of unvacillating mental preparedness," as claimed in the second NSC-20 draft.[148] All of us who lived through the Cold War take this preparedness for granted. But the point to note here is that a democracy would need to effect a program of "preparedness" exactly because it had no built-in formula of "complete identification" as totalitarian states could have. Moreover, a democracy, possessing powerful forces of opinion drawing it away from such a stance, requires special vigilance.

By building a 'total preparedness' approach to foreign policy, the problem with Western agency would be attenuated, since the program of security could prevail over choices, alternatives, and challenges. One way to understand this response to self-threat is as the final strategic reduction of the West itself—and liberal order—as a capability of readiness and strength, rendering intentions rather moot as in the case of the Soviet state. The fear of themselves (e.g., their potential weakness and tolerance) would be contained in that it would be no easy matter for parliaments and democratic public to opt out of, intentionally, a "long term state of readiness."[149] Thus, we see the reason for the proscribed policy course in NSC-20/4 of expanding pressure on the Soviet state, discussed immediately above. A militarizing campaign of pressure was far less risky for the political life of the Atlantic community than alternatives such as serious negotiations with the Soviet Union.

The notion that fear and anxiety have shaped U.S. foreign policy has been put forth by commentators for years.[150] This fear has typically been viewed more strictly as a function of changes in external forces that render the West more vulnerable (e.g., the "missile gap"). Far less attention has been paid to what I have emphasized here, a fear of the self.[151] By emphasizing this fear and, thereby, contextualizing the Soviet threat as such, we gain some insight into what the authors of NSC-68, writing over a year later than those of NSC-20, meant when they stated for dramatic, edifying purposes: "Even if there were no Soviet Union we would face the great problem of the free society, accentuated many fold in this industrial age, of reconciling order, security, the need for participation, with the requirements of freedom."[152] These were indeed the problems of agency in liberal modernity.

Integration and Militarization in Western Europe

Reflect for a moment on the position of U.S. policymakers. They faced a plurality of states, each with democratic publics, powerful interest groups, and politicians in precarious positions of power. The policymakers of these liberal states, therefore, had to ensure that their state and society had the autonomy to set the terms of its social existence so that the various interests could be navigated. If these states had been nonliberal and authoritarian they would no doubt also seek to set those terms autonomously as well. Indeed, it is not at all clear that negotiation or cooperation would be any harder or easier, since centralized power could easily lead to a recalcitrance over a given issue deemed vital that may not be tenable in a liberal state. It is likely to depend on the specific situation. The crucial difference for liberal states is that they comprise multiple domains of liberal modernity, within each of which actors must be autonomous enough to shape and contest practices and relations. For authoritarian states, facilitating the determination and contestation of the character and terms of market relations, civil rights, and democratic governance by relatively autonomous actors is a problem. For liberal states it is part of organized political life. If autonomy has any real meaning for an authoritarian state, it is the autonomy of the state per se that matters. The practical implications of this is that, for issue areas such as trade, a liberal state has to come to terms with its own market actors, their specific interests, and relations with other market actors including labor and the perceived demands and interests of a broader democratic public, and then deal with other states with the same pressures and so on. Of course, all states have domestic interests with which to contend.[153] But only liberal states legitimize, within distinct limits, the relative autonomy of different actors across a wide array of domains within which the question of justice and right are at least capable of being politicized. They face the further problem that outcomes and processes in one domain are intertwined with those of another, as any politician who has had to explain economic crises to an electorate could attest. International order-makers are thus forced to devise mechanisms for allowing states to navigate these pressures. Yet, at the same time, the international coordination and construction of relations and policy—i.e., order-making—must proceed, at least so that strength can be augmented within a relevant zone of order.

This is the quandary. We have nodal points of strength, based on the legitimacy of the very forces of liberal life discussed above, that can undermine strength and give one grounds for deep self-doubt and fear. We have states that want autonomy and yet lack confidence in their ability alone or together (through integration) to make themselves secure. States—coming back full circle—are not in a position to impose this security-making on societal actors that covet (along with policymakers) their economic development, the progress of which is in turn important for (economic) security.

As Harriman's comments earlier underscore, it must have been very tempting for U.S. policymakers to turn to the Atlantic alliance for a way to deal with these tensions. Many of the reasons why I have already considered. Indeed, it was exactly because liberal order-building engendered so many forces and tensions that there could never be any single force or factor to which the increasing militarization of relations could be attributed. This is the reason why I have adopted a functional approach. What would it mean to say that the militarization of the West was caused by something? As I hope the complexity of the above analysis conveys, that militarization was tied to so many processes and outcomes that looking for "the cause" of NATO is like looking for the cause of a state.[154] It is not just that things were overdetermined. Western militarization was occurring in the variegated context of liberal order-building. Here and there policymakers advanced militarization by such acts as reaching out for the political dimensions of NATO, avoiding unwanted consequences through military aid, "war-itizing" peacetime, and so on.

In the remainder of this section, I want to push the connection between integration and security a bit further to show that the transformation of the U.S. external state into a predominantly military presence—marked vividly, for example, by the displacement of U.S. economic recovery missions by U.S. military aid missions—flowed specifically out of the search for a way to come to terms with the quandaries inherent in the pursuit of liberal strength.

To start, Vandenberg feared that U.S. military aid would undermine Western Europe's own efforts at security-building. The trick for him would lie in "making . . . military aid wholly supplementary to the self-help and mutual aid defense programs of these other countries. In other words, it must be their last reliance rather than their first reliance in their own physical defenses."[155] Yet making it a "first reliance" was a compelling strategy in the context of the construction of international liberal order. Western European states would not have to face the pressures of constructing unified European strength. They could import it. By curtailing, as explored above, their own direct responsibility for their own security, and avoiding a program of extensive intra-European security cooperation to deal with both Germany and the Soviet Union, Western European states limited the necessity of having to make the greater sacrifices in state autonomy that would accompany an effort to build inter-European organs of military and economic power sufficient to resist perceived threats. The political effect of the U.S. nuclear deterrent was "to limit the extent of military, political, and economic cooperation and neglect the development of war plans."[156] Moreover, as a basic institutional frame, NATO could allay the tension between diverging state interests and the demands of economic and political collaboration inherent in an international liberal order. Instead of constructing an extensive cooperative institutional order, Western European states cooperated with each other and the U.S. just enough to help construct a militarized U.S. hegemonic center. While, in the ensuing decades, Western European states did manage to cooperate in NATO, this cooperation was minimal in comparison with what would have been necessary without the U.S. Even as late as the end of the 1980s, Barry Buzan could observe that "U.S. hegemony both underwrites much of the political and military coordination achieved by Western Europe, and prevents the development of higher levels of Western European cohesion."[157] Rather than displacing the political-economic integration that was the goal of the ERP—which was something that both Kennan and John Foster Dulles feared—it simply deferred it.[158]

It is important to keep in mind that NATO did not in itself simply prevent or prompt the integration of Western Europe. Its ramifications for European integration were much more complex. First, it made it possible for Western European states that were pursuing integration in other dimensions to proceed without confronting head on, and in a compressed time frame, the pressures of more in-depth integration along political and economic lines.[159] In effect, by allaying these pressures as well as many of the differences between states in Western Europe touched on above, NATO left open the possibility of establishing economic cooperative institutions such as the European Coal and Steel Community that were integrative and yet violated only minimally sovereign state interests. NATO afforded states the time to work out differences between them.[160] This matters profoundly for liberal states, which face politically mobilized groups and democratic publics. Thus, cooperation could continue to take place in the wake of the ERP on an inter-state basis, rather than necessitating supranational institution-building.

Second, it limited the necessity of Western European states themselves creating a strong link between the spheres of security and economy. That link turned out to be left, as Charles Maier points out, to the U.S. to make with limited success in the early 1950s in its effort to get Europe to increase its defense contribution.[161] By limiting cooperation mostly to the economic sphere Western European states ensured that it would take place in the context of interstate relations. It is the state in international liberalism that has stood at the juncture of international exchange and the national market economy. To have injected heavy demands for security cooperation into this configuration would have necessitated the construction of common security organs such as those associated with the failed European Defense Community (EDC), the French effort (beginning in 1950) to lay the groundwork for a cooperative European military force. It also would have required a coordination of fiscal and welfare policies that would have considerably constrained the scope of Western European states. With the U.S. taking responsibility for this linkage, Western Europe could trade off the necessity of constructing heavy, collaborative security mechanisms for lighter forms of U.S. hegemonic encroachments and interventions, which could be resisted without necessarily sacrificing European security. Harriman perhaps said it best when he argued at the fall 1949 meeting of ambassadors: "The Atlantic Pact concept should be the umbrella under which all measures agreed upon should be taken; that security, and not economic integration or political integration, should be the point of departure of our policy."[162]

In effect, what NATO did was provide a "space" for Western European states to work out their political and economic difficulties at both the national and international levels, especially, as Maier has observed, through the "politics of productivity." As an alliance in which power was overlaid from above by the U.S., NATO removed much of the security question from the domain of democratic debate and contestation (an outcome that might have come back to haunt these states in the 1980s as pan-European social movements did contest "the security question" loudly). Indeed, this was a major political manifestation of the curtailment of direct responsibility for security in Western Europe. While Western European states would exercise influence over the character of NATO strategy and weapon deployments throughout the Cold War, ultimate responsibility for the production and maintenance of the security system per se did not lie with these states.[163] As such, NATO permitted Western European states to narrow the content of inter-state and -society relations to the technologies of production and to mechanisms of liberal monetary and trade policy. These states would not need to depend on each other for much else. Acheson articulated this strategy in 1951 when he told Congress that "behind the shield of military power which we and our allies are creating, the techniques of growth and expansion are being maintained intact."[164] Indeed, the post-World War II period has witnessed in Europe the highest degree of institution-building in history, leading to the European Community. But the scope of such institutions has been mostly limited to technical-economic issues. (The difficulty of moving beyond this horizon formed in part the basis for a loss of faith in the possibilities of political integration in the 1960s.) This has preserved the sovereignty of the state over social and political policy. As a result, the embedded liberalism observed by Ruggie was facilitated by the alliance. Given the common discipline of a Cold War and the reduction of inter-state relations to political-strategic concerns, a narrow technological focus in the economic sphere, which, as Maier shows, reduced the vulnerability of liberal politics at the state level, was more tenable.

The provision of confidence through NATO and military aid represented a process of relieving Western European states of the necessity of having to provide for their own security. They did not need to become deeply involved in securing the region as might otherwise have been necessary. Strategy could be displaced to the global confrontation of the U.S. and the Soviet Union. Western Europe could concentrate on its domestic political and economic difficulties. As David Calleo points out, being distanced from "high politics" provided Western Europe opportunity to trade with Eastern Europe and the Soviet Union, since tensions were not as likely to interfere as in the case of U.S.-East trade. Calleo also shows that NATO allowed Western European states to free up resources not only for their own economic concerns, but also for their own military concerns: Britain could focus on Commonwealth defense, while France could focus on its colonies. And the emergent West German state had more room to consider rearmament within the NATO framework.[165] In response to this very possibility, France could successfully propose the Schuman Plan in order to forge common economic ties with Germany and the rest of Europe. NATO allowed for the European Coal and Steel Community to be separated from the direct pressures of security, and provided a common bond for economic integration.[166] Thus, the irony is that the militarization of Western European relations allowed states there to construct a space at the domestic and interstate levels that was distanced from the realm of security.

The reliance of the liberal core chiefly on U.S. military power and leadership meant that the transformation from economic to military security could occur with a minimum of international institution-building, even cooperative military institution-building. In this transformation the U.S.

external state in Europe was transformed from the ECA into the Mutual Security Agency and varied U.S. expenditures in the region were transformed into military procurements. Except for standard diplomatic machinery, the U.S. external state in Europe was more or less reduced to NATO and covert organs such as the CIA. In this respect, the institutional legacy of the ECA was indeed limited as many in Congress had intended.

Conclusions

The authors of NSC-68 seemed to comprehend very well the vulnerability of a liberal order to its own political dynamics and the benefits of an emphasis on military power. The slow and open nature of democratic government and the relations between such governments made "superior" military power a necessity to compensate for the advantages that secretive and speedy dictatorial governments were thought to possess. A decided military advantage lowers the risks for especially vulnerable liberal democracies of operating "on a narrow margin of strength."[167] In a very real sense, the authors of NSC-68 wanted to replicate the advantages of authoritarian systems—their secrecy and minimum consultation with democratic publics and other governments—by constructing a military security sphere that was similarly insulated.[168] Not only in Western Europe, but also in the U.S., the realm of security grew to be increasingly insulated from the pressures of democratic processes. This development should serve as a warning to those who would place their faith in democracy as a check on the military sphere of states. One thing that was so brilliant about NSC-68 was the way that the authors could locate a huge militarization program in the context of liberal order and its principles. They could rely on the ability of liberal states to accommodate such a program based on the way that spheres of social practice—in this case security—could be defined out of the reach of liberal principles. Kennan's alternative to the call in NSC-68 for a massive military build-up of conventional and nuclear forces, i.e., to re-emphasize "economic, diplomatic, and psychological instruments of containment,"[169] was misplaced given the political dynamics that stood behind liberal militarization.

A rising predominance of strategic-military relations in the liberal order would naturally provide fertile ground for moves toward the formation of an actual military organization as the North Atlantic Treaty was transformed "from a psychological shield into a military one" (i.e., NATO).[170] The militarization of political relations in 1949 and 1950 meant that the liberal uniaxis would be highly sensitive to strategic-military events such as the Soviet atomic bomb and the Korean War. That is, given the constriction of the international political realm associated with the strategic reduction, there were few modes of political adjustment available in the alliance—and between it and the Soviet Union—to provide a basis for response to changes and shifts in the strategic-military realm. With NATO as the only institution of political cohesion for the liberal order in Europe, no real alternative realms of response to Soviet foreign policy at the end of the 1940s existed other than the military-strategic. The preferred answer was to help push militarization further along, especially in the face of increasingly salient self-fears. As the authors of NSC-68 understood, the North Atlantic Treaty lacked a real military organization to tie states together in organizational-material terms. This lack made the alliance vulnerable because of a perceived potential absence of resolve that might pave the way for European declarations of neutrality:

> The frustration of Kremlin design . . . cannot be accomplished by us alone. . . . Strength at the center, in the United States, is only the first of two essential elements. The second is that our allies and potential allies do not as a result of a sense of frustration or of Soviet intimidation drift into a course of neutrality eventually leading to Soviet domination.[171]

Military commitments would have to be increased for Western Europe as well as the United States. Western Europe would be militarized in a material-organizational as well as an international political-strategic form. Doubling back in a circular fashion, the militarization of political relations in Western Europe resonated throughout the world: indeed, a major reason for fighting the Korean war was to solidify "American prestige and the credibility of its commitments," above all, in Europe.[172] Ultimately, it doubled back on itself again, as Lawrence Kaplan points out, by serving "to denigrate the possibilities for detente which the death of Stalin and subsequent changes in the Soviet Union after 1953 might have allowed."[173]

The issues raised in this chapter can help to clarify some of the stakes in the debate over whether the militarization of containment began before or after the commencement of the Korean War.[174] Any judgment depends on what militarization is understood to be. It is clear that the actual deployment of weapons and troops (or military build-up) did not reach the levels we associate with the Cold War until the Korean War. However, along the dimensions of militarization I have stressed in this study there was considerable progress. Military-strategic relations become an increasingly salient dimension of international relations among states and societies. The emergence of NATO as the only extensive institutional link between the U.S. and Western Europe, the increasing emphasis on military over economic security, and the casting of a U.S. nuclear deterrent over Europe are among the transformations discussed above that marked the militarization of the politics of international liberal relations prior to the Korean War. It was these very transformations that permitted states in Western Europe to distance themselves from security concerns. That distance, tested as it has been by the Bosnian crisis, still haunts Western Europe and the Atlantic alliance more generally.

Abstracting out the attributes and effects of military force as it emerged in the making of liberal order, three dimensions come into view:

1. Military force achieves and maintains international order without encompassing a wide range of social practices. As the currency of systemwide political relations, it minimizes direct entrance into the economic and political practices associated with the domains of liberal modernity. Thus, it can be perceived by agents in a liberal order as a realm of international politics, which interferes minimally in liberal practice and leaves them the most space for action.

2. It minimizes permanent institution-building. Deploying military force and establishing military institutions is much easier than creating formal social and political institutions. When crises do arise, military force is a particularly attractive form of power to have at the ready. This attribute corrects for the lack of mediative institutions at the international level.

3. Military force minimizes the degree to which basic international political bonds can be politically contested. Given the "concentrated-coercive" nature of military organization,[175] liberal domain actors at the international and domestic levels—such as democratic publics—generally have a minimum of access to the relevant decisionmaking apparatus. This insulation minimizes the claims that individuals, groups, representative bodies, and states can make on the military force deployed by a hegemon in a liberal order. As a result, there is little chance of agents mak-

ing demands on the organs of military force, which might otherwise lead to more authoritative and broad-scoped institutional relationships.[176]

When these dimensions are considered in toto, they imply that the creation of space for agents in Western Europe depended on limiting access to the very social form (military power) that produced that space. The transfer of authority in exchange for security, a well-ordered society, and juristic freedoms is a familiar trade-off in the construction of a Western polity. But even the individuals who hypothetically choose out of fear, according to Locke, to construct political society and renounce individual sovereignty retained, collectively, ultimate sovereignty and established a representative legislature.[177] While Western European policymakers and sometimes even protesting democratic publics shaped Cold War security structures, these forces were nothing like the access available to resourceful groups and individuals to shape state policy in other realms. The difference between the Lockean trade-off and that of international liberal order may stem from the character of fear. Fear in Locke's state of nature was based on the vulnerability of the individual in a potentially hostile environment. Fear in the making of international liberal order was based on a fear of the self and those threats engendered by the very formation of a political society.

5

✳

Conclusion

This study began and was completed during what is called the "post-Cold War period." Like many others, I entered this period with a sense of optimism about leaving behind the limitations on international political life associated with forty years of cold war. I soon found myself lapsing into bouts of pessimism about the renewed energy being dedicated to that perennial goal of international political life: international order. The basis for that pessimism was that policymakers—and even scholars—had little interest in confronting what forty years of order-making could actually teach them. Those lessons seem to have been displaced by the euphoric myth that 1989 was a new "year zero" for understanding and ordering the world, and that the end of the Cold War also meant the end of the old order and the necessity to think hard about it.

Although we are in a political environment very different from that of the 1940s, many of the Cold War's essential components endure, including NATO, the perpetuation of a global U.S. military network, massive arms exports from the West, and a Europe still hesitant about providing for its own security. More generally, the construction of most of the pillars of contemporary international life depended, to varying degrees, on the early postwar effort to fashion an international order. These include the UN, a human rights regime, international economic institutions, European integration, decolonization, a proliferation of states, democratization, and liberalization.

The eventful beginnings and unfolding of order-making in the middle of the twentieth century are therefore ignored at a cost. We would fail to understand, for example, why, in the postwar growth—if not revolution—of international institution-building, institutions would be limited in their political and social scope and engaged in reinforcing the status of the sovereign state as the primary form of political agency across the globe.[1] In the realism that dominated international thought in the U.S. during the Cold War this outcome would be viewed as a function of anarchy in the international system. However, postwar realism would fail to explain why, in the first place, so much institution-building occurred during the war—before the Soviet Union emerged as a threat and while the U.S. was only in the process of constructing its role as a hegemon.[2] More fundamentally, anarchy—which derives from a world of sovereign states and the absence of powerful and authoritative international institutions—is exactly what needs to be explained. In contrast, this book has shown how patterns of postwar institution-building and the reinforcement of state sovereignty flow from three interrelated dimensions of postwar liberal order-building. One is the way that states—strong or weak—were designated as central constituents of order in a political tradition, liberalism, that prized the state as the locus of effective and, more optimistically, just social relations. Another is the commitment in policymaking to constructing thin and temporary institutions that I have identified as part of an overall pattern of minimalization in the making of liberal order. Finally, there is the reliance on military power as the central currency of order-wide political relations rather than simply as a means to secure the liberal world against external and internal threats.

The U.S. commitment to maintaining a network of global military power of Cold War proportions is likely to continue well into the twenty-first century. Critics of current leadership in the West who are anxious to see a strong commitment to humanitarian intervention may disapprove of the scope of this network. But their calls for more rather than less intervention where it is deemed necessary are likely to be met, if at all, through the operation of this network. Only further study will show whether the very conditions and conflicts that call out for intervention become crises in part because of the lack of robust and effective international institutions that might become engaged early on politically and thereby obviate the need for military action at a later stage. There is, however, no simple trade-off here. As this study has shown, no matter what the original intentions, commitments to political-economic structures and institutions can shape and expand military-security commitments in decisive ways. In general, international political-economic relations and security outcomes are linked to a greater extent than our intellectual traditions might otherwise lead us to believe.

But these points still rest on an implicit sense that the international community under the leadership of a liberal core of states and societies can set the terms for international order in the twenty-first century. This assumption ignores one of first goals of this study: to establish that social fabrics like liberal modernity—formed across centuries rather than decades—are not simply constructed by cores or hegemons and are not simply subject to ordering from above, but rather are dependent on a wide range of historical forces and agents.

Policymaking and research today will need to become far more sensitive to these wider historical contexts in all their complexity and mutability, even if only further liberalization is seen to be at stake. However daunting the mid-century task of order-building, it had the advantage of being part of a wider liberal moment in history. The successful completion of the Second World War was itself a crucial condition of that moment, as it freed states and societies from wartime controls, opened the way to postwar reconstruction, and forced leaders to think seriously about what type of principles and institutions would populate a postwar world. Although liberal principles and institutions have gained a new vitality after the Cold War, it is far from clear that we comprehend even the basic character of our current moment and therefore what the limits and possibilities of political agency are.

The above points also skirt the question of how well we understand the international political stakes in the commitment to build or maintain an order, particularly a liberal one. From the vantage point of the end of the twentieth century, it might appear to many that the attempt to build an order that was global in scope in the aftermath of war was not just overly ambitious, but actually dangerous. As this book has argued, it was the West's project of international liberal order, not a Soviet socialist order, that was the overarching framework for the settlement of the Second World War. The initial attempt to incorporate the Soviet Union within the emerging order generated tensions that led to the confrontation that became the Cold War. Above all, the Soviet Union was in a unique position to challenge the task, led by the U.S., to define the relations and boundaries of liberal order. This effort at definition was formidable and precarious in itself, especially since it entailed the incorporation of a diverse range of states and societies with their own national agendas and sets of specific interests. Indeed, order-making produced tensions among the states and societies within liberal order, especially regarding the problem of reconciling order and autonomy. These tensions compelled U.S. policymakers to turn increasingly to military-strategic means in the exercise of U.S. leadership. Tensions also revolved around a reluctance within the U.S. itself about its emerging hegemony that made attractive to policymakers the recourse to a form of power (i.e., military) that seemed to require a minimum of lasting political engagements. Reinforcing this growing recourse to military power was the adoption of strategies or doctrines, such as containment, that, despite policymakers' initial efforts to avoid exactly this outcome, in the end entailed taking a predominantly military approach to order-making.

Must the pursuit of order be accompanied by the pain, waste, and inequity that have come to be associated with forty years of Cold War? Those looking at things from the long history of the formation of European states and a European state system—with its bloody wars and tyrannies—might be inclined to answer yes. They would be both right and wrong. Clearly, the processes of state-formation and international order-making share, for instance, a profound connection to war and its manifold repercussions. But state-formation and order-making are also very different. Internationally, relations are ordered among a plurality of political authorities. Domestically, the formation of a state means the establishment of order through a single authority. Drawing any equivalence between the two processes has to be done carefully.

State-formation and international order-making share something deeper than the repercussions of war. It was the pursuit of exclusive authority, the contests over its control, and the conflicts with other polities over the scope of their authority that contributed to the blood and waste of European history. What perhaps makes international order into something dangerous is the extent to which its builders attempt to construct a single, universal web of relations among and across a plurality of polities and societies. International order itself may not be the problem. Rather the problem may be the attempt to establish a predominant, exclusive order, of global dimensions, against other potential orders and those forces that might challenge the terms of that order.

To say that the creation of a postwar international liberal order was dangerous is not to concentrate blame for the Cold War on the West. Most readers will readily recognize that in the preceding pages the Soviet Union is depicted as an aggressive, if not expansionist, state. Its historic aggression can rightly be condemned morally, as can that of the West. But such condemnation must be distinguished from the question of attributing forty years of Cold War to one set of agents or another.[3] I have tried to show how complex the history of the rise of that confrontation is and how cautious we would have to be to affix blame to any party to it. The point has been to emphasize the importance of liberal order-building in shaping that confrontation, not to make any final, condemning judgment on its agents based on that importance.

If the debate about the meaning and lessons of the Cold War are circumscribed to the narrow pursuit of blame, then a significant intellectual resource will be squandered. From the perspective of this study, it is far more productive to conclude by drawing out some basic insights about contemporary U.S. foreign policy- and order-making.

Liberal Identities, Liberal Dilemmas

Two very different liberal identities have been at work in this study. One is the masterful, active agent, reaching out globally, taking responsibility for the shaping of international life. The other is the more fearful, relatively inactive agent, obsessed with its own domestic life, interests, and quarrels. One is the innovative producer, the other is the passive consumer. One is the deliberate and purposeful campaigner, the other the drifting and uncertain reactor. These two identities have repeatedly surfaced in commentary on liberal modernity across two centuries, from Alexis de Tocqueville's observation that democracies wage war well but make foreign policy badly, to Carl Schmitt's disillusionment with endless deliberations of liberal parliaments, and to John Dewey's hopes for robust democratic experimentation, both domestic and international. Today, we have commentators who are frustrated by an apparent failure of Western leadership and resolve, in contrast to those who fear the costs of continued U.S. leadership. Others, such as Tony Smith, remind us of the great liberalizing mission that has organized heroic U.S. activism across a century.

Rather than being absolute, the two identities are likely to coexist in splendid dialectic in a liberal state, society, or international order. In this sense, the portrait of the post-World War II period as a triumph of inter-nationalism over isolation in the U.S.—recast most recently, both force-fully and thoughtfully, by the late Eric Nordlinger[4]—is misrepresentative. Postwar U.S. foreign policy was a combination of the two. This mixture was in place from the beginning of the period. Recall the wartime faith of policymakers that a system of liberal economic exchange would lead to a relatively self-regulating war settlement, within which a UN capable of channeling international politics into peaceful dialogue would be backed up by the regional power of the U.S., Britain, the Soviet Union, and China. Underlying the system would be the return of stability and political strength, especially in Europe, that would make U.S. intervention super-fluous and the pursuit of an "isolationist internationalism" possible. It was a system, it turned out, that could not produce the order promised by its own discourse of security, rights, democracy, and markets. Although the faith was abandoned, the notion that order and strength could be con-structed while keeping limits on U.S. involvement was not.

The pursuit of limits in the context of activism is perilous. Options for action in international institutional and diplomatic arenas are narrowed. This undercuts efforts to deal with problems of order already on the table and those that might arise in the near future. We saw this unfold in the case of economic security. The pursuit of economic security created commitments with which the circumscribed mechanisms and institutions of economic security could not contend. We, therefore, should be suspicious of calls for a return to an economic-security focus after the Cold War. Such efforts, cou-pled with a generally widespread current belief that the U.S. needs to exer-cise restraint, could be a redux to watch out for. The same goes for the much heralded foreign policy doctrine centered on the expansion of markets and democracy. What commitments does this expansion entail? How will ten-sions, conflict, and reversals in democratization be responded to?

But then, think of the dilemmas U.S. policymakers faced in struggling to build international order. On the one hand, political institutions in which agents have access and influence over outcomes (especially through repre-sentation) are quintessentially liberal. On the other hand, such access and influence can threaten order by preventing decisive action as agents deliber-ate over and contest policies. The authors of NSC-68, one recalls, under-stood this. There is also the complicating dilemma that the construction of effective international institutions to provide for global forms of gover-nance, important to life within states and societies, can also limit the capacity of states to set the terms of their own social existence. Such construction is, therefore, likely to be resisted by some. Add to this the dilemma that the constraint of the precious few institutional possibilities for governance because of this resistance or for the sake of decisive action can, in the end, limit agency, particularly in the case where such institutions would be essential for achieving a desired outcome. One can perhaps understand how attractive the recourse to military power could be in the making of order,[5] especially when it seemed to policymakers such as Averell Harriman to be uniquely capable of contending with some of the dilemmas of order-making, while opening up space for states and societies struggling to set the terms of their own social existences. We might wonder, as institutions such as the Organization for Security and Cooperation in Europe (OSCE) appear to languish, whether the recent efforts to expand NATO and build a "Partnership for Peace" will succumb to the same recourse to military power for the states and societies of Eastern Europe. During the early Cold War, the very creation of space for liberalization and even integration through military umbrellas seemed to limit the construction of institutions at the global level. We do not know if this so more generally, but the issue deserves further thought and research.

The building of liberal order, then, is plagued with dilemmas. Although we can imagine that many of these dilemmas are not unique to what I have labeled a liberal order, the dilemmas are likely to be experienced in a liberal order far more intensely. Just think of the dilemma associated with the building of strength and stability through liberalization. You facilitate the democratic claims and contestations of agents within a given society. This can help legitimate your order-making efforts. But it can also promote voices within the democratic process that can challenge the terms of international order.[6] Or consider the dilemma, wherein the very attempt to nurture independent sources of strength creates dependencies on aid and leadership that undermine the prospects for such sources to emerge as independent. Moreover, such independent strength could also create fear that solidarity in the liberal order would be compromised, along with the leadership supposedly working toward independent sources of strength in the first place.

By pointing to the many dilemmas and contradictions that populate international liberal order, I do not wish to imply that the alternative to militarization and even Cold War is a straightfoward attempt to confront the tensions of order-making head on and seek some form of resolution on some higher political-institutional plane. That alternative would require that the dilemmas of liberal order, especially those bearing on the autonomy of agents to set the terms of their own social existence, could be overcome or mediated somehow prior to the establishment of working institutions. For example, a community of common interest would need to exist that was robust enough to bring agents into a consistent constellation. Or we would have to assume that every institution would permit the kind of adaption between autonomy and governance that the embedded militarization described in this book allowed.[7] It may be far better to recognize that dilemmas are not subject to resolution and that the attempt to overcome them—minimally, to find a workable way to manage them—is not a wise course.

But it is not easy to give up on the attempt to overcome dilemmas in the context of order-making. The whole point of making a systemwide order is to bring the elements subject to order into some kind of workable relationship to one another. This is what marks liberal order-making as modern. It is a large-scale organization of agency. Such an organization is meant to facilitate agency and to prevent such agency from being stymied by dilemmas thrown in its way.[8] What then could it mean to call for a moratorium on the overcoming of dilemmas? Would this moratorium merely result in inaction and drift? (In the Bosnian civil war, the West has had its face rubbed in dilemmas and the impediments they create for agency.) There is no easy answer to these questions. I can here only suggest some possible starting points for thinking about them.

Order, Fear, and Complexity

Central to the postwar fears described in this book was the fear that states and societies in the liberal order could not handle the tensions, dilemmas, and contradictions inherent in the making of order. This was self-fear. Courage for some, in this context, could mean facing and overcoming the dilemmas by building strength, solidarity, and—yes—a degree of hard-nosed realism that would make the wide-scale production and use of violence feasible. But is this really courage when it is based upon the fear of a liberal order about its own potential impotence and ineffectiveness? The alternative is courage based on resistance to such fears in the first place. Consider the words of political philosopher Judith Shklar:

> Tolerance consistently applied is more difficult and morally more
> demanding than repression. . . . Courage is to be prized, since it both

prevents us from being cruel, as cowards so often are, and fortifies us against fear from threats, both physical and moral. This is, to be sure, not the courage of the armed, but that of their likely victims. . . . The alternative then set, and still before us, is . . . between cruel military and moral repression and violence, and a self-restraining tolerance that fences in the powerful to protect the freedom and safety of every citizen, old or young, male or female, black or white. Far from being an amoral free-for-all, liberalism is, in fact, extremely difficult and constraining, far too much so for those who cannot endure contradiction, complexity, diversity, and the risks of freedom.[9]

Shklar points to a courage that is cognizant of the power of fear, even self-fear. Instead of reacting to that power and even, as I argued in chapter 4, fearing that states and societies will not fear enough, the courageous would endeavor to remove as much as possible the reasons for fear in the first place, and ensure proper mechanisms of protection against abuse by concentrations—or what I have called nodal points—of power. In the end, making an order means defining limits. The difference between one liberal order and another, a better and a worse one, could depend on how much tolerance is allowed within such boundaries. This would mean that risks would be taken by order-makers and that the existence of dilemmas would be treated as part of what a more tolerant, constrained, and less militarized liberal order is about. Order-makers would risk a robust democratic commitment to facilitating the unimpeded access of diverse actors to state power and international institutions in the hope that the payoff of legitimation would offer the strength necessary to resist anti-democratic forces. Such a commitment would not, "unrealistically," have required abandoning the defense of Europe or a—more modest—military machine to do so.

Shklar's words also suggest a very different approach to order that bears directly on the question of a moratorium on the slaying of dilemmas. An order that allows for "contradiction, complexity, diversity, and the risks of freedom" is one in which practices, processes, and outcomes are recognized as always contestable and subject to revision. In contrast, in the order-making described in this book, there was an attempt to bring actors and their relations—despite their complex diversity—into an organized constellation with relatively clear identities and definitions of acceptable practices. This suggests that there are two basic ways to respond to complexity. One is to look for paths of closure that set boundaries as best possible to issues of who should do what, where, and with whom. The other way to respond to complexity is to simply accept it and find mechanisms, options, and even strategies for pursuing one's interests, if not also order, within it. This approach is the far more difficult and courageous one.

However, the notion that there is actually a choice to be made after the Cold War between these starting points for U.S. policymaking is somewhat disingenuous, if the premises of this study are taken seriously. The possibility of minimizing complexity—or, more importantly, its perception—even by attempting to reduce diversity and contradiction in order-making, may have been unique to the moment of the 1940s. Then, the war had laid open opportunities to define relations and set boundaries. Especially important was the way that the war signaled to many at the time that the project of building international order along liberal lines was the common project of the leading powers. The Soviet challenge to that project, if anything, reinforced its palpability. This same type of relatively coherent experience of history and legitimation of agency on a global scale does not exist today. If the 1940s was a sort of concentrated "big bang" of international order, then U.S. policymakers are now experiencing the uncertainties of far more diffuse and differentiated constellations of actors, interests, identities, and problems. It is not simply that there no longer is a Soviet threat to concentrate interests and identities. Years before that threat disappeared, the order as it had been built in the 1940s was growing increasingly diffuse. An acute example of this is the U.S. departure in the early 1970s from the original Bretton Woods agreements. We can even ask if a liberal order, as it has been discussed in this book, still exists. This is a question that has no easy answer. But the very fact that I can feel justified in asking it is one sign of just how ambiguous things are. Despite the growing salience of the single term, globalization, to characterize much of our current "post-Cold War moment," the term refers to seemingly contrary processes, including integration and fragmentation; diffusion and concentration; and localization and transnationalization.

I would not want to imply that our current post-Cold War moment is so diffuse and thick with a diversity of processes, agents, their interests, and problems (e.g., environmental degradation and collapsing states) that it is less open compared to the start of the post-World War II moment, when international life was likely experienced by policymakers as more susceptible to order-making. (If anything, there certainly were fewer states around for policymakers to worry about.) The current relative thickness and diffuseness may indicate that it makes a lot less sense to talk now about any overarching international order. Instead, the possibility that a variety of orders are operating in different domains, regions, or even locales should be recognized. Against this prospect, the declaring of a "New World Order" indeed seems foolish. We would need a decidedly decentralized understanding of order, which would reject the notion that the international realm could be ordered on truly large-scale, momentous—and, therefore, modern—lines. It would mean that U.S. policymakers would have to recognize that international life is not "project-ready" the way some might nostalgically believe it was in the 1940s. The dust of change is unlikely to settle down into a discernible and manageable pattern. Those patterns have historically depended on limits to the number and type of actors as well as the range of issues drawn into order-making, as was the case in the 1940s. I do not believe these limits can be set or sustained at the end of the twentieth century. While the task of reorganizing or even inventing forms of agency and authority in our current historical moment still lies before us, we should not expect the arrival of a new Kennan to put it all into a single, coherent perspective or doctrine such as containment. Yet the habit of waiting for a coherent story to be told is not easily shaken. Such a habit is yet one more hangover from the Cold War. Getting past it is at least one way that a moratorium on overcoming the dilemmas of grand order-making might commence.

A Foreign Policy of the Local

But what would a foreign policy that began with these assumptions about complexity and a plurality of orders look like, how would it be executed, and what reasons would one have for thinking it could be politically feasible? It may make sense to take seriously the notion that U.S. policymakers would be best off not pursuing a single set of foreign policy principles or doctrines. Instead, they could allow themselves to build foreign policies around the specific conditions and dynamics of each situation, problem, or even opportunity that they, U.S. civil society, or even the international community identifies as relevant to U.S. interests and security. (Of course, a crucial question will be how these are identified.) This type of specificity would allow for the application of a plurality of foreign policy mechanisms—including diplomacy, military coercion, aid, and institution-building—in the context of a plurality of foreign policy approaches—including isolationist, regionalist, multilateralist, and internationalist. After a century

of foreign policy-making, the U.S. state has built up a considerable repertoire of approaches and mechanisms—both good and bad—that can be
exploited selectively in an environment that is as diverse as it is unstable. We
might call this a foreign policy of the local.

In the 1940s Kennan drew a distinction between two trends in U.S. foreign policy.[10] One was the universalizing attempt to establish an international order shaped by law and norms of peaceful coexistence within an
international society of states. The other trend was based on the recognition that what counts is the play of national interests and power dynamics
within a given situation and geographical locale. This is nothing but the
classic distinction between idealism (or liberalism) and realism. It fails to
note two things I have stressed in this book: the important role of norms
in local situations and the play of power dynamics in the making of international order. Kennan's universal-particular distinction also overlooked
how a doctrine for exercising power, such as containment, could itself take
on universal dimensions that could open the way for all sorts of particular
or local power solutions with disastrous consequences, which Kennan himself later bemoaned. What happened, one should recall, was that specific
situations were not really considered in their specificity, but rather in
regard to how local sources of power and authority could serve the general
doctrine of containment. The flexibility associated with containment was
not applied to the question of whether or not containment should guide
policy, but only to the question of which agent or source of strength would
best carry it out (authoritarian or not). A foreign policy of the local, in
contrast, would insist that principles could be local as well as global,
depending not simply on the power dynamics of a situation, but also on
how U.S. policymakers and the public see themselves in relation to a
region, locale, specific issue, or global threat.

For some commentators and policymakers this would be tantamount to
legitimizing drift, indecision, and inaction. For other commentators and
policymakers a foreign policy of the local would be seen as potentially
opening the way to all sorts of unwarranted and costly interventions and
engagements. But a sense of drift emerges only as a function of the desire
for a coherent global policy. Once this is recognized as no longer appropriate, much of the sting of the charge of drift fades. Moreover, concerns with
both inaction and overreaction miss the point that each potential engagement would have to be judged as to its compellingness and feasibility in the
context of resources and potential effectiveness. We would have to give up

our quest for an overarching principle or doctrine that automatically rules on a situation as deserving engagement or not.

I realize that what has traditionally made a problem, issue, or region a compelling site for U.S. involvement has been a general definition of U.S. interests and identity. But what a foreign policy of the local would depend on is asking questions about U.S. interests and identity with regard to each situation, problem, or opportunity. In this sense, we would build a specific (or local) U.S. identity around each specific situation and order. (For example, the U.S. might have an identity of open borders regarding immigration, but one of closed borders regarding drug smuggling.) We would stop trying to define a single, overarching identity that would undergird the U.S. perception of the world and define the place of a U.S. state and society within it. Both that state and society and that world are far too complex and changeable for any one definition to cover. Such complexity defies the simple question of whether the U.S. should be an isolationist or internationalist power. In the end, however, there is no denying that such an approach is riskier regarding both the possibility of too much involvement and too little. There are grounds for self-fear. But rather than dwell on the risks we might summon the courage to take them in the way that Shklar argues liberalism calls for.

A foreign policy of the local would require that the U.S. state give up any dreams of a global liberal order of the sort described in this book.[11] But it need not abandon its liberalism. If the U.S. is serious about its liberalism, then it could redirect it toward the individuals, families, collectives, and neighborhoods struggling to make themselves freer and more secure. Human rights—not just civic and political, but also social, economic, and cultural ones—would be central. The postwar liberal order was directed mostly at states and the strength—and, where feasible, the freedom and security—they could provide. A new challenge for those committed to international liberalism would be to place the problem of the distribution of opportunities and resources at the local level in a far more central position. Along these lines the World Bank has already adopted a policy of micro-financing, emphasizing loans to small enterprises including family ones. At the same time, a foreign policy of the local would look to build up the strength of non-state actors (from neighborhood and market associations to NGOs and IGOs), helping along a decentralization of power in the international system. But such decentralization need not be viewed in zero-sum terms relative to states. Non-state and state actors could form fruitful partnerships in dealing with problems and opportunities for developing more equitable and secure lives throughout the world. Many NGOs, for instance, emerge out of U.S. civil society, so that a foreign policy of the local would, by avoiding predetermined policy, open space for them to shape U.S. foreign policy on the basis of their extensive knowledge and practical engagement in specific situations.

To a great extent the foreign policy of the local is already in operation in the specific U.S. policies generated toward countries and regions and in the growing importance of NGOs, for instance, in humanitarian aid. Moreover, at least the value of avoiding grand order-making is already recognized by the U.S. administration. In a recent speech to Freedom House, President Clinton declared:

> [T]here seems to be no mainframe explanation for the PC [personal computer] world in which we're living. We have to drop the abstractions and dogma, and pursue, based on trial and error and persistent experimentation, a policy that advances our values of freedom and democracy, peace and security.[12]

Accomplishing this will not be easy in that grand principles have been rhetorically useful justifications for action and inaction on the part of policymakers. But in a political environment no longer very trusting of the grand schemes and abstractions of states, there may be more than a little political sense in emphasizing a foreign policy approach that highlights decentralization, efficacy, experimentation, local entrepreneurial effort, and caution regarding commitments. A foreign policy of the local does require greater and more in-depth thought and analysis, if not more sensitivity to local situations. It will require that we go back each time to rethink our identity and relationship to a situation, locale, or region. But if we take what former Secretary of Defense Robert McNamara says seriously about the lessons of Vietnam, then this analysis of and sensitivity to the local could be crucial in avoiding new debacles.[13]

With the end of the Cold War, the U.S. was left with what I have called an external state—organs deployed to administer and order relations in the international realm—built up in the pursuit of international order and the waging of Cold War. On one level, recent debate over U.S. foreign policy and international involvement has been about the question of what the nature of that external state should be or even whether the U.S. should still have one. Before organs such as the U.S. Agency for International Development are closed down the broader question of what type of foreign policy approach the U.S., as a liberal state and society, wants to take should be considered. If the pursuit of a grand, globalizing order no longer makes sense, the U.S. needs to ask on what terms as a state and society it wants to exist in the world; for surely, whatever it does, the U.S. has no choice but to be there.

NOTES

Introduction

1. A recent example is Richard Bellamy, *Liberalism and Modern Society*.

2. Acheson, *Present at the Creation: My Years in the State Department*.

3. Mann, *The Sources of Social Power*, p. 26. On the efficiency of military organization see Finer, *The Man on Horseback*, pp. 6–20; and Perlmutter, *The Military and Politics in Modern Times*. See the discussion of their views in Giddens, *The Nation-State and Violence*, pp. 249–50.

4. This phrase is obviously a play of the phrase, "embedded liberalism," coined by John Gerard Ruggie, in "Embedded Liberalism." Ruggie took his cue from the argument of Karl Polanyi in *The Great Transformation*, p. 56, that a social order, such as an economy, can either operate according to the terms that are set by a broader context of social relations and thereby be embedded in that context; or can become separated from that context and begin to set the terms for social relations more broadly, becoming thereby disembedded. Ruggie argued that international liberal economic practices and principles—that in a nineteenth-century context were disembedded—could be embedded in the twentieth century in broader concerns with the domestic stability and well-being of societies affected by them.

5. The play between the two modes is explored with a focus on foreign policy-making in Hollis and Smith, *Explaining and Understanding*. See also Puchula, "The Pragmatics of International History."

6. Gadamer, *Truth and Method*, p. 146.

7. Ricoeur, "The Model of the Text."

8. Weber, *Theory of Social and Economic Organization*, pp. 95–98.

9. Ibid., pp. 96–97.

10. Habermas, *The Logic of the Social Sciences*, p. 67; Taylor, "Interpretation of the Sciences of Man;" and Ricoeur "The Model of the Text."

11. For a similar sense of interpretation see Heikki Patomaki, "How to Tell Better Stories About World Politics."

1. "A Certain Overlordship"

1. A controversial recognition of this shift is Fukuyama, "The End of History?" pp. 3–18. See also Gaddis, *The United States and the End of the Cold War*, ch. 9; Deudney and Ikenberry, "The International Sources of Soviet Change," pp. 73–118; Kegley, "The New Global Order," pp. 21–40; and Hoffmann, "What Should We Do in the World," pp. 719–32. The struggle of Eastern Europe with the transition to liberalization is considered in Bunce, "Rising Above the Past," pp. 395–430.

2. See the discussion in Tony Smith, *America's Mission*, pp. 13–19.

3. See the extensive theoretical exploration of this question by Doyle, "Kant, Liberal Legacies, and Foreign Affairs," pp. 205–35, 323–53; and idem, "Liberalism and World Politics," pp. 1151–69. See also Russett, *Controlling the Sword*, ch. 5; idem, *Grasping the Democratic Peace*; and Bueno de Mesquita and Lalman, *War and Reason*. Empirical investigations include Small and Singer, "The War-Proneness of Democratic Regimes, 1816–1965"; Chan, "Mirror, Mirror on the Wall . ."; Weede, "Democracy and War Involvement"; Maoz and Abdolali, "Regime Type and International Conflict, 1816–1976." See also Levy, "The Causes of War: A Review of Theories and Evidence," p. 270.

4. The book that still remains his most influential is Wallerstein, *The Modern World-System*. On ideational and cultural developments see idem, *The Capitalist World-Economy*.

5. Ruggie, "Continuity and Transformation," pp. 131–59.

6. Krasner, "Westphalia and All That."

7. Walker, *Inside/Outside*.

8. Cox, *Production, Power, and World Order*, pp. 217–18.

9. Berman, *All That is Solid*, ch. 1, captures the play between despair and hope for Marx, Weber, and other relevant writers.

10. Herf, *Reactionary Modernism*; and Nandy, *Traditions, Tyranny and Utopias*.

11. Eisenstadt, "A Reappraisal of Theories of Social Change and Modernization," in *Social Change and Modernity*, p. 423.

12. The Weberian and Baudelaireian experience of modernity are contrasted in Lash and Friedman, "Introduction: Subjectivity and Modernity's Other." Marx was also very aware of this flux which he saw as the result of capitalism's constant making and remaking of the world. See Berman, *All That Is Solid*.

13. The possibility of a post-Fordist, high technology, late-twentieth-century capitalism underscores the unique dimensions of industrialism as a mode of modernity. See Harvey, *Condition of Postmodernity*.

14. In contrast, philosopher Alastair MacIntyre in *After Virtue* uses the term liberal modernity to denote that modernity is liberal, the exact opposite of my use.

15. Though, of course, this is done sometimes. One example is Ruggerio, *European Liberalism*, p. 51, who conceives of liberties forming a system.

16. The term "liberal-capitalist state" is best understood as conveying the close intersection and historical proximity of the two forms, rather than their indistinguishableness.

17. Polanyi, *The Great Transformation*, pp. 56–76.

18. When Smith, *America's Mission*, p. 7, refers to this international dimension it is as a world view on the part of (U.S.) liberal democratic actors which he calls "liberal democratic internationalism." It is not a view that is inherent in being a liberal democrat. Otherwise, all liberal democrats and liberal democratic states the world over would be liberal democratic internationalists.

19. Deutsch, *Political Community*, p. 134.

20. Adler and Barnett, "Governing Anarchy," p. 76.

21. For discussion of the play between liberal and illiberal ways of making social existence see Holmes, *The Anatomy of Antiliberalism*.

22. In the work of John Gray, who has become a sharp critic of American liberal theory, there was a distinct transformation from a view that argued in his *Liberalism*, for the recognition of a fundamental liberal identity based on four elements (individualism, egalitarianism, universalism, and meliorism); to one that finds no continuous liberal tradition but only liberal civil societies, in his *Liberalism: Essays in Political Philosophy*; and on to one that asks in *Post-Liberalism: Studies in Political Thought* that we drop the qualifier "liberal" and focus instead on civil societies per se which may take place in illiberal contexts. I will argue that civil society and practices and principles associated with a diverse liberal tradition can occur in social spaces that may or may not be liberal. Thus, I find points of agreement in Gray's two latter texts. But Gray is directing his attention to political theory and our purposes are different, however much we share a concern with overcoming a sense of singularity in the liberal tradition. The sense of diversity is also noted in Smith, "Unfinished Liberalism," who is actually defending liberal theory in the U.S. from Gray's attacks.

23. A core, of course, can be identified within the context of a single liberal political theory. One articulation of a core in what is claimed to be a specifically American version of liberalism is in Dworkin, "Foundations of Liberal Equality."

24. Wittgenstein, *Philosophical Investigations*, pp. 31–36.

25. On the way that forms of organization can circulate globally see Meyer and Scott, *Organizational Environments*.

26. These were originally applied to the analysis of international relations by James Rosenau, who noted its widespread use in the study of U.S. politics. Rosenau, "Pre-theories and Theories." See also Keohane and Nye, *Power and Interdependence*, pp. 64–65; Mansbach and Vasquez, *In Search of Theory*, ch. 2; Vasquez, *The Power of Power Politics*, pp. 59–61; and Keohane, *International Institutions*, pp. 57–58. While Rosenau thought that issue areas were determined by state and nonstate actors—a view adopted by Mansbach and Vasquez—Keohane and Nye have argued that issue areas ultimately depend on state policies and perceptions for their emergence and substantiation.

27. Walzer, *Spheres of Justice*, pp. 17–20, 316–18; and idem, "Liberalism and the Art of Separation." Such 'spheres of operation' carry with them unique distributive principles and contexts of 'social meanings.' In a complex modern society, it is possible to restrain power by preventing its accumulation and spillover across spheres.

28. Walzer, "Liberalism and the Art of Separation," p. 327. Nonetheless, the borders and content of Walzer's spheres are very much open to contest. See Walzer, *Spheres of Justice*, ch. 13.

29. Indeed, the term 'sphere' implies the existence of a demarcated space, rising out of its association with globes. The term 'domain' is more properly associated with a region or range of elements that emerge as a result of a function or activity such as rulership. The distinction between domains and spheres is parallel to the distinction made by Perry Anderson between respectively the overlapping and "parcellized sovereignty" of disparate political units in the medieval world and the firm boundaries of absolutist states in the early modern period. Anderson, *Lineages of the Absolutist State*, p. 16. See also Ruggie, "Continuity and Transformation."

30. Although Walzer recognizes that there can be considerable interaction and spillover across spheres, he ultimately associates a liberal modern society with the very capacity to establish separations or walls.

31. Foucault, "The Subject and Power," p. 210.

32. See Foucault, *Power/Knowledge*, pp. 122–123; and idem, "Questions of Method," pp. 100–117.

33. For example, Foucault shows in his *The History of Sexuality* how the engagement of the medical field with the "problem" of sex in the eighteenth and nineteenth centuries molded the emerging domain of sexuality in decisive ways. He called his method, in which he traced the effects of these ruptures, 'geneology.' Foucault, *The History of Sexuality*, vol. 1, p. 30.

34. See for instance Kenwood and Lougheed, *The Growth of the International Economy, 1820–1980*; McKinlay and Little, *Global Problems*, ch. 5; and Murphy, *International Organization and Industrial Change*.

35. These sketches will be incomplete and unlikely to satisfy the political theorist, jurist, or economic historian who makes an intellectual home among the topics covered. I am willing to risk disapproval in the hope that the specialist reader will understand that I seek only to supplement a hitherto abstract discussion and to help justify why I have identified these five elements as the predominant mediums of liberal modernity.

36. A seminal approach to that history is Ruggiero, *European Liberalism*.

37. English foreign trade, for example, doubled in the first half of the eighteenth century. See Deane and Cole, *British Economic Growth 1688–1959*, p. 48. Although foreign trade is generally seen as occurring within the context of mercantilist policies, it is fairly clear that the Dutch in the seventeenth century practiced what could be understood as free trade policies. See Wallerstein, *The Modern World System II*, p. 61. For some of the ways that an international market economy differs from a mercantile one see Gilpin, "Economic Interdependence," pp. 19–66.

38. See Ruggiero, *European Liberalism*, p. 49.

39. On France see ibid., pp. 171–72, 187. On Germany see Rohr, *Social Liberalism in Germany*, pp. 82, 91.

40. Some of the dimensions of this interdependence are sketched in Gilpin, "Economic Interdependence," pp. 19–66.

41. Pollard, *The Integration*, pp. 25–26.

42. Henderson, *The Zollverein*, pp. 40–44.

43. See for example Hilgerdt, "The Case for Multilateral Trade," pp. 393–407.

44. Stein, "The Hegemon's Dilemma," p. 368.

45. In the relatively recent past "liberal protectionism" has emerged as a new way to protect individual industries. See Aggarwal, *Liberal Protectionism*.

46. Although, as noted by Albert Hirschman, *The Passions*, p. 121, the eighteenth-century Scottish thinker Adam Ferguson thought that a strong preference for the orderly administration of economic life could lead to a willingness to compromise liberty.

47. See Polanyi, *The Great Transformation*; and Gilpin, "Economic Interdependence," pp. 27–39, for a comparison between the mercantile and the liberal economic systems.

48. On German liberal reluctance see James Sheehan, *German Liberalism*, p. 30.

49. Polanyi, *The Great Transformation*, ch. 12.

50. Hobsbawm, *Industry and Empire*, pp. 27–28. On the emergence of the freedom of contract in Britain see Atiyah, *Freedom of Contract*.

51. Trebilcock, *Industrialization*, pp. 142–52, 185.

52. See Pollard, *The Integration*, p. 29. The best history of the formation of the Zollverein remains, Henderson, *The Zollverein*.

53. Many of these changes are charted in Hamerow, *New Europe*, pp. 274–75.

54. On Britain see Mathias, *The First Industrial Nation*, pp. 37–38, 350–53. On France see Cameron, *France and Economic Development*, p. 35.

55. Hobhouse, *Liberalism*, p. 108.

56. That story is told extremely well by Polanyi, *The Great Transformation*. A more recent exploration of the link between democracy and markets is Lindblom, *Politics and Markets*.

57. The locus classicus of republicanism in its classical form is Machiavelli, *The Prince and the Discourses*. This tradition is explored comprehensively in Pocock, *The Machiavellian Moment*. See also Skinner, "Political Liberty," pp. 225–50; Doyle, "Liberalism and World Politics," pp. 1151–69; and Habermas, "Three Normative Models of Democracy."

58. Skinner, "Political Liberty," p. 238.

59. This is done by Everdell, *The End of Kings*, pp. 3–13; and Deudney, "Dividing Realism," p. 50, p. 36.

60. How wide this franchise and what other conditions go along with any definition of democracy vary widely. Huntington, *The Third Wave*, p. 16, turns to the criteria relevant to the nineteenth century offered by Jonathan Sunshine, "Economic Causes and Consequences of Democracy," pp. 48–58. These are: 1) voting eligibility of fifty percent of adult males; and 2) an executive power based either on a parliamentary majority or regular popular elections.

61. Hobsbawm, *The Age of Capital*, p. 107, for example, argues that industrialization made it inevitable that the masses would have to be politically enfranchised, an outcome liberals were not prepared to resist.

62. The relationship between liberalization and democratization is explored in Huntington, *Third Wave*, pp. 121–29.

63. Collins, *The Age of Progress*, pp. 10–11.

64. Hamerow, *New Europe*, pp. 292–300.

65. See for example Watson, "British Parliamentary System," p. 104.

66. Ibid., pp. 107–8, 118–19.

67. Dahl, *Polyarchy*, pp. 1–14.

68. Habermas, *The Structural Transformation*, p. 83.

69. A brief analysis of the emergence of rights in Britain is in Marshall, *Class, Citizenship, and Social Development*, pp. 78–105, especially p. 81. A more general portrait is offered in Anderson and Anderson, *Political Institutions*. pp. 238–41, 274–85.

70. See Brownlie, "The Expansion of International Society," p. 360; and Iwe, *The History and Contents of Human Rights*, p. 117.

71. Schwarzenberger, *A Manual of International Law*, p. 13.

72. Kant, "Perpetual Peace," pp. 284–86.

73. Gong, *Standard of 'Civilization'*, p. 91.

74. Mill, *Utilitarianism*, pp. 486–87. The link between the nationalism and progress in liberal doctrine is explored by Hobsbawm, *Nations and Nationalism*, ch. 1; and Mayall, *Nationalism*, pp. 42–43.

75. Tamir, *Liberal Nationalism*, ch. 3, distinguishes between this liberal democratic strain in self-determination—which she labels as self-rule—and the more cultural dimensions within which members of a nation seeks "to preserve their distinct existence, and to manage communal life in accordance with their particular way of life (p. 69)." I continue to focus on the former sense because, as Tamir herself makes clear (p. 57), it is the most prevalent one. Whether her effort and those of sympathetic others are articulating a shift in the domain remains to be seen.

76. Johnson, *Self-Determination*, p. 77. Johnson, ibid., p. 94, distinguishes the early form of self-determination based on popular sovereignty from its later form based on the nation. Cobban, *The Nation State*, p. 44, exhorts us to avoid assuming that the link between free or even democratic institutions is based on any "innate interdependence." In 1862, Lord Acton saw a clash between the nation and the rights of individuals. See Manning, *Liberalism*, p. 94. This same theme has been addressed by Cobban, *National Self-Determination*, p. 106; Arendt, *The Origins of Totalitarianism*, pp. 230–31; and Mayall, *Nationalism and International Society*, p. 75.

77. See Macartney, *National Minorities*, p. 109. On the Serbian revolt see Collins, *Age of Progress*, p. 296.

78. Hobsbawm, *Nations and Nationalism*, p. 32.

79. Cobban, *National Self-Determination*, pp. 47–48, traces what he sees as a "temporary eclipse" for the principle of nationality in this period.

80. This change is traced by Jackson, *Quasi-States*, pp. 41, 75–78; Hobsbawm, *Nations and Nationalism*, pp. 26, 40, 101, 170–71.

81. Arguing that sovereignty predates liberalism and is, therefore, a nonliberal element of international life, is as nonsensical as arguing that markets, because their existence predates liberalism, are also nonliberal. Moreover, by the time the reader comes to the conclusion of this book, it should be fairly clear that the making of liberal order has been a potent force underwriting the centrality of the sovereign state. The possibility of an alternative outcome is indicated by the fate of states and their sovereignty in postwar Eastern Europe.

82. This transformation is discussed in Barkin and Cronin, "The State and the Nation," pp. 123–24.

83. Jackson, *Quasi-States*, p. 152.

84. The thought of these four authors constitutes the substance of the theoretical discussion in Vincent, *Nonintervention*, ch. 3.

85. See, for example, Cohen, "Toward a Liberal Foreign Policy," pp. 67–86.

86. In Michael Doyle's work the play between doctrine and institutions is very strong. See his "Liberal Legacies."

87. One particularly strong version of this understanding is Gilpin, *U.S. Power*.

88. The contrast of liberalism, Marxism, and Neorealism is frequently employed in international relations textbooks and across a wide array of works. One prominent example of such a contrast is Gilpin, *The Political Economy*. See also McKinlay and Little, *World Order*.

89. This is most clearly discussed in McKinlay and Little, *World Order*. In addition, while most students of the apparent peace among liberal democracies have not directly addressed the issue of international order, scholars such as Ernst-Otto Czempiel, "Governance and Democratization," have explored some of the relevant implications, especially the notion that the potential proliferation of liberal democratic states can open the way for a more peaceful international order.

90. A good example of this is Hoffmann, *Primacy or World Order*.

91. Recently, this purposiveness has increasingly been articulated as instances of international or global governance where "[g]overnance is essentially purposive and should be distinguished from order which does not require conscious purpose or intention." Biersteker, "The 'Triumph' of Neoclassical Economics," p. 102.

92. The possibility of having a descriptive sense of order is discussed in Hoffmann, "Report of the Conference."

93. Bull, *Anarchical Society*, p. 8. See Biersteker, "Neoclassical Economics" for further elaboration on the two senses of order.

94. Bull identified these goals as the maintenance of 1) the system and society of states, 2) the independence of the units in that system, and 3) a general condition of peace among them where feasible. Although these might appear to be very general goals, they describe an order of externally sovereign states with sufficient common interest in the maintenance of a generally peaceful international society. A change in any of these goals would surely alter the character of the order.

95. Cox, *Production, Power, and World Order*, p. 127. It should be pointed out that Cox uses order in a number of other senses (e.g., world order and social order) as well.

96. Rosenau, "Governance, Order, and Change," p. 5.

97. Ibid., p. 12.

98. Krasner, *Structural Conflict*, p. 61.

99. Ruggie, "Embedded Liberalism," pp. 195–231.

100. This is part of the seminal definition offered by Krasner, ed., *International Regimes*, p. 2.

101. This is one way to read the monumental work by Moore, *The Social Origins of Dictatorship and Democracy*.

102. Sayer, *Capitalism and Modernity*, p. 24, identifies these two forms as the "key elements of "modern capitalism."

103. It, of course, is possible to speak of a capitalist order in the depictive sense in the same way we may speak of a capitalist system. One example of this is Wallerstein's world capitalist system, which is viewed depictively as well as purposively.

104. See Cox, *Production, Power, and World Order*, ch. 5.

105. While Cox, ibid., pp. 134–43, offers a trenchant analysis of the political struggle to make liberal states in Europe in the nineteenth century, he seems to imply that what he calls a liberal world order flows comparatively easily, especially from the interests of the hegemonic British state.

106. In the face of declining U.S. hegemony the tensions between these two forms became an important dimension of international relations scholarship over the last decade. Robert Keohane's seminal work, *After Hegemony*, directly addressed the question of how states, in the absence of the concentrated agency associated with hegemony, could cooperate through mutual adjustment of interests in the context of cooperative arenas such as international regimes.

107. Bull, *Anarchical Society*, p. 20.

108. Falk, "Contending Approaches."

109. Hoffmann, "Conditions of World Order," p. 456.

110. Alker, "Dialectical Foundations," 69–98. Biersteker, "Neoclassical Economics," p. 111, points out that "different world orders simultaneously coexist and overlap with one another with varying degrees of accommodation and contradiction." Alker is collaborating with Biersteker, Tahir Amin, and Takashi Inoguchi on a project titled, "The Dialectics of World Order."

111. Jackson, *Quasi-States*, pp. 10, 36, 40.

112. A similar use of the term "partial" in both its senses is found in Sunstein, *The Partial Constitution*. Note that the notion of partiality runs counter to the ways that liberalism is typically associated with neutrality.

113. See Braudel, *On History*, pp. 74–76, 92–97.

2. *"Stupendous Forces Are Loose"*

1. G. John Ikenberry, asks straightforwardly, "how does one explain the Anglo-American postwar settlement?" in Ikenberry, "Creating Yesterday's New World Order," p. 58.

2. Murphy, *International Organization and Industrial Change*, p. 226.

3. Maier, "The Two Postwar Eras," pp. 327–52.

4. Carr, *The Twenty Years' Crisis*, p. 224.

5. Polanyi, *The Great Transformation*, ch. 19.

6. See Hintze, *The Historical Essays of Otto Hintze*; Weber, *General Economic History*; Downing, *The Military Revolution*; Giddens, *The Nation-State and Violence*; Mann, *Social Power*; Shaw, *Post-Military Society*; Tilly, ed., *The Formation of National States*; and Skocpol, *States and Social Revolutions*.

7. Marwick, *War and Social Change*; and McNeill, *The Pursuit of Power*.

8. Gilpin, *War and Change*, pp. 116–23.

9. The point is a comparative one. There has been significant discussion of this type of impact in the histories of postwar periods and in treatments of the transformative dimensions of apparent historical breakpoints such as Westphalia. But it has been more modest compared to the study of domestic impact. Also, in a recent essay, "Westphalia and All That," Stephen Krasner cautions us to be weary of claims regarding supposed breakpoints such as Westphalia.

10. One initial thrust along these lines is made by Ruggie in "Territoriality and Beyond," through a differentiation of the international political ramifications of various types of war.

11. Carr, *The Twenty Years' Crisis*, p. 40.

12. The relationship between heroic rhetoric and liberalism is briefly considered in Latham, "Liberalism's Order / Liberalism's Other."

13. See also Ikenberry, "Creating Yesterday's New World Order," pp. 82–83.

14. David Kennedy, "The Move to Institutions," traces a quite similar experience of a historical moment around World War I, where the rupture and chaos of the war is followed by the establishment of a new type of (institutionalized) order around the settlement of the war and the founding of the League of Nations.

15. Nietzsche, *The Birth of Tragedy*.

16. Durkheim, *The Elementary Forms of the Religious Life*, pp. 455, 460.

17. Freud, *New Introductory Lectures*, p. 65.

18. Weber, *Theory of Social and Economic Organization*, p. 361.

19. Lefebvre, *La somme et le reste*. See also Zolberg, "Moments of Madness."

20. Turner, *Dramas, Fields, and Metaphors*, ch. 7.

21. Maier, "Empires or Nations?" also draws this parallel.

22. Maier, "Two Postwar Eras."

23. Hobsbawm, *The Age of Extremes*, p. 141.

24. The role of surviving elites is central to arguments made in Maier, "Two Postwar Eras."

25. Larson, *Origins of Containment*, pp. 22–23, 328, incorporates in her discussion of the advantages of including variables from the international level the point made by Eulau, "Multilevel Methods," pp. 47–48, that placing a given entity at one level in the wider explanatory context of a 'higher' level is more productive. She also incorporates the advice to consider the "operational environment" of policymaking offered by Harold and Margaret Sprout, "Environmental Factors," pp. 41–56. While Larson in my view corrects the Sprouts by holding that factors of which policymakers are not necessarily conscious can form part of an environment, her criticism of international level explanations as underdetermining fails to consider the possibility that such explanations can, as in this study, be cast in more substantive terms and be more directly linked to the level of agency and the specific ways that such agency unfolds. In general, Larson wants to explain the "timing" of the emergence of cold war thinking; I am more concerned with the character of postwar international politics and its militarization.

26. On the effects of World War II see Kolko, *The Politics of War*, pp. 618–26; and Steel, *Pax Americana*, pp. 5, 21.

27. PPS 4, July 1947, in Etzold and Gaddis, eds., *Containment*, p. 109.

28. See the discussion of "the revolt against the West" in Jackson, *Quasi-States*, pp. 82–85.

29. Grosser, *The Western Alliance*, ch. 1.

30. Davis, *The Cold War Begins*, pp. 5–6, 12, 370–71.

31. See, for example, the discussion in DePorte, *Europe Between the Superpowers*, ch. 4.

32. In contrast, Kolko, *Politics of War*, pp. 252, 624–25, sees the postwar order as a failure of liberal principles. I would rather see the compromises of liberal principles as exactly what a liberal order is about.

33. Cited in DePorte, *Europe Between the Superpowers*, p. 81.

34. Ikenberry, "Origins of American Hegemony," p. 382; and Gardner, *Covenant with Power*, ch. 4, emphasize the "self-regulating" nature of liberal multilateralism as the basis for minimizing U.S. direct involvement in Europe. Such a view underplays the extent to which the U.S. was involved early on to an unprecedented extent. It thereby tends to read history backward from a point later in the 1940s when the U.S. appeared to be much more engaged via the ERP and NATO. That there was an ultimate goal of a minimizing, self-regulating international economy that made involvement more palatable domestically is consistent with the arguments here, but it does not emphasis sufficiently the forces that were brought to bear on this involvement by the necessity of a war settlement.

35. Ruggie, "Territoriality and Beyond," p. 168

36. Many arenas—especially international organizations—are simultaneously agents, depending on the dimension under consideration. States exhibit this duality as well in that they can act in the international arena and also be the site for groups to contest and cooperate regarding policy-formation. On the dual character of states see Wendt, "The Agent-Structure Problem," p. 339, n.6.

37. On this see Weber, *Social and Economic Organization*, ch. 1.

38. Vandenberg, *Private Papers*, p. 97.

39. Ibid., p. 149.

40. Polanyi, *Great Transformation*; and Dewey, *Liberalism and Social Action*.

41. Vandenberg, *Private Papers*, p. 132.

42. See Ruggie, "International Structure," where he points out, p. 32, that "the fabric of international life is made up of micro cases. . . [I]f change comes it will be the product of micro practices."

43. Giddens, *A Contemporary Critique*, p. 35.

44. Braudel, *On History*, pp. 74–75.

45. See, for example, Ruggie's edited volume, *Multilateralism Matters*.

46. Giddens, *A Contemporary Critique*. p. 27. Wendt, "Agent-Structure Problem," surveys the numerous scholars who have developed structurationist approaches. What is being suggested here is the possibility of a dialectical relationship between international conditions, or structures, and U.S. hegemonic state agency.

47. Carlsnaes, "The Agency-Structure Problem," stresses the dimension of time as an important element in the play between structure and agency. Clearly the unfolding of the liberal order-building *process* as the terrain of the structure-agency interaction renders time as an essential element.

48. For a discussion of hegemonic stability theory see Gilpin, *Political Economy of International Relations*, pp. 72–80. See also Keohane, *After Hegemony*, p. 32. On the consistency of a liberal order with the U.S. liberal state and society see Ikenberry, "Origins of American Hegemony," pp. 382–83.

49. Ikenberry, "Origins of American Hegemony," p. 375.

50. For different, but not unrelated reasons, Larson, *Origins of Containment*, p. 20, criticizes the realist international systemic explanation as well for being underdetermining because "it cannot explain how particular states will react to the pressures and possibilities inherent within the structure of the system."

51. Post-revisionists explicitly are committed to a "multicausal" approach which takes history, politics, structure, and perceptions into consideration. See Gaddis, "Post-

Revisionist Synthesis." They purposely avoid setting these factors in an overall systemic explanation to which one might otherwise ascribe some determinism.

52. McCormick, *America's Half-Century*; and idem, "World Systems."

53. Wallerstein, *Modern World System II*, pp. 38–60.

54. On the Gramscian school see Gill, ed., *Gramsci, Historical Materialism and Inter-national Relations*.

55. Cox, "Gramsci, Hegemony and International Relations," p. 171.

56. Cox, "Toward a Post-Hegemonic Conceptualization," p. 140.

57. Cox, *Production, Power, and World Order*, ch. 7.

58. Ibid, p. 150.

59. Ling, "Hegemony and the Internationalizing State," has also questioned this sense of hegemony through a consideration of alternative models of order in East Asia.

60. Gilpin, *War and Change*, p. 116. Lea Brilmayer adopts this definition of hegemony straight away in *American Hegemony*.

61. *Compact Oxford English Dictionary*, p. 753.

62. Interestingly, prior to the nineteenth century hegemony was sometimes understood to mean a preponderant presence that could set the terms of existence. The *Compact Oxford English Dictionary*, p. 753, shows from 1567, "Aegemonie or Sufferaigntie of things growing upon ye earth." See also Williams, *Keywords*, p. 144.

63. See, for example, Gilpin, *War and Change*, p. 13.

64. Ikenberry and Kupchan, "Socialization and Hegemonic Power."

65. Bull, *Anarchical Order*, pp. 214–16.

66. Doyle, *Empires*, p. 40.

67. Hegemonic stability theory does not face this issue because it collapses state agency and hegemony into one another.

68. Djilas, *Conversations with Stalin*, p. 114.

69. This point is made very well by Maier, "The Two Postwar Eras and the Conditions for Stability in Twentieth Century Western Europe."

70. Nettl, "The State."

71. France, by virtue of its colonial empire and occupation duty also qualified, but to a far lesser degree than these three states.

72. Petras, et al., *Class, State, and Power*, p. 3.

73. Indeed, Robert Cox's concept of the "internationalization of the state" points to the way that states of all types can become "transmission belts" between domestic spheres and the increasingly globalized forces in the external realm. Cox, "Social Forces."

74. Yergin, *Shattered Peace*, pp. 5–6. See other formulations in Schurmann, *Logic of World Power*, p. 105; Barnet, *Roots of War*, p. 25; and Neu, "National Security Bureaucracy."

75. Putnam, "Diplomacy and Domestic Politics."

76. See most recently Snyder, *Myths of Empire*, ch. 7, for an analysis of the contours and ramification of this battle. While Snyder, ibid., pp. 257–58, does recognize that domestic politics is only one contributor, he does not take into specific consideration the extent to which the U.S. was caught up in the process of constructing a global international system based on principles as well as interests which I call international liberalism. For earlier formulations of the nationalist versus internationalist contest regarding the immediate postwar external commitment see Schurmann, *The Logic of*

World Power, part 1; Cumings, *Roaring of the Cataract*, pp. 23, 90–91; Eden, "The Diplomacy of Force," pp. 180–89; Justus Doenecke, *Not to the Swift*, chaps. 3–5, 8; Hartmann, *Truman and the 80th Congress*, p. 162; and Block, *Origins of International Economic Disorder*, pp. 70–93.

77. Freeland, *The Truman Doctrine*. As we shall see regarding liberal relations in Western Europe, the exaggerated Soviet threat may have helped achieved a domestic political closure through consensus that avoided submitting the terms of policy to democratic debate with each change in international conditions and Soviet policy. Thus, program was emphasized over process. See Gaddis, *Long Peace*, ch. 3, on this point.

78. Some of the ramifications of this temporariness from the perspective of national planning are considered in Lowi, *The End of Liberalism*, pp. 161–74. See also Hartmann, *Truman and the 80th Congress*, p. 162.

79. Arkes, *Bureaucracy*, p. 203, explores many of the dimension of the temporary status of the ERP.

80. The implications of this format for external state-building are considered in chapter 4.

81. This conceptual "catch up" is conveyed nicely in Dyson, *The State Tradition*, part 1. See also the argument in Krasner, "Westphalia and All That."

82. See Joyce and Gabriel Kolko, *The Limits of Power*, and Block, *Origins*.

83. Some notable works in this area are Goldstein and Keohane, eds., *Ideas and Foreign Policy*; Klotz, *Norms and International Relations*; Katzenstein, ed., *Culture and National Security*; Lapid and Kratochwil, eds., *The Return of Culture and Identity in IR Theory*; and Campbell, *Writing Security*.

84. Sociologists such as Ann Swidler, "Culture in Action," have questioned the notion of explaining social life by locating underlying interests as the "engine of action" associated with the Weberian tradition. Instead, Swidler and others would have us look at the "strategies of action" through which people organize their lives and sometimes even construct their interests in the first place.

85. This argument will be mostly focused on the relationship between interests and ideational forces that emerge directly out of discussions about the Cold War, international liberalism, U.S. hegemony, and post-World War II security. For more general theoretical and methodological discussions on the relevance of ideational factors see the works cited in note 83, above.

86. Carr, *The Twenty Years' Crisis*, pp. 86–87.

87. See Gaddis, "The Corporatist Synthesis," p. 361, where he questions the lack of opportunity in corporatist historical approaches for viewing moral dimensions as anything more than a cloak. Also see idem, *The Long Peace*, p. 51, for a discussion of American wartime idealism in part "as a way to sanctify the wielding of power." However, Gaddis, ibid., p. 59, does go on to recognize that the commitment to self-determination had a substantial dimension to it in postwar relations in that it was consistent with the development of strong allies—a point that will be explored further below. The notion that liberal principles are moral cloaks is also advanced by historians more closely associated with revisionist tradition: see Cumings, *Roaring of the Cataract*, p. 66; and McMahon, *Colonialism and Cold War*, p. 305, where he describes the American commitment to independence in Indonesia as rhetorical. The idealistic basis of U.S. expansion is one of the main themes in Kennan, *American Diplomacy*. On the notion that col-

lective security principles in the U.N. were used by Roosevelt as a cover for military base appropriations see Dallek, *The American Style of Foreign Policy*, pp. 152–53.

88. Lundestad, "Moralism, Presentism, Exceptionalism," pp. 534–35, draws this connection between the two positions, represented on the one hand by Herbert Feis and on the other by William A. Williams. See also Freeland, *Origins of McCarthyism*, pp. 57–58.

89. See Davis, *Cold War Begins*, p. 392; and DePorte, *Europe Between the Superpowers*, pp. 78–80.

90. This argument is made by Rotter, *Path to Vietnam*, pp. 1–9.

91. See Gardner, *Covenant with Power*; and Gaddis, *Long Peace*, p. 220, on the Wilsonian endeavor to "integrate power with morality."

92. The most thorough exploration of the role of liberal principles and practice in Eastern Europe is Lundestad, *The American Non-Policy*.

93. Connolly, *The Terms of Political Discourse*, p. 63.

94. Maier, "The Politics of Productivity."

95. Mearsheimer, "The False Promise," informs us that "the most basic motive driving states is survival. States want to maintain their sovereignty," p. 10.

96. Lippmann, in Wolfers, *Discord and Collaboration*, p. 150. See discussion of these in Buzan, *People, States and Fear*, pp. 16–25.

97. Thucydides, *Peloponnesian War*, pp. 341–48.

98. Ibid., p. 347

99. See Walzer, *Just and Unjust Wars*, pp. 5–12, for a discussion of whether underlying the "necessity" of attacking Melos is a set of moral questions.

100. The notion, advanced by Waltz, *Theory of International Politics*, pp. 26–27, that power imbalances precipitate the pursuit of empire is similar to the notion that natural fathers of small children dominate the latter as parents. Despite the obvious links of natural fathers to their children and their grossly unbalanced power advantages, everything depends, first and foremost, on a given father's engagement in the project of parenthood. A project of this sort is not merely an internal attribute of a given father, it is an external engagement in a social context and this is not subject to the charge of reductionism that Waltz is so apt to level against nonsystemic or systematic explanations. Of course, physical preponderance is a (necessary) factor for fathers and empires. But it is not decisive in that what counts is the actual engagement in the project of fatherhood or empire.

101. See Wendt, "Anarchy is What States Make of It."

102. I can imagine some readers jumping up and proclaiming that this writer has missed a—or even *the*—paramount lesson of twentieth-century security. Nuclear weapons transport the concern with physical survival into the heavens. After being forced to dive under my desk in primary school nuclear attack drills hundreds of times, I understand the appeal of this claim. But this emphasis misses the point. What nuclear weapons do is increase the socially embedded stakes of survival by threatening the very existence of a society, a "civilization," or even a species, humankind. A sniper at my door is a threat that is far more circumscribed to the physical realm than nuclear war, which is on the other end of the spectrum, given its potential to destroy an entire society, if not global civilization. The connections between individual, national, and international security is explored cogently by Buzan, *People, States and Fear*.

103. Waltz, *Theory of International Politics*, pp. 138–46.

104. Ruggie, "Continuity and Transformation," p. 138, finds it dubious.

105. Goldstein and Keohane, eds., *Ideas and Foreign Policy*. As implied in chapter 1, the essay by Krasner, "Westphalia and All That," does engage the historical context of an emerging Western modernity in Europe. However, because Krasner sets sovereignty up as a discrete ideational variable relative to changes in material conditions as well as practices, his approach is consistent with the framework of that volume, which is decidedly micro-ideational.

106. Buzan, *People, States and Fear*, pp. 19–20.

107. Buzan, *People, States and Fear*, p. 7. On essentially contested concepts see Gallie, "Essentially Contested Concepts," and Connolly, *The Terms of Political Discourse*.

108. Aron, *Politics and History*, p. 177.

109. Buzan, *People, States and Fear*, p. 272.

110. See V.R. Berghahn, *Militarism*, pp. 7–8. Much of my understanding of the history of the use term is owed to Berghahn's book.

111. Vagts, *History of Militarism*, p. 17.

112. Hintze, *Historical Essays*.

113. See, for example, Kaldor and Eide, eds., *The World Military Order*.

114. Ross, "Dimensions of Militarization."

115. The occlusion of societal, political, and ideological militarization in Ross's formulation is criticized by Shaw, *Post-Military Society*, p. 13.

116. Thee, "Militarization."

117. Stambuk, *American Military Forces Abroad*, pp. 4–6.

118. Stinchcombe, *Constructing Social Theories*, pp. 83–106; and Cohen, *Karl Marx's Theory of History*, chaps. 9, 10.

119. See Malinowski, *A Scientific Theory of Culture*; Parsons, *The Social System*; and Haas, *The Uniting of Europe*.

120. Contingency and agency intersect. Both Stinchcombe, *Constructing Social Theories* and, of course, Cohen, *Marx's Theory of History* point to the consistencies of historical and functional approaches.

121. Elster, "Marxism," p. 82.

122. Burley, "Regulating the World," draws a picture of U.S. wartime planning that should be treated as only a starting point for a liberal order-building process that was shaped by events and negotiations that are the focus of historians such as Michael Hogan.

123. Unger, *False Necessity*, p. 334, struggles with similar issues.

124. A basic reason why this functional explanation differs from functionalism per se is that the latter tends to assume the stable existence of society or order and then goes about explaining the presence of specific social elements (e.g., the raindance) in terms of their contribution to that stable existence. If they do not so contribute they are dysfunctional.

125. See Morgenthau, *Politics Among Nations*.

126. See for example, Gilpin, "The Richness of the Tradition," and Buzan, et al. *The European Security Order Recast*.

127. Buzan, et al., *The European Security Order Recast*, p. 1.

128. Waltz, *Theory of International Relations*, pp. 170–71.

129. Ibid, pp. 168–173.

130. Lebow, "The Long Peace," p. 257–58.

131. See Evangelista, "Stalin's Postwar Army Reappraised," and below.

132. A neorealist who does enter the history and focuses exactly on that proximate army is Wagner, "What is Bipolarity?" Wagner, however, does not distinguish between a concern with the political ramifications of a perceived threat in Europe and the perception on the U.S.'s part that a threat existed. He also tends to assume a U.S. interest in the fate of the region. This is something that must be explained.

133. In "Continuity and Transformation," Ruggie has shown how the logic of Waltz's approach emphasizes the reproduction of a system, not its transformation.

134. On the zero-sumness of the relationship see Waltz, *Theory of International Politics*, p. 1.

135. Fischer, *Historians' Fallacies*, p. 147.

136. Waltz, *Theory of International Politics*, pp 199–202.

137. Ibid., p. 191.

138. Gilpin, *War and Change*, pp. 13, 30, respectively.

139. Ibid., p. 33.

140. Krasner, "State Power and the Structure of International Trade."

141. See Eden, "The End of U.S. Cold War History?," Cumings, "Revising Postrevisionism," and Hogan and Paterson, *Explaining the History of American Foreign Relations*.

142. Williams, *Tragedy of American Diplomacy*; and LaFeber, *America, Russia, and the Cold War*.

143. Block, *The Origins of International Economic Disorder*, p. 10.

144. McCormick, *America's Half-Century*, p. 48, tells us U.S. policymakers "had a vision of how to reorder and manage the world-system."

145. Hogan, "Corporatism," p. 235.

146. Gaddis, "The Emerging Post-Revisionist Synthesis."

147. Leffler, *Preponderance of Power*.

148. Leffler, "National Security," p. 203.

149. Leffler *Preponderance of Power*, p. 19.

150. There is Leffler, "The American Conception of National Security," "Adherence to Agreements," and "The United States and the Strategic Dimensions." Leffler's perspective, however, changed over that decade.

151. Leffler, "National Security," p. 91, 205.

152. The dynamics of "securitizing" issues is explored by Waever, "Securitization and Desecuritization."

153. Leffler, *Preponderance of Power*, pp. 3–10.

154. For a different sense of why it is not the whole story which stresses the capitalist economic interests often occluded by Leffler see Cumings, "Revising Postrevisionism."

3. An Enemy Is Better Than a Friend

1. Notter, *Postwar Foreign Policy Preparation*, p. 464.

2. See Shoup and Minter, *Imperial Brain Trust*; and Council on Foreign Relations, *War and Peace Studies*.

3. Cited in Divine, *Second Chance*, p. 247.

4. United Nations, *Charter*, ch. 6 (article 33), p. 19.

5. For an analysis of some of those doctrines see Latham, "Getting Out From Under."

6. Morgenthau, *Scientific Man*, p. 119.

7. Cited in Divine, *Second Chance*, p. 315.

8. Clifford, "American Relations," p. 476.

9. For an in-depth consideration of the analogy between domestic and international order see Suganami, *The Domestic Analogy*.

10. Bull, *Anarchical Society*, p. 13.

11. See, for example, Meyer, "World Policy." Meyer has made this reproduction of state practices central to his life's work.

12. Messer, *End of an Alliance*, p. 189.

13. An exploration of this question in the immediate post–World War II period is in Ruggie, "Embedded Liberalism."

14. See McMahon, *Colonialism and Cold War*, p. 305; and Rotter, *The Path to Vietnam*, pp. 176–77.

15. Mastny, "Stalin and the Militarization," p. 109. Ironically, in a not so dissimilar fashion Kolko and Kolko, *Limits of Power*, p. 17, claim that many American policymakers saw no place for the Soviet Union in a free market world.

16. Cited in Gaddis, "The Insecurities of Victory," p. 244.

17. Although he is mainly concerned with what he calls a capitalist world economy, rather than an international liberal order as it is more broadly defined here, Bruce Cumings discusses the demarcation of geopolitical regions in *Roaring of the Cataract*, p. 763; and idem, "The Origins and Development," pp. 1–40.

18. Paterson, *Meeting the Communist Threat*, p. 129, points out "[i]n most cases agreements were not broken, but rather interpreted differently by both sides."

19. Messer, *End of an Alliance*, pp. 108–09.

20. Etzold and Gaddis, eds., *Containment*, p. 60. See also Paterson, *Meeting the Communist Threat*, p. 115.

21. Kuniholm, *Cold War in the Near East*, p. 300, contrasts the apparent *fait accompli* in eastern Europe with the contestation in the Northern Tier region composed of Iran, Turkey, and Greece, where the "parameters had yet to be defined."

22. In his early work, John Lewis Gaddis argued for a strong distinction between Communist ideology and the Soviet Union as a threatening power to the West, the latter of which he believed was more important. See Gaddis, "Was the Truman Doctrine a Real Turning Point?" p. 392. Brands, *The Specter of Neutralism*, p. 310, adopts this view and bases it on the fact that the U.S. ignored ideological differences and established relations with Tito and pursued a Sino-Soviet split. But I would argue that it was exactly because the Soviets challenged the West with a decidedly nonliberal ideology and set of practices that made the opportunity potentially to split the adversary so attractive in the first place. Gaddis has since departed from his earlier view on the role of ideology in challenging the West and now places a great deal of emphasis on it. See Gaddis, "The Cold War," pp. 234–46.

23. See Schwartz, *America's Germany*, pp. 28–29.

24. Some of the ways Britain affected especially monetary practices is covered in Gardner, *Sterling-Dollar Diplomacy*; on the influence of Britain in the security area see Folly, "Breaking the Vicious Circle," pp. 59–77; on France's impact on security see Harrison, *The Reluctant Ally*. For an excellent overall analysis of this issue that takes liberalism quite seriously see Risse-Kappen, *Cooperation Among Democracies*.

25. Department of State, *Foreign Relations of the United States (FRUS), 1941*, vol. 1. p. 367.

26. United Nations. *Charter*, ch. 7 (article 51), p. 27.

27. See for example, *FRUS, 1945*, vol. 5, pp. 263–64.

28. Gaddis, *Origins of the Cold War*, pp. 17, 225.

29. As Barry, "Superfox," p. 143, makes clear, "objectionable counterfactuals can be characterized in general terms as ones where the antecedent cannot be imagined without also requiring other changes, prior or concomitant, that are of such nature as to make nonsense of it." In this case it is the extent of necessary changes that renders the counterfactual nonsensical. See also Tetlock and Belkin, eds. *Counterfactual Thought Experiments*, pp. 19–21.

30. A good survey of what was thought in both Germany and Britain on the Concert order is Holbraad, *Concert of Europe*. For an understanding of the growing range of phenomena being ordered across the nineteenth and twentieth centuries see Murphy, *International Organization and Industrial Change*, p. 199.

31. Murphy, *International Organization and Industrial Change*.

32. The word community is formed ultimately by the amalgam of the Latin prefix *com* meaning "together" and *munis* meaning "under obligation." Williams lays out the history of the word and its cognates in *Keywords*, pp. 70–76.

33. For an exploration of those possibilities see Linklater, "Problem of Community;" and Latham, "Liberalism's Order / Liberalism's Other."

34. Deutsch, et al., *Political Community*, pp. 5, 129.

35. Ibid., pp. 123–28.

36. The notion of nascent community is considered in Adler and Barnet, "Governing Anarchy," pp. 86–89.

37. Cited in LaFeber, *The Origins of the Cold War*, p. 41.

38. Ibid., pp. 44–45.

39. Cited in Gardner, *Sterling-Dollar Diplomacy*, p. 1. The obvious analogy is the book that enters the public domain as an object of reading, interpretation, and debate by others, which no longer can be rightfully said to be possessed by the author, but rather by her public.

40. Lundestad, "Empire by Invitation."

41. See Waltz, *Theory of International Politics*, pp. 168–76.

42. Besides Lundestad, "Empire by Invitation?" and Folly, "Breaking the Vicious Circle," the plural nature of liberal system-construction is noted by Gaddis, "Turning Point," p. 392; Hogan, *The Marshall Plan*, pp. 123–24; and Ikenberry, "Origins of American Hegemony," pp. 391–94.

43. See NSC-68 reprinted in Etzold and Gaddis, eds., *Containment*, p. 441.

44. Rawls, *Political Liberalism*, p. xviii.

45. Ibid., p. 50.

46. The status of Europe as a "Third Force" and potential challenger will be explored below.

47. The vulnerability of democracies, as opposed to liberal orders, especially in the area of foreign policy and war-making, has been noted since Alexis de Tocqueville in *Democracy in America*, pp. 236–50. As we shall discuss below, this theme was central to NSC-68. A more recent version of the argument is made by Jean-François Revel in *How Democracies Perish*. For Revel—and the authors of NSC-68—the point is that the criticism and plurality of voices in a democracy make them fragile and impotent in the face of threats. My argument regarding liberal order is obviously different.

48. This incident is described by Messer, *End of an Alliance*, p. 76. Leffler, *Preponderance*, p. 40, points out that Secretary of State Byrnes's willingness to accommodate Soviet interests in eastern Europe depended on Soviet acceptance of "liberal economic and political principles."

49. See Hixson, *George F. Kennan*, p. 53, for such a depiction.

50. This is conveyed in Policy Planning Staff (PPS) Paper 23 in Etzold and Gaddis, eds., *Containment*, pp. 114–25, especially pp. 120–21, where it is recommended that the U.S. "do everything possible from now on to coordinate . . . policy toward Germany with the views of Germany's immediate western neighbors." Who must "make their full contribution and bear their full measure of responsibility."

51. Some of the pluralistic elements of the ERP is captured in Arkes, *Bureaucracy*, ch. 7.

52. The third element was ultimately recognized by others in the State Department, among them Charles Bohlen, as risking the demarcation of a separate sphere of influence, which will be discussed below. See Gaddis, *Long Peace*, pp. 51–52.

53. The "boundary setting" implications and increasing irreversibility of Germany's division is considered in Maier, " 'Pax Americana,' " p. 5.

54. Although the process of separation represented a devolution of available channels of negotiation between the Soviets and the West, the status of "separation" is not meant to imply that the Soviets were thoroughly cut off from the liberal world. After all, they and the emerging Eastern bloc remained in the United Nations and international economic exchanges continued between East and West. More importantly, while its position was increasingly distanced from the liberal world, the Soviet Union was still capable of exerting a negative pressure on the delineation of liberal relations from that position in ways which will be explored below.

55. For the play between security and modernity across the centuries and its impact on thought see Toulmin, *Cosmopolis*, especially p. 42, where he argues that Descartes search for certainty led him to the individual cognito.

56. Mill, *Utilitarianism*, p. 67.

57. Zygmunt Bauman, has argued that "[t]he other of order is not another order: chaos is its only alternative." *Modernity and Ambivalence*, p. 7. But he fails to note that the extent to which an order can be challenged and negated by the establishment of an other order. I am trying to show that this latter challenge became palpable only as the Soviets were increasing separated from liberal order. Until then their challenge was far more tied to the possibility of thrusting liberal order into chaos.

58. Cited in Gaddis, "Insecurities of Victory," p. 271.

59. Paterson, *Communist Threat*, ch. 3, attempts to critically evaluate the emerging perception of a Soviet threat as though it were on a single trajectory of development.

60. See Sherry, *Preparing for the Next War*, pp. 159–78.

61. This point is made by Gimbel, "Cold War Historians," pp. 86–102; see also Pollard, *Economic Security*, p. 105.

62. Melvyn Leffler, "The United States," p. 288, argues that even the 1948 Czech coup did not generate a sense of a threat of war in the U.S. administration. Also see Kennan's November 1947 draft of Policy Planning Staff (PPS) 13, entitled, "Resumé of World Situation," in Etzold and Gaddis, eds., *Containment*, pp. 90–97.

63. On Truman's "hard-line" see Messer, *End of an Alliance*, p. 184.

64. FDR's qualified recognition of Soviet dominance in eastern Europe is discussed by Gaddis, "Turning Point," pp. 387–88. Harbutt, *The Iron Curtain*, p. 283, also conceives of the main lines of tension in the Cold War as stemming from the way the Soviets stepped out of the Eastern European region.

65. The importance of the perception of an internal threat is explored by Leffler, "The American Conception," pp. 363–65; Kolko and Kolko, *Limits of Power*, p. 499; and Smith, "From Disarmament to Rearmament," p. 359.

66. See Schwartz, *America's Germany*, p. 92, on the U.S. fear of East-West trade regarding especially western Germany.

67. See Kuniholm, *Cold War in the Near East*, on the pressures the Soviet applied in the eastern Mediterranean. The Soviet questioning of the British role in Greece in 1946 is discussed by Kofas, *Intervention and Underdevelopment*, p. 61.

68. See the "Report of the Special 'Ad Hoc' Committee of the State-War-Navy Coordinating Committee," April 21, 1947 in *FRUS, 1947*, vol. 3, pp. 208–9, 216–19; and "Policy with Respect to American Aid to Western Europe," in Etzold and Gaddis, eds., *Containment*, pp. 102–13.

69. Gaddis, *Strategies of Containment*, p. 4.

70. The status of the Truman Doctrine as the first publicized containment policy is addressed in Pollard, *Economic Security*, p. 130. The early dimensions of containment prior to mid-1947 are explored in Gaddis, *Strategies of Containment*, chaps. 1, 2.

71. Etzold and Gaddis, eds., *Containment*, pp. 88, 173–203.

72. Watson, *The Evolution of International Society*, p. 14.

73. Cited in Holbraad, *The Concert of Europe*, p. 138.

74. Berlin, *Four Essays on Liberty*, pp. 121–22.

75. Ibid., p. 131.

76. Of course, as implied above, liberal hegemonic leadership endeavors to set the terms of the relations that open up these possibilities.

77. Some of the different forces at play regarding the state in liberal and nonliberal international economies are explored by Kahler, "Survival of the State."

78. The importance I am attributing to state sovereignty in liberal order is not simply a matter of sneaking the realist concern with sovereignty in to drive explanations. My point is that state sovereignty took on specific force and salience through the liberal moment and the making of liberal order. In fact, if anything, liberalism is far more attached to the sovereign state than realism could ever hope to be. I explain why in "Getting Out From Under."

79. One fascinating articulation of this view is Perroux, "Economic Space: Theory and Applications."

80. Even if both the invitation for and appeal to Soviet participation were disingenuous, the point is that the potential for Soviet inclusion existed. The question of sincerity of the U.S. invitation to all European states is considered in Lundestad, *American Non-Policy Towards Eastern Europe*, pp. 402–5; Dallek, *American Style*, p. 173; and Van Der Beugel, *From Marshall Aid*, pp. 44–45. See also the PPS paper, "Policy with Respect to American Aid to Western Europe," in Etzold and Gaddis, eds., *Containment*, p. 106. On the Soviet rejection of participation see Halle, *The Cold War*, p. 135; Paterson, *Communist Threat*, p. 30; LaFeber, *America, Russia, and the Cold War*, p. 60; and Arkes, *Bureaucracy*, p. 202.

81. See Hogan, *Marshall Plan*, pp. 80, 268; Maier, "Supranational Concepts," p. 34; and Milward, *Reconstruction of Western Europe*, p. 400.

82. Rappaport, "The United States and European Integration," pp. 141–42, provides a fuller discussion of Britain's reason for rejection of the Schuman Plan.

83. This of course was a central concern in Polanyi, *The Great Transformation*. Although Britain's economy was in many respects socialist, a significant portion was organized as a market, and it clearly participated in international economic exchange. See Shonfield, *Modern Capitalism*, pp. 88–99.

84. Of course the fact that American foreign policy was so crucial to liberal order construction makes its adjustments at this level an important arena of analysis for the system in general. See Schurmann, *The Logic of World Power*, pp. 186ff; and Cumings, *Roaring of the Cataract*, ch. 1.

85. My understanding of the U.S. role in Indonesian independence is based above all on McMahon, *Colonialism and Cold War*, pp. 140–316.

86. Etzold and Gaddis, eds., *Containment*, p. 259.

87. Hirschman, *Exit, Voice, and Loyalty*.

88. See Colbert, "The Road Not Taken," pp. 608–28, for a more detailed discussion of many of the factors mentioned in this paragraph. On the relation between Indochina and European international politics and economy more generally see Rotter, *Path to Vietnam*, pp. 4–9.

89. Colbert, "Road not Taken," p. 624.

90. Mehta, "Liberal Strategies of Exclusion," p. 435.

91. "Memorandum by Assistant Secretary of State for Economic Affairs," *FRUS, 1948*, vol. 1, p. 558. That Thorpe was not alone in this thinking is made clear in the many references to related points made by Thorpe's contemporaries found in Gaddis, *Long Peace*, p. 259, n.53, n.54.

92. "Memorandum by Assistant Secretary of State for Economic Affairs," *FRUS, 1948*, vol. 1, p. 558.

93. Both principles, and their perceived importance for "the viability of political systems" are explored in Gaddis, *Long Peace*, p. 59. The second point is addressed by Lundestad, "Empire by Invitation," p. 263. An early formulation along these lines which stresses that there is a limit to intervention because of the necessity of obtaining popular support for international programs is in Van Der Beugel, *Marshall Aid*, pp. 220–21. Some of the consensual dimensions of hegemony more generally are explored by Cox, "Gramsci, Hegemony and International Relations," pp. 162–75. Not

surprisingly, Lea Brillmayer, *American Hegemony*, p. 199, points out that popular sovereignty is especially important to her theory of liberal consent because it: 1) legitimizes what the state consents to; and 2) rebuts claims that decisions are imposed by external actors.

94. "Memorandum by Assistant Secretary of State for Economic Affairs," *FRUS, 1948*, vol. 1, p. 558.

95. This was recalled by Averell Harriman, European Cooperation Agency ambassador and is cited in Burr, "Marshall Planners," p. 512.

96. Miller, *The United States and Italy*, ch. 8.

97. See Lundestad, *America's Non-Policy Towards Eastern Europe*, pp. 313–17.

98. See, for example, the November 1947, "Resumé of World Situation," in Etzold and Gaddis, eds., *Containment*, pp. 91, which calls for "strengthening local forces of independence."

99. "Report of the Special 'Ad Hoc' Committee," *FRUS, 1947*, vol. 3, pp. 208–09.

100. See for example Woods and Jones, *Dawning of the Cold War*, pp. 24–28; Dallek, *American Style*, p. 159; and Yergin, *Shattered Peace*, ch. 1, on the so-called Riga axioms.

101. Yergin, *Shattered Peace*, p. 11.

102. See Gaddis, "Turning Point," pp. 387–88; Dallek, *American Style*, p. 181; Leffler, "Adherence to Agreements," p. 92; and Anderson, *United States, Great Britain, and the Cold War*, p. ix.

103. Gaddis, *Origins of the Cold War*, pp. 281–90; see also Messer, *End of an Alliance*, pp. 82–83.

104. On the domestic forces see Gaddis, *Origins of the Cold War*, pp. 281–90; and Messer, *End of an Alliance*, pp. 82–83. For a review of some of the ways that both sides violated the Yalta accord see Leffler, "Adherence to Agreements," p. 104.

105. The emphasis on the use of the hardline to generate domestic support for external commitments is explored in Freeland, *Origins of McCarthyism*.

106. Leffler, "Adherence to Agreements," p. 94.

107. See Dallek, *American Style*, pp. 161–65. This logic is also evident in parts of NSC-68, in Etzold and Gaddis, eds., *Containment*, pp. 426, 441.

108. Quoted in Kuniholm, *Cold War in the Near East*, p. 298.

109. Kennan, *Measures Short of War*, p. 11.

110. "Report of the Special 'Ad Hoc' Committee," *FRUS, 1947*, vol. 3, pp. 217.

111. NSC-68, reprinted in Etzold and Gaddis, eds., *Containment*, p. 425.

112. This positioning of the Soviets is explored in Gimbel, *Origins of the Marshall Plan*, pp. 130ff.

113. Gaddis, *Strategies of Containment*, p. 74.

114. Schelling, *The Strategy of Conflict*, pp. 3–4; and Hart, *Strategy*, p. 335.

115. See the September 1946 lecture by George Kennan entitled, "Measures Short of War," reprinted in *Measures Short of War*, pp. 3–17.

116. See, for example, Yergin, *Shattered Peace*, pp. 141–46, 169, 295. Gaddis, *Long Peace*, ch. 3, is concerned with showing that spheres resulted from historical conditions and thus were hardly inevitable or desired.

117. On the Near East see Kuniholm, *Cold War in the Near East*, p. 377; on Africa see Harbutt, *Iron Curtain*, p. 269; and on Germany and the early avoidance of spheres in Europe see Gaddis, *Long Peace*, p. 53.

118. On the Paris conferences see Harbutt, *Iron Curtain*, p. 274; and Messer, *End of an Alliance*, pp. 193–94. On Yalta and Eastern Europe see Leffler, "Adherence to Agreements," pp. 88–123. The play between what appeared to be FDR's secret acceptance of Soviet dominance in Eastern Europe at Yalta and his public declaration of having defeated the temptation of spheres is considered in Gardner, *Spheres of Influence*.

119. Gaddis, *Long Peace*, pp. 49–52, traces these arguments between Kennan and Bohlen. Also see Lundestad, *America's Non-Policy Towards Eastern Europe*, pp. 73–75, for a consideration of Stimson's and Wallace's pro-spheres view. An early advocate of separate spheres who believed their clear definition would lead to less room for conflict was Walter Lippmann. See Dallek, *American Style*, pp. 133.

120. See Lundestad, *America's Non-Policy Towards Eastern Europe*, p. 100–101.

121. Cited in Gaddis, "Insecurities of Victory," p. 271.

122. In this respect, the Marshall Plan was more a commitment to a regional economy than to global multilateralism. See Maier, "Supranational Concepts," p. 30; and Block, *Origins of International Monetary Disorder*, p. 240, n.38.

123. Gimbel, *The Origins of the Marshall Plan*, p. 139. On use of the Soviet threat in general to keep the West together see Milward, *Reconstruction of Western Europe*, p. 283; and Kaplan, *The United States and NATO*, p. 72.

124. See Lundestad, *America's Non-Policy Towards Eastern Europe*, p. 104. The logic of Western consolidation was captured by Kennan and the Policy Planning Staff in "Policy with Respect to American Aid to Western Europe" (PPS 1), in mid-1947, reprinted in Etzold and Gaddis, eds., *Containment*, pp. 102–7. An earlier portrayal of this logic was in Clark Clifford's September 1946 report to the president, "American Relations."

125. See Maier, "Making of 'Pax Americana," p. 4; and Messer, "Paths not Taken," pp. 297–320.

126. The best discussion of this alternative is Gaddis, *Long Peace*, ch. 3.

127. Ireland, *Entangling Alliance*, p. 65, makes this observation.

128. Cited in Etzold and Gaddis, eds., *Containment*, pp. 91–93. See also Ikenberry, "Origins of American Hegemony," p. 386.

129. As we will explore further below, this dynamic underlaid much of the impetus for the "empire by invitation" extended to the U.S.

130. Gaddis, *Long Peace*, pp. 64–65, explores the tension over the U.S.-Soviet face-off in Germany and how it served to supply an additional impetus to the empire by invitation.

131. PPS 37, August, 1948, in Etzold and Gaddis, eds., *Containment*, pp. 135–44. Note also the discussion in Hixson, *George F. Kennan*, pp. 81–87; and Schwartz, *America's Germany*, pp. 35–40.

132. See Schwartz, *America's Germany*, p. 39.

133. On the Truman administration's use of failure see Freeland, *Origins of McCarthyism*, p. 9. Gaddis, *Long Peace*, p. 61, for instance argues that the failure of the emergence of a European "Third Force" led to the U.S. military commitment. An argument for viewing the necessity of the European Recovery Program as stemming from the failure of the multilateral economic system planned for during World War II is made by Ikenberry, "Origins of American Hegemony," pp. 371, 385. General failure of the instruments of system construction is a important aspect of the arguments in Kolko and Kolko, *Limits of Power*, pp. 329, 710.

134. A recent example is Reiff, *Slaughterhouse: Bosnia and the Failure of the West*.

135. See the discussion above about employing counterfactuals in the context of historical situations involving a wide array of complex factors.

136. See Leffler, "Strategic Dimensions of the Marshall Plan," p. 300, for a portrayal of the failure perceived by Acheson in the spring of 1950.

137. For example, see Milward, *Reconstruction of Western Europe*, p. 48; and Hogan, *Marshall Plan*, pp. 30–33.

4. *"The Requirements of Freedom"*

1. Etzold and Gaddis, ed., *Containment*, pp. 435–36.

2. Although this commitment has been recognized across the historiography of the Cold War, the most concentrated consideration is Pollard, *Economic Security*, pp. 4, 55–57, 133. Pollard points out that the call for a militarized version of containment contained in the 1946 report to the president by Clifford, "American Relations," was shelved. The report (p. 479), however, not only recognized the value of economic security but also argued that supplying "military support in case of attack is a last resort; a more effective barrier to communism is strong economic support."

3. Quote from Department of State, *FRUS, 1949*, vol. 1, pp. 254–55. See also Pach, "Arming the Free World," p. 389; and Kaplan, *A Community of Interests*, pp. 21–22. The containment logic of economic security is considered in Messer, "Paths not Taken," p. 298; and, of course, Pollard, *Economic Security*, p. 133.

4. On Eastern Europe see Lundestad, *America's Non-Policy Towards Eastern Europe*, p. 223.

5. Cited in Gardner, *Sterling-Dollar Diplomacy*, p. 9.

6. Cited in Pollard, *Economic Security*, p. 13.

7. Gaddis, *Strategies of Containment*, p. 83.

8. The dynamics of this concentration are explored by Freeland, *Origins of McCarthyism*, ch. 5. See Arkes, *Bureaucracy*, p. 102, on the congressional pro-business approach in the Marshall Plan and its basis in the "trade leads to security" formula.

9. The commitment to work with Western Europe regarding both the domestic and international economic dimensions was predicated, in part, on its feasibility. In other words, as I argued above, economic and political conditions conducive to liberalization were already in place to some degree in Western Europe. In Asia, in contrast, a Marshall Plan-type program was rejected in part because of a perceived lack of feasibility. See Borden, *The Pacific Alliance*, p. 110.

10. Clifford, "American Relations," p. 479. See also Woods and Jones, *Dawning of the Cold War*, p. 155. Milward, *Recovery of Western Europe*, pp. 59–60, explores some of the reasoning behind integration as a spur to economic growth and thus "pluralist democracy" in Europe.

11. Cited in Gardner, *Sterling-Dollar Diplomacy*, p. 11. That type of faith was also echoed in the thought of David Mitrany. See his *Working Peace System*.

12. See Maier, "Politics of Productivity," p. 31; and Hogan, *The Marshall Plan*, pp. 134–51. Arkes, *Bureaucracy*, pp. 312–16, shows that while ECA head Paul G. Hoffmann tried to emphasize that he was strictly interested in economic factors, he did

realize that the ERP had a political dimension. The point is that the range of such a politics was constricted.

13. See Maier, "Politics of Productivity."

14. These agreements are analyzed masterfully by Albert Hirschman in *National Power and the Structure of Foreign Trade*.

15. There are, of course, many ways of being political, a term that is essentially contested. Some of the many ways are considered in Charles Maier's introduction to his edited volume, *Changing Boundaries of the Political*, and in Connolly, *Political Discourse*, where the term's contested status is made clear.

16. Kennan, *Measures Short of War*, p. 296.

17. Ibid., p. 11.

18. The difference was captured in theoretical terms by the distinction referred to above between negative and positive liberty. Berlin, *Essays on Liberty*, p. 166, recognized that these are only two types of attitudes toward the ends of life and that specific situations would mix both types of liberty.

19. There is no historical precedent for such an open order. However, the point of such a counterfactual is to underscore the salience of limits and closure in the building of liberal order, not to demonstrate its feasibility.

20. Interestingly, the philosopher Richard Rorty, who has made much of the link between liberalism and solidarity, for instance in his *Contingency, Irony, and Solidarity*, has been criticized for being a Cold War liberal by Richard Bernstein, *The New Constellation*, ch. 8.

21. Some thinking along these lines is found in Linklater, *Men and Citizens*.

22. See Sherry, *Preparation for the Next War*, pp. 199–204, on the expansion of bases and the world peace mission accepted by the Joint Chiefs of Staff. See also Paterson, *Communist Threat*, p. 43, on the new forward defense strategic thinking. See Leffler, "Adherence to Agreements," p. 112, on the retention of World War II bases in the context of NATO. And see Herkin, *Winning Weapon*, on the increasing importance of the A-bomb in U.S. strategic thinking. On the differences between the prewar and postwar U.S. military posture see Lundestad, "Empire by Invitation," p. 265.

23. Leffler, "Was 1947 a Turning Point," p. 28, reviews these strategic expansions in 1947.

24. This point is observed in Pach, "Arming the Free World," pp. 304, 369.

25. See Leffler, "American Conception of National Security."

26. The overemphasis Leffler places on military planning forms part of Gaddis's critique of his approach; see Gaddis, "Comments."

27. As planners themselves came to realize, making this separation was far from simple. Congressional intentions are discussed in Arkes, *Bureaucracy*, p. 111.

28. See Green, "The Cold War Comes to Latin America," pp. 158–60.

29. See the "Report of the Special 'Ad Hoc' Committee of the State-War-Navy Coordinating Committee," April 21, 1947 in *FRUS, 1947*, vol. 3, p. 206. The same point is made in Gaddis, *Strategies of Containment*, p. 63.

30. That historical time can differ, especially in so crucial a period as the immediate postwar years, is a point observed by Grosser, *Western Alliance*, p. 59. On the broader theoretical implications of differences in political time see Maier, "The Politics of Time," pp. 151–78.

31. Kirkpatrick, "Dictatorships and Double Standards."

32. Jackson, *Quasi-States*.

33. On the minimal importance of shared international values see Kratochwil, *Norms, Rules and Decisions*, pp. 64–66.

34. The state centrism of the liberal tradition is generally explored in Latham, "Getting Out From Under."

35. Cited in Gaddis, "The Insecurities of Victory," p. 267, n.110.

36. Jones, *Fifteen Weeks*, pp. 166–67.

37. Cited in ibid., pp. 270, 273.

38. Kennan's views on Spain are discussed in Hixson, *George F. Kennan*, p. 58. On the inclusion of Italy in NATO see Smith, "From Disarmament to Armament," p. 362.

39. Quoted in Steel, *Walter Lippmann*, pp. 438–39. In August 1948, for example, Kennan claimed that he could not articulate the specific aims of Soviet containment. See NSC 20/1, in Etzold and Gaddis, eds., *Containment*, pp. 173–202.

40. Cited in Kennan, *Memoirs*, pp. 321—22.

41. On Acheson's defense of the Truman Doctrine see Woods and Jones, *Dawning of the Cold War*, p. 149. The designation of containment as a "flexible policy" is discussed in ibid., p. 143.

42. One criticism Kennan lodged in early 1948 against U.S. foreign policy was that its universal approach "tends to rule out political solutions (that is, solutions relating to the peculiarities in the positions and attitudes of the individual peoples)." "Review of Current Trends: U.S. Foreign Policy," in Etzold and Gaddis, eds., *Containment*, pp. 97–98. Although Kennan recognized that both universalistic and particularistic approaches were embedded in American foreign policy, such a view overlooks the way that a universal principle allows for particular solutions to be handled by the "individual peoples" themselves.

43. This "freedom of action" was observed by Gaddis, "Turning Point," p. 399.

44. On the weakness of the Greek economy and the limited efforts to apply economic security see Wittner, *American Intervention in Greece*, pp. 184, 226–27; and Amen, *American Foreign Policy*, pp. 195ff. On the early reservations about the representative nature of the Greek government see Kofas, *Greece During the Cold War*, p. 64. On the risks not taken on a political settlement and the recourse to violence and authoritarianism, see Wittner, *American Intervention in Greece*, pp. 121, 134, 268; and Jones, *"A New Kind of War,"* pp. 47ff. Kennan's warning on supporting authoritarian governments is addressed in Gaddis, *Strategies of Containment*, p. 40. See also the discussion of U.S. policymakers' fear of the vulnerability of unstable democratic governance and the recourse to authoritarian forces in Smith, *America's Mission*, pp. 184–88.

45. See Amen, *American Foreign Policy in Greece*, for a detailed discussion of these organs.

46. These justifications are brought out in Wittner, *American Intervention in Greece*, p. 73; and Amen, *American Foreign Policy in Greece*, p. 79.

47. Barnett, "The New United Nations Politics," p. 87.

48. See Lippmann, *The Cold War*, ch. 1.

49. Some of this activity is summarized in Paterson, *On Every Front*, pp. 62–63. The general origins of clandestine political operations and the CIA is summarized in Leary, *The Central Intelligence Agency*, pp. 36–49.

50. For a discussion that emphasizes the security motives at work in the expansionary and globalist aspects of containment see Tucker, *The Radical Left*, pp. 107–11.

51. Gallagher and Robinson, "The Imperialism of Free Trade," p. 13.

52. On exclusionary terms and means see Mehta, "Liberal Strategies of Exclusion."

53. This is discussed in Tilly, *Coercion, Capital, and European States*, p. 24.

54. This tendency has not escaped the notice of historians and political scientists alike. Besides historians such as Gaddis, political scientists such as Hadley Arkes, *Bureaucracy*, and Theodore Lowi, *End of Liberalism*, ch. 6, have sounded the same theme.

55. By authority, following the definition of Kratochwil, *Norms, Rules and Decisions*, I mean the degree to which there is "acceptance of decisions as authoritative which are either rendered by dispute-settling organs or which have been made collectively (pp. 62–63)." Scope refers to the degree to which policy and decisionmaking—both within and across a wide range of issue areas—falls under an institution's governance.

56. See Grosser, *Western Alliance*, pp. 61–63.

57. A provocative exploration of some of the ways that containment helped set the terms of U.S. identity is in Campbell, *Writing Security*, pp. 175–79.

58. See Hixon, *George F. Kennan*, pp. 94–95.

59. Klein, *Strategic Studies and World Order*, pp. 114–18.

60. McNamara, *In Retrospect*, p. 322.

61. NSC-68, in Etzold and Gaddis, eds., *Containment*, pp. 393–94. As Gaddis, "Turning Point," p. 401, shows, this dynamic was also understood by Acheson by 1949, as he tried to counter both Kennan's and Bohlen's emphasis on Soviet intentions over capabilities.

62. Kratochwil, "The Challenge of Security in a Changing World," p. 127.

63. See Kratochwil, *Rules, Norms, and Decisions*, p. 258, for a general discussion of the stress that structural realism places on capabilities over politics; the same point is brought out from another angle by Ashley, "The Poverty of Neorealism," p. 291.

64. Cumings, *Roaring of the Cataract*, pp. 66–70. On the British view see Woods and Jones, *Dawning of the Cold War*, p. 103.

65. See the discussion in Kaplan, *The United States and NATO*, pp. 31–32.

66. Vandenberg, *Vandenberg Diaries*, p. 341.

67. This understanding of the status of the confrontational nature of international liberalism contrasts with that of Michael Doyle, "Liberal Legacies," part 2, p. 324, who sees it as inherently bombastic and marked by missionary zeal. Cf. also Gaddis, *Origins of the Cold War*, p. 352, on the Truman Doctrine as overly confrontational because of its ideologically conflictual nature.

68. On the limited organizational "instrumentalities" see Wittner, *American Intervention in Greece*, p. 104. On the consideration and rejection of the option of sending troops see Jones, *"New Kind of War,"* p. 92.

69. See Lundestad, *America's Non-Policy Towards Eastern Europe*, pp. 63, 223, 254–55, 331, on the limits in Eastern Europe and Messer, *End of an Alliance*, p. 198, on the Middle East.

70. The limits of U.S. intervention in India is addressed in Brands, *Specter of Neutralism*, p. 48. The U.S. deference to Britain in their traditional spheres is considered by Kuniholm, *Cold War in the Near East*, pp. 97, 227, 242–43. A discussion of the limited troop commitment is in Wells, "The First Cold War Buildup," p. 182.

71. The Europe first strategy is portrayed by Gaddis, *Long Peace*, p. 56. See also Kennan's November 1947 "Resume of the World Situation," in Etzold and Gaddis, eds., *Containment*, p. 91.

72. Address before the Delta Council in Cleveland on May 8, 1947, reprinted in Jones, *Fifteen Weeks*, p. 279.

73. Lippmann, *The Cold War*, p. 24.

74. Kolko and Kolko, *Limits of Power*, p. 711. A major theme throughout Lippmann, *The Cold War*, is how the universalism of containment would put stress on U.S. resources as the entire liberal world became a potential point for the application of counterforce.

75. See Lundestad, "Empire by Invitation," p. 267; Hogan, *Marshall Plan*, p. 443; and Paterson, *Communist Threat*, p. 34.

76. "Review of Current Trends: U.S. Foreign Policy," in Etzold and Gaddis, eds., *Containment*, p. 227.

77. Maier, "Making of 'Pax Americana,' " p. 42.

78. On Turkey, see Leffler, "Strategy, Diplomacy, and the Cold War," p. 818. On the effort to trade aid for base rights see Ireland, *Entangling Alliance*, pp. 125–27; and Kaplan, *Community of Interests*, pp. 36ff. On military advisers see ibid., pp. 60ff. On European resistance see ibid., pp. 61–2, 139; and idem, *The United States and NATO*, p. 39.

79. The extent to which Western European states gave up control of their security is explored in Buzan, "The Future of Western European Security," p. 29; and in Kaplan, *The United States and NATO*, pp. 5–12. Many aspects of the sometimes ambiguous relationship between sovereignty and security are explored in Stambuk, *American Forces Abroad*, pp. 7–12, 161–64. As Sherry, *Preparing for the Next War*, p. 42, shows, as early as 1944, FDR had been willing to order a study on air bases that was to "ignore considerations of national sovereignty."

80. Beugel, *Marshall Aid*, p. 216.

81. Cited in Hobsbawm, *Nations and Nationalism*, p. 30.

82. Cited in Jones, *Fifteen Weeks*, p. 280.

83. For a discussion of the reasons for U.S. support of integration see Rappaport, "The United States and European Integration," pp. 121–22; Hogan, *The Marshall Plan*, p. 90; Kaplan, *Community of Interests*, p. 7; and Calleo, *Beyond American Hegemony*, p. 30.

84. Haas, "International Integration," p. 366.

85. See Rappaport, "The United States and European Integration," p. 132.

86. Congressional resistance is considered in Ikenberry, "Origins of American Hegemony," pp. 388–89.

87. On the expectations of the disappearance of the ERP see Arkes, *Bureaucracy*, pp. 203, 301; and Milward, *Reconstruction of Western Europe*, p. 169. The perception of the temporariness of Europe's problems and their status as an emergency are discussed in Milward, ibid., p. 219; and Maier, "Supranational Concepts," p. 29.

88. On the ramifications of the business emphasis in the ERP see Arkes, *Bureaucracy*, p. 329. See also Wilkins, *The Maturing of Multinational Enterprise*, pp. 287–323, on the general scope of the postwar activity of multinational corporations (MNCs). One area of MNC involvement not discussed here is the American occupation of Germany. See Eisenberg, "U.S. Policy in Post-War Germany."

89. See Arkes, *Bureaucracy*, pp. 157, 299, 215, 301, 325.

90. Hogan, *Marshall Plan*, p. 136.

91. See ibid., pp. 143–51, where many of the aspects of this participation—the chief goal of which was to incorporate labor into the recovery effort—are explored.

92. Vandenberg, *Private Papers*, p. 395.

93. Ibid., p. 382.

94. Ibid., pp. 392–93.

95. On the limited leverage of the ERP see Milward, *Reconstruction of Western Europe*. p. 125; and Arkes, *Bureaucracy*, pp. 311, 326. European resistance and alternatives are also discussed in Milward, pp. 120, 173; and Hogan, *Marshall Plan*, pp. 123–24.

96. This constitutes the main theme of Freeland, *Origins of McCarthyism*, ch. 5; see also Jackson, "Prologue to the Marshall Plan."

97. Integration as a political goal of the Marshall Plan is considered in Milward, *Reconstruction of Western Europe*, p. 56. On the promotion of U.S. interests in general see Freeland, *Origins of McCarthyism*, p. 56; Block, *Origins of International Monetary Disorder*, pp. 83–84; and Kolko and Kolko, *Limits of Power*, pp. 436ff. The specific outcomes in Italy and France are detailed in Leffler, "Strategic Dimensions of the Marshall Plan," pp. 280–81; Jackson, "Prologue to the Marshall Plan," p. 1046; and Maier, "Supranational Concepts," pp. 32–33.

98. See Gimbel, *Origins of the Marshall Plan*, p. 4, on the incorporation of Germany; LaFeber, *America, Russia, and the Cold War*, p. 62; Maier, "Supranational Concepts," p. 31; and Leffler, "Strategic Dimensions of the Marshall Plan," pp. 282–83.

99. See Arkes, *Bureaucracy*, pp. 216–18, on the encouragement of East-West trade in the ERP. The dualistic multilateral and bipolar character of the ERP is discussed in Woods and Jones, *Dawning of the Cold War*, p. 246. The ramifications of the ERP for Eastern Europe as seen by the administration is treated in Lundestad, *America's Non-Policy Towards Eastern Europe*, p. 104; and Leffler, "Strategic Dimensions of the Marshall Plan," p. 283. In effect, a certain degree of closure was necessary regarding East-West multilateral economic relations before they could be carried on into the future.

100. NSC-20/1, in Etzold and Gaddis, eds., *Containment*, pp. 182–83.

101. The most complete treatment of these dimensions is Leffler, "Strategic Dimensions of the Marshall Plan," and idem, *Preponderance of Power*, ch. 5. See also Jackson, "Prologue to the Marshall Plan;" and Ambrose, *Rise to Globalism*, pp. 92–93.

102. Milward, *Reconstruction of Western Europe*, pp. 5, 54.

103. "Report of the Special 'Ad Hoc' Committee of the State-War-Navy Coordinating Committee," April 21, 1947, in Department of State, *FRUS, 1947*, vol. 3, pp. 204–19.

104. See also the comments by Jackson, "Prologue to the Marshall Plan," p. 1055. On strategic materials see Kaplan, *Community of Interests*, pp. 13–14. Wallace and Baruch's observations are treated by Kaplan, p. 13; and Hogan, *Marshall Plan*, p. 94. The links between economic and military security made in the Senate are considered in Arkes, *Bureaucracy*, p. 110.

105. Smith, "From Disarmament to Rearmament," p. 359.

106. Acheson is quoted in LaFeber, "NATO and the Korean War: A Context," p. 463. Lovett is quoted in Pach, "Arming the Free World," pp. 364–65.

107. Cited in Smith, *The United States, Italy and NATO*, p. 105.

108. Vandenberg, *Private Papers*, p. 475.

109. NSC 14/1, in Etzold and Gaddis, eds., *Containment*, p. 130.

110. See Hogan, *The Marshall Plan*, pp. 189, 313, on the rearmament-integration link and coordination.

111. See May, "The American Commitment to Germany," p. 438.

112. Etzold and Gaddis, eds., *Containment*, pp. 158–59.

113. On these points see Kaplan, *The United States and NATO*, pp. 4, 104, 128, 152, 173; idem, *Community of Interests*, pp. 74–76; Schwartz, *America's Germany*, p. 115; Ireland, *Entangling Alliance*, p. 183; Leffler, "Strategic Dimensions of the Marshall Plan," p. 295; Lundestad, "Empire by Invitation," p. 272; and May, "America's Commitment to Germany," pp. 432–33.

114. Cited in Kaplan, *The United States and NATO*, p. 71.

115. Kaplan, *Community of Interests*, p. 41.

116. Bohlen's views are cited in Folly, "Breaking the Vicious Circle," pp. 70–71; and Gaddis, *Long Peace*, ch. 3.

117. Etzold and Gaddis, eds., *Containment*, pp. 154–55.

118. Taft's views are in Doenecke, *Not to the Swift*, pp. 162–63. On the way NATO overcame the potential for a return to isolationism see May, "America's Commitment to Germany," pp. 431–36.

119. The extent to which isolationist military approaches influenced the Truman administration's military planning is explored in Sherry, *Preparing for the Next War*, pp. 49, 203–4, 229–32; Doenecke, *Not to the Swift*, p. 165; Rosenberg, "America's Atomic Strategy," p. 69; and Eden, "Capitalist Conflict," p. 253.

120. When Acheson signed the North Atlantic Treaty he claimed that it might correct the failure of the ERP to unify Europe through the U.S. connection. See Kaplan, *The United States and NATO*, pp. 5–6; Freeland, *Origins of McCarthyism*, p. 323; LaFeber, *America, Russia, and the Cold War*, p. 84; and Joffe, "Europe's American Pacifier."

121. On British resistance to economic integration see Hogan, *The Marshall Plan*, p. 75; and Ireland, *Entangling Alliance*, pp. 165–66. On French reluctance regarding Germany see Schwartz, *America's Germany*, p. 38; Kaplan, *United States and NATO*, pp. 135–38; Joffe, "Europe's American Pacifier," pp. 69–70; Gaddis, *Long Peace*, p. 66; Ireland, pp. 67–71, 109, 175. On the undermining of confidence see Hogan, pp. 310–12; and LaFeber, "NATO and the Korean War," p. 362.

122. See Kaplan, *The United States and NATO*, pp. 135–38; and Ireland, *Entangling Alliance*, p. 67.

123. Doenecke, *Not to the Swift*, p. 154. The irony that a U.S. push for a strong independent West Germany to minimize U.S. involvement in Europe had led to increased Western European demand for U.S. involvement is noted by Ireland, *Entangling Alliance*, pp. 75–76.

124. "Summary Record of a Meeting of United States Ambassadors at Paris, October 21–22," in *FRUS, 1949*, vol. 4, p. 482.

125. This complexity is one reason why I have viewed those forces mostly through the lens of U.S. policymakers. The other reason is the sheer salience of the U.S. perspective, which, nonetheless, was only one among many. On this issue see the Introduction above.

126. Etzold and Gaddis, eds., *Containment*, pp. 203–11.

127. Ibid., p. 207.

128. Ibid., p. 205.

129. Ibid., p. 204.

130. Ibid., p. 209.

131. Cited in Leffler, *Preponderance of Power*, p. 218. See the excellent study by Avi Shlaim, *The United States and the Berlin Blockade*.

132. Frémeaux and Martel, "French Defense Policy," p. 96.

133. Etzold and Gaddis, eds., *Containment*, p. 150.

134. Kennan, *Memoirs*, pp. 408–09.

135. *FRUS, 1947*, vol. 3, p. 216.

136. This memo is discussed in Steel, *Walter Lippmann*, p. 460.

137. In this view, he was generally in accord with Kennan's Program A discussed in the last chapter.

138. Leffler, *Preponderance of Power*, pp. 212–13; and Wall, *The United States and the Making of Postwar France*, pp. 133–34.

139. The story and politics surrounding the Soviet bomb is superbly told and analyzed in Holloway, *Stalin and the Bomb*.

140. On these efforts see, for example, Leffler, *Preponderance of Power*, p. 215.

141. Etzold and Gaddis, eds., *Containment*, pp. 204–05.

142. Ibid., p. 209.

143. Smith, *The United States, Italy and NATO*, p. 66.

144. Etzold and Gaddis, eds., *Containment*, p. 210.

145. Ibid., p. 208.

146. Ibid., p. 175.

147. Ibid., p. 174. This is not, however, an accurate quote of Clausewitz.

148. Ibid., p. 298.

149. Ibid., p. 300.

150. Examples include Johnson, "Periods of Peril," p. 952; Nordlinger, *Isolationism Reconfigured*, pp. 268–70; and Stueck, *Road to Confrontation*, p. 257.

151. A very nuanced discussion of vulnerability that does take self-fearing (without using the term) into account along with other forms of vulnerability is in Buzan, *People, States and Fear*, ch. 3.

152. Etzold and Gaddis, eds., *Containment*, pp. 401, 412.

153. See, for example, the excellent analysis of this problem in Putnam, "Diplomacy and Domestic Politics."

154. Some of the broader theoretical issues at stake in this sense of explanation are developed in Patomäki, "How to Tell Better Stories About World Politics."

155. Vandenberg, *Private Papers*, p. 479.

156. Kaplan, *Community of Interests*, p. 72. See also Hogan, *The Marshall Plan*, p. 443; and Calleo, *Beyond American Hegemony*, p. 19.

157. Buzan, "Western European Security," p. 36.

158. On Kennan's views see Gaddis, *Long Peace*, pp. 63–64. On Dulles see Kaplan, *The United States and NATO*, p. 185.

159. The "disguised integration" especially of the early NATO is analyzed in Stambuk, *American Forces Abroad*, pp. 167–72. See also Kaplan, *The United States and NATO*, p. 128. Hogan, *The Marshall Plan*, pp. 80, 443, points out also that the collaboration over collective security "overshadowed" but never replaced the trend toward increasing unity. There also was, of course, a slow progression of increasing security collaboration in NATO through the years, but the failure of the European Defense

Community (EDC), the "withdrawal" of France, and the continued American dominance point away from integration in any meaningful sense. See also the essays in Heller and Gillingham, eds., *NATO: The Founding of the Atlantic Alliance.*

160. The role of NATO as a facilitator of further cooperation in the economic sphere is noted by Beugel, *Marshall Aid*, p. 257. Some interesting reflections on the emergence of a "liberal time" and its allocative nature is in Maier, "Politics of Time," p. 165.

161. Maier, "Making of 'Pax Americana,' " pp. 42–54; and idem, "Finance and Defense," pp. 335–51. On some of the theoretical issues surrounding this link see Gowa, "Bipolarity, Multipolarity, and Free Trade."

162. *FRUS, 1949*, vol. 4, p. 494.

163. On this influence see Risse-Kappen, "Long-Term Future of European Security," p. 57.

164. Acheson's comments were made in, U.S. Congress, House Committee on Ways and Means, *Extension of the Reciprocal Trade Agreements Act*, p. 7. Acheson also claimed that the U.S. must "maintain as spacious an environment as possible in which free states might exist and flourish." Cited in Freeland, *Origins of McCarthyism*, p. 322. For a discussion of the importance of productivity see Maier, "Politics of Productivity"; Hogan, *The Marshall Plan*, ch. 1; and Kaplan, *Community of Interests*, p. 77.

165. Calleo, *Beyond American Hegemony*, pp. 19, 35.

166. The use of the Schuman Plan to link France and Germany is considered in Ireland, *Entangling Alliance*, pp. 168–75; Wiggershaus, "The Decision for a West German Defense Contribution," p. 199; and LaFeber, *America, Russia, and the Cold War*, p. 86.

167. Etzold and Gaddis, eds., *Containment*, pp. 403–4, 422.

168. See Russett, *Controlling the Sword*, for some of the problems and possibilities of democratic control of the military.

169. Gaddis, "The Soviet Threat Reconsidered," p. 169.

170. Smith, "From Disarmament to Rearmament," p. 359.

171. Etzold and Gaddis, eds., *Containment*, p. 414.

172. Cumings, *Roaring of the Cataract*, p. 48. See also Lloyd Gardner, "Commentary," pp. 61–62.

173. Kaplan, *The United States and NATO*, p. 11.

174. See, for example, Jervis, "Impact of the Korean War," who argues that the Korean War was the crucial turning point; and LaFeber, "NATO and the Korean War," who points to patterns of militarization that reflected a general systemic crisis as well as events that occurred previous to the Korean War such as the Soviet A-bomb.

175. Mann, *Sources of Social Power*, p. 26.

176. Holm, "The Democratic Victory," argues that even democratic states try to shield foreign policy from democratic processes.

177. Locke, "The Second Treatise of Government," especially chaps. 9 and 10. On the play between sovereignty and security see Ullman, "Redefining Security."

5. Conclusion

1. The European Union might be taken as an exception to this outcome. However, this would overlook a chief observation of chapter 4: the limited scope of institutions at

the international level allowed Western European states to pursue this exception at the regional level.

2. Realists could look to other theoretical approaches to address this anomaly, such as liberal interdependence theory. But that move would only reinforce the limits of the realist approach itself as it has been historically articulated. Those limits are discussed in Baldwin, ed., *Neorealism and Neoliberalism*. To what extent a constructivist or historicist realism can emerge—with which the analysis of this book would be a part—remains to be seen. See Buzan, Jones, and Little, *The Logic of Anarchy*.

3. There seems to be a revival of this activity since the end of the Cold War. Some recent discussions of this issue include Leffler, "Inside Enemy Archives;" Macdonald, "Communist Bloc Expansion in the Early Cold War;" and Miner, "Revelations, Secrets, Gossip and Lies."

4. Nordlinger, *Isolationism Reconfigured*.

5. That recourse regarding the Gulf War is explored in Tucker and Hendrickson, *Imperial Temptation*.

6. Those, such as Carl Schmitt, *The Concept of the Political*, who see only weakness in liberalism along these lines fail to note the legitimizing strength liberalization can create. It is the two sides that create the paradox.

7. The term embedded militarization, as defined in the introduction to this book, is meant to convey that militarization developed within the context of the liberal order-building process.

8. The relationship between dilemmas, or aporias, and modern agency is explored in Bauman, *Postmodern Ethics*, esp. pp. 8, 11.

9. Shklar, *Ordinary Vices*, pp. 4–5.

10. See George F. Kennan, *American Diplomacy, 1900–1950*, pp. 83–89; and PPS-23, reprinted in Etzold and Gaddis, eds., *Containment*, pp. 97–100.

11. The contemporary problem with continuing with business as usual along these lines is discussed in Hoffmann, "Crisis of Liberal Internationalism."

12. Remarks by the President, Freedom House Speech, October 6, 1995, Washington, D.C.

13. McNamara, *In Retrospect*.

BIBLIOGRAPHY

Acheson, Dean G. *Present at the Creation: My Years in the State Department*. New York: Norton, 1969.

Adler, Emmanuel. "Seasons of Peace: Progress in Postwar International Security." In *Progress in Postwar International Relations*, pp. 128–73. Edited by Emmanuel Adler and Beverly Crawford. New York: Columbia University Press, 1991.

Adler, Emanuel and Michael N. Barnett. "Governing Anarchy: A Research Agenda for the Study of Security Communities." *Ethics and Inernational Affairs* 10 (1996): 63–98.

Aggarwal, Vinod K. *Liberal Protectionism: The International Politics of Organized Textile Trade*. Berkeley: University of California Press, 1985.

Alker, Jr., Hayward R. "Dialectical Foundations of Global Disparities." *International Studies Quarterly* 25 (March 1981): 69–98.

Allen, David and Michael Smith. "Western Europe in the Atlantic System." *Review of International Studies* 16 (January 1990): 19–37.

Allison, Graham T. *Essence of Decision: Explaining the Cuban Missile Crisis*. Boston: Little, Brown, 1971.

Allison, Graham T. and Morton H. Halperin. "Bureaucratic Politics: A Paradigm and Some Policy Implications." In *Theory and Policy in International Relations*, pp. 40–80. Edited by Raymond Tanter and Richard Ullman. Princeton: Princeton University Press, 1972.

Almond, Gabriel. "Capitalism and Democracy." *PS: Political Science and Politics* 24 (September 1991): 467–74.

Ambrose, Stephen. *Rise to Globalism: American Foreign Policy Since 1938*, rev. 4th ed. New York: Penguin Books, 1985.

Amen, Michael Mark. *American Foreign Policy in Greece 1944/1949: Economic, Military and Institutional Aspects*. Frankfurt am Main: Peter Lang, 1978.

Anderson, Eugene and Pauline Anderson. *Political Institutions and Social Change in Continental Europe in the Nineteenth Century*. Berkeley: University of California Press, 1967.

Anderson, Perry. *Lineages of the Absolutist State*. London: New Left Books, 1974.

Anderson, Terry. *The United States, Great Britain, and the Cold War 1944–1947*. Columbia: University of Missouri Press, 1981.

Angell, Norman. *The Great Illusion*. New York: Garland Press, 1972.

Arendt, Hannah. *The Origins of Totalitarianism*. San Diego: Harcourt Brace Jovanovich, 1973.

Arkes, Hadley. *Bureaucracy, the Marshall Plan, and the National Interest*. Princeton: Princeton University Press, 1972.

Aron, Raymond. *Politics and History*. New Brunswick, NJ: Transaction Books, 1984.

Ashley, Richard. "The Poverty of Neorealism." In *Neo-Realism and Its Critics*, pp. 255–300. Edited by Robert Keohane. New York: Columbia University Press, 1986.

Atiyah, P. S. *The Rise and Fall of Freedom of Contract*. Oxford: Clarendon Press, 1979.

Ball, Nicole. *Security and Economy in the Third World*. Princeton: Princeton University Press, 1988.

Baldwin, David A., ed. *Neorealism and Neoliberalism: The Contemporary Debate*. New York: Columbia University Press, 1993.

Barkin, J. Samuel and Bruce Cronin. "The State and the Nation: Changing Norms and the Rules of Sovereignty in International Relations." *International Organization* 48 (Winter 1994): 107–30.

Barnet, Richard. *Roots of War*. New York: Penguin Books, 1972.

Barnett, Michael. "The New United Nations Politics of Peace: From Juridical to Empirical Sovereignty." *Global Governance* 1 (Winter, 1995): 79–97.

Barnett, Michael and Alexander Wendt. "The Systemic Sources of Dependent Militarization." In *The Insecurity Dilemma: National Security of Third World States*, pp. 97–119. Edited by Brian L. Job. Boulder, CO: Lynne Rienner, 1992.

Barry, Brian. "Superfox." *Political Studies* 28 (March 1980): 136–43.

Bartlett, Christopher. "Statecraft, Power and Influence." In *Britain Pre-eminent: Studies of British World Influence in the Nineteenth Century*, pp. 179–93. Edited by Christopher Bartlett. New York: St. Martin's Press, 1969.

———. "Britain and the European Balance." In *Europe's Balance of Power, 1815–1848*, pp. 145–63. Edited by Alan Sked. New York: Barnes & Noble, 1979.

Bauman, Zygmunt. *Modernity and Ambivalence*. Cambridge: Polity Press, 1991.

———. *Postmodern Ethics*. Oxford: Blackwell, 1993.

Bellamy, Richard. *Liberalism and Modern Society*. University Park: The Pennsylvania State University Press, 1992.

Bentham, Jeremy. "Plan for an Universal and Perpetual Peace." In *Peace Projects of the Eighteenth Century*, pp. 1–44. New York: Garland Publishing, 1974.

———. *An Introduction to the Principles of Morals and Legislation*. Edited by J. H. Burns and H. L. A. Hart. London: Methuen, 1982.

Berghahn, Volker R. *Militarism: The History of an International Debate, 1861–1979*. Cambridge: Cambridge University Press, 1981.

Berlin, Isaiah. *Four Essays on Liberty.* New York: Oxford University Press, 1969.

Berman, Marshall. *All That Is Solid Melts Into Air.* New York: Penguin Books, 1982.

Bernstein, Richard J. *The New Constellation: The Ethical-Political Horizons of Modernity/Postmodernity.* Cambridge: MIT Press, 1992.

Bertrand, Maurice. "Some Reflections on Reform of the United Nations." In *International Institutions at Work,* pp. 193–219. Edited by Paul Taylor and A. J. R. Groom. New York: St. Martin's Press, 1988.

Biersteker, Thomas J. "The 'Triumph' of Neoclassical Economics in the Developing World." In *Governance Without Government,* pp. 102–31. Edited by James N. Rosenau and Ernst-Otto Czempiel. Cambridge: Cambridge University Press, 1992.

Block, Fred L. *The Origins of International Economic Disorder: A Study of United States International Monetary Policy from World War II to the Present.* Berkeley: University of California Press, 1977.

Borden, William. *The Pacific Alliance: United States Foreign Economic Policy and Japanese Trade Recovery, 1947–1955.* Madison: University of Wisconsin Press, 1984.

Boyer, Yves and Diego A. Ruiz Palmer. "Prospects for Enhanced Defense Cooperation Within the Atlantic Alliance." In *Beyond Burdensharing: Future Alliance Defense Cooperation,* pp. 27–57. Edited by William B. Taylor, Jr. Brussels: The Alliance Papers, 1989.

Brands, H. W. *The Specter of Neutralism: The United States and the Emergence of the Third World, 1947–1960.* New York: Columbia University Press, 1989.

Brandt, Willy. *North-South: A Program for Survival.* London: Pan Books, 1980.

Braudel, Fernand. *On History.* Chicago: University of Chicago Press, 1980.

Breunig, Charles. *The Age of Revolution and Reaction, 1789–1950,* 2nd ed. New York: W. W. Norton, 1977.

Bridge, F. R. and Roger Bullen. *The Great Powers and the European States System 1815–1914.* London: Longman, 1980.

Brilmayer, Lea. *American Hegemony: Political Morality in a One-Superpower World.* New Haven: Yale University Press, 1994.

Brownlie, Ian. "An Essay on the History of the Principle of Self-Determination." In *Grotian Society Papers 1968,* pp. 90–99. Edited by C. H. Alexandrowicz. The Hague: M. Nijhoff, 1970.

——. "The Expansion of International Society: The Consequences for the Law of Nations." In *The Expansion of International Society,* pp. 357–69. Edited by Hedley Bull and Adam Watson. Oxford: Clarendon Press, 1984.

Brzoska, Michael and Thomas Ohlson. "Arms Production in the Third World." *Bulletin of Peace Proposals* 17 (1886): 265–68.

Bueno de Mesquita, Bruce and David Lalman. *War and Reason.* New Haven: Yale University Press, 1992.

Bull, Hedley. *The Anarchical Society: A Study of Order in World Politics.* New York: Columbia University Press, 1977.

Bullen, Roger. "The Great Powers and the Iberian Peninsula." In *Europe's Balance of Power, 1815–1848,* pp. 54–77. Edited by Alan Sked. New York: Barnes & Noble, 1979.

Bunce, Valerie. "Rising Above the Past: The Struggle for Liberal Democracy in Eastern Europe." *World Policy Journal* 7 (Summer 1990): 395–430.

Burley, Anne-Marie. "Regulating the World: Multilateralism, International Law, and the Projection of the New Deal Regulatory State." In *Multilateralism Matters: The Theory and Praxis of an Institutional Form*, pp. 125–56. Edited by John G. Ruggie. New York: Columbia University Press, 1993.

Burr, William. "Marshall Planners and the Politics of Empire: the United States and French Financial Policy." *Diplomatic History* 15 (Fall 1991): 495–522.

Buzan, Barry. "Economic Structure and International Security: The Limits of the Liberal Case." *International Organization* 38 (Autumn 1984): 597–624.

———. "The Future of Western European Security." In *European Polyphony: Progress Beyond East-West Confrontation*, pp. 16–45. Edited by Ole Waever, Pierre Lamaitre, and Elzbieta Tromer. London: Macmillan, 1989.

———. *People, States and Fear: The National Security Problem in International Relations*, 2nd ed. Chapel Hill: The University of North Carolina Press, 1991.

Buzan, Barry; Morten Kelstrup, Pierre Lemaitre, Elzbieta Tromer, and Ole Waever, eds. *The European Security Order Recast: Scenarios for the Post-Cold War Era*. London: Pinter Publishers, 1990.

Buzan, Barry; Jones, Charles; Little, Richard. *The Logic of Anarchy: Neorealism to Structural Realism*. New York: Columbia University Press, 1993.

Calleo, David. *Beyond American Hegemony: The Future of the Western Alliance*. New York: Basic Books, 1987.

———. "NATO and Some Lessons of History." In *NATO at Forty: Change, Continuity, & Prospects*, pp. 155–178. Edited by James R. Golden, Daniel J. Kaufman, Asa A. Clark IV, and David Petraeus. Boulder, CO: Westview Press, 1989.

———. "Rebalancing the U.S.-European-Soviet Triangle." In *Europe and America Beyond 2000*, pp. 36–62. Edited by Gregory F. Treverton. New York: New York University Press, 1990.

Cameron, David R. "The 1992 Initiative: Causes and Consequences." In *Euro-Politics: Institutions and Policymaking in the "New" European Community*, pp. 23–74. Edited by Alberta Sbragia. Washington, D.C.: The Brookings Institution, 1992.

Cameron, Rondo. *France and the Economic Development of Europe, 1800–1914: Conquests of Peace and Seeds of War*. Princeton: Princeton University Press, 1961.

Campbell, David. *Writing Security: United States Foreign Policy and the Politics of Identity*. Minneapolis: University of Minnesota Press, 1992.

Carlsnaes, Walter. "The Agency-Structure Problem in Foreign Policy Analysis." *International Studies Quarterly* 36 (September 1992): 245–70.

Carr, E. H. *The Twenty Years' Crisis: 1919–1939*. New York: Macmillan, 1939.

Cecco, Marcello de. *Money and Empire: The International Gold Standard, 1890–1914*. Oxford: Basil Blackwell, 1974.

Cerny, Philip G. "European Defense and the New Détente: the Collapse of the Cold War System." *West European Politics* 13 (October 1990): 139–151.

———. "Plurilateralism: Structural Differentiation and Functional Conflict in the Post-Cold War World Order." *Millennium* 22 (Spring 1993): 27–52.

Chan, Steve. "Mirror, Mirror on the Wall . . . Are the Freer Countries More Pacific?" *Journal of Conflict Resolution* 28 (December 1984): 617–48.

Chernoff, Fred. "Cooperation in the Western Alliance: Why States Work Together." Paper delivered at the Annual Meeting of the International Studies Association, Atlanta, Georgia, March 1992.

Clifford, Clark. "American Relations with the Soviet Union [1946]." Reprinted in Arthur Krock, *Memoirs: Sixty Years on the Firing Line*, pp. 419–82. New York: Funk & Wagnalls, 1968.

Cobban, Alfred. *The Nation State and National Self-Determination.* London: Collins, 1969.

Cobden, Richard. "England, Ireland, and America." In *The Political Writings of Richard Cobden*, vol. 1, pp. 7–34. New York: Kraus, 1969.

Cohen, G. A. *Karl Marx's Theory of History: A Defence.* Princeton: Princeton University Press, 1978.

Cohen, Marshall. "Toward a Liberal Foreign Policy." In *Liberalism Reconsidered*, pp. 67–86. Edited by Douglas MacLean and Claudia Mills. Totowa, NJ: Rowan & Littlefield, 1983.

Cohen, Raymond. "Reappraisal of the Theory that Democracies Do Not Go to War with Each Other." *Review of International Studies* 20 (July 1994): 207–23.

Colbert, Evelyn. "The Road Not Taken: Decolonization and Independence in Indonesia and Indochina." *Foreign Affairs* 51 (April 1973): 608–28.

Collins, Irene. *The Age of Progress.* New York: St. Martin's Press, 1964.

The Compact Oxford English Dictionary. 2nd Edition. Oxford: Clarendon Press.

Connolly, William E. *The Terms of Political Discourse.* Princeton: Princeton Univeristy Press, 1974.

Cooper, Richard N. *The Economics of Interdependence: Economic Policy in the Atlantic Community.* New York: McGraw-Hill, 1968.

———. "Trade Policy Is Foreign Policy." *Foreign Policy* No. 9 (Winter 1972/1973): 18–36.

———. "Prolegomena to the Choice of an International Monetary System." *International Organization* 29 (Winter 1975): 63–98.

Council on Foreign Relations. *The War and Peace Studies of the Council on Foreign Relations, 1939–1945.* New York: Council on Foreign Relations, 1946.

Cox, Robert W. "Gramsci, Hegemony and International Relations: An Essay in Method." *Millennium* 12 (Summer 1981): 162–75.

———. "Social Forces, States and World Orders: Beyond International Relations Theory." In *Neorealism and its Critics*, pp. 204–52. Edited by Robert Keohane. New York: Columbia University Press, 1986.

———. *Production, Power, and World Order: Social Forces in the Making of History.* New York: Columbia University Press, 1987.

———. "Toward a Post-Hegemonic Conceptualization of World Order: Reflections on the Relevancy of Ibn Khaldun." In *Governance Without Government: Order and Change in World Politics*, pp. 272–94. Edited by James N. Rosenau and Ernst-Otto Czempiel. Cambridge: Cambridge University Press, 1992.

Cromwell, William C. *The United States and the European Pillar: The Strained Alliance.* New York: St. Martin's Press, 1992.

Cumings, Bruce. "The Origins and Development of the Northeast Asian Political Economy: Product Cycles, Industrial Sectors and Political Consequences." *International Organization* 38 (Winter 1984): 1–40.

———. *The Origins of the Korean War.* Vol. 2: *The Roaring of the Cataract, 1947–1950.* Princeton: Princeton University Press, 1990.

———. " 'Revising Postrevisionism,' or, the Poverty of Theory in Diplomatic History." *Diplomatic History* (Nov–Dec, 1993): 539–69.

Czempiel, Ernst-Otto. "Governance and Democratization." In *Governance Without Government: Order and Change in World Politics*, pp. 272–294. Edited by James N. Rosenau and Ernst-Otto Czempiel. Cambridge: Cambridge University Press, 1992.

Dahl, Robert. *Polyarchy*. New Haven: Yale University Press, 1971.

Dallek, Robert. *The American Style of Foreign Policy: Cultural Politics and Foreign Affairs*. New York: Oxford University Press, 1983.

Davis, Mike. "The Political Economy of Late-Imperial America." *New Left Review* No. 143 (January-February 1984): 6–38.

Davis, Lynn E. *The Cold War Begins*. Princeton: Princeton University Press, 1974.

Deane, Phyllis and William A. Cole. *British Economic Growth 1688–1959*. New York: Cambridge University Press, 1969.

DePorte, A. W. *Europe Between the Superpowers: the Enduring Balance*. 2nd ed. New Haven: Yale University Press, 1986.

Deudney, Daniel. "Dividing Realism: Structural Realism Versus Security Materialism on Nuclear Security and Proliferation." *Security Studies* 2 (Spring/Summer 1993): 7–36.

Deudney, Daniel and G. John Ikenberry. "The International Sources of Soviet Change." *International Security* 16 (Winter 1991/92): 73–118.

Deutsch, Karl. S. Burrel, R. Kann, M. Lee, M. Lichterman, R. Lingren, F. Lowenheim, and R. Van Wagenen. *Political Community and the North Atlantic Area*. New York: Greenwood Press, 1957.

Dewey, John. *Liberalism and Social Action*. New York: G. P. Putnam's Sons, 1935.

Djilas, Milovan. *Conversations with Stalin*. New York: Harcourt, Brace & World, 1962.

Divine, Robert A. *Second Chance: The Triumph of Internationalism in America During World War II*. New York: Athenium, 1967.

Doenecke, Justus. *Not to the Swift: The Old Isolationists in the Cold War Era*. Lewisburg: Bucknell University Press, 1979.

Donnelly, Jack. "International Human Rights: A Regime Analysis." *International Organization* 40 (Summer 1986): 599–642.

———. *Universal Human Rights in Theory and Practice*. Ithaca: Cornell University Press, 1989.

———. "Progress in Human Rights." In *Progress in Postwar International Relations*, pp. 312–58. Edited by Emanuel Adler and Beverly Crawford. New York: Columbia University Press, 1991.

Doran, Charles. *The Politics of Assimilation: Hegemony and Its Aftermath*. Baltimore: John Hopkins University Press, 1971.

Downing, Brian M. *The Military Revolution and Political Change*. Princeton: Princeton University Press, 1982.

Doyle, Michael W. "Kant, Liberal Legacies, and Foreign Affairs." *Philosophy and Public Affairs* 12 (Summer and Fall 1983). Parts 1 and 2: 205–235, 323–353.

———. "Liberalism and World Politics." *American Political Science Review* 80 (December 1986): 1151–69.

———. *Empires*. Ithaca: Cornell University Press, 1986.

Durkheim, Emile. *The Elementary Forms of the Religious Life*. Translated by Joseph Swain. New York: Collier Books, 1961.

Dworkin, Ronald. "Liberalism." In *Private and Public Morality*, pp. 113–43. Edited by Stuart Hampshire. Cambridge: Cambridge University Press, 1978.

——. "Foundations of Liberal Equality." In *The Tanner Lectures on Human Values*, pp. 1–119. Salt Lake City: University of Utah Press, 1990.

Dyson, Kenneth H. F. *The State Tradition in Western Europe*. New York: Oxford University Press, 1980.

Eden, Lynn. "Capitalist Conflict and the State: The Making of United States Military Policy in 1948." In *Statemaking and Social Movements: Essays in History and Theory*, pp. 233–61. Edited by Charles Bright and Susan Harding. Ann Arbor: University of Michigan Press, 1984.

——. "The Diplomacy of Force: Interests, the State, and the Making of American Military Policy in 1948." Ph.D. dissertation, University of Michigan, 1985.

——. "The End of U.S. Cold War History?" *International Security* 18 (Summer 1993): 174–207.

Eide, Asbjorn and Marek Thee, eds. *Problems of Contemporary Militarism*. New York: St. Martin's Press, 1980.

Eisenberg, Carolyn. "U.S. Policy in Post-War Germany: The Conservative Restoration." *Science and Society* (Spring 1982): 24–38.

Eisenstadt, S. N. "A Reappraisal of Theories of Social Change and Modernization." In *Social Change and Modernity*, pp. 412–430. Edited by Hans Haferkamp and Neil J. Smelser. Berkeley: University of California Press, 1992.

Elrod, Richard. "The Concert of Europe: A Fresh Look at an International System." *World Politics* 28 (January 1976): 159–74.

Elster, Jon. "Marxism, Functionalism, and Game Theory" *Theory and Society* 7 (July 1982): 453–495.

Etzold, Thomas and John Lewis Gaddis, eds. *Containment: Documents on American Policy and Strategy, 1945–1950*. New York: Columbia University Press, 1978.

Eulau, Heinz. "Multilevel Methods in Comparative Politics." *American Behaviorial Scientist* 21 (September/October 1977): 39–62.

Evangelista, Matthew. "Stalin's Postwar Army Reappraised." *International Security* 7 (Winter 1982–83): 110–68.

——. *Innovation and the Arms Race: How the United States and the Soviet Union Develop New Military Technologies*. Ithaca: Cornell University Press, 1988.

Everdell, William. *The End of Kings: A History of Republics and Republicans*. New York: Free Press, 1983.

Falk, Richard. "Contending Approaches to World Order." *Journal of International Affairs* 31 (Fall/Winter 1977): 171–98.

Farwell, Byron. *Queen Victoria's Little Wars*. New York: Harper & Row, 1972.

Federation of American Scientists. "Arms Sales Monitor." No. 11/12 (January/February 1992).

Feis, Herbert. *From Trust to Terror: The Onset of the Cold War, 1945–1950*. New York: Norton, 1970.

Finer, Samuel E. *The Man on Horseback*. London: Pall Mall, 1962.

Fischer, David Hackett. *Historians' Fallacies: Toward a Logic of Historical Thought*. New York: Harper and Row, 1970.

Folly, Martin. "Breaking the Vicious Circle: Britain, The United States, and the Genesis of the North Atlantic Treaty." *Diplomatic History* 12 (Winter 1988): 59–77.

Forsyth, Murray. "The Tradition of International Law." In *Traditions of International Ethics*, pp. 23–41. Edited by Terry Nardin and David Mapel. Cambridge: Cambridge University Press, 1992.

Foucault, Michel. *Language, Counter-Memory, Practice*. Ithaca: Cornell University Press, 1977.

———. *The History of Sexuality*. Vol.1: *An Introduction*. New York: Vintage Books, 1980.

———. *Power/Knowledge: Selected Interviews and Other Writings, 1972–1977*. Edited by Colin Gordon. New York: Pantheon Books, 1980.

———. "The Subject and Power." In *Beyond Structuralism and Hermeneutics*, pp. 209–26. Edited by Hubert L. Dreyfus and Paul Rabinow. Chicago: University of Chicago Press, 1982.

———. "Questions of Method: An Interview with Michel Foucault." In *After Philosophy: End or Transformation*, pp. 100–117. Edited by Kenneth Baynes, James Bohman, and Thomas McCarthy. Cambridge: MIT Press, 1987.

Fox, Edward Whiting. *History in Geographic Perspective: The Other France*. New York: Norton, 1971.

Freeland, Richard. *The Truman Doctrine and the Origins of McCarthyism: Foreign Policy, Domestic Politics and Internal Security, 1946–1948*. New York: Knopf, 1972.

Frémeaux, Jacques and André Martel "French Defense Policy: 1947–1949." In *Western Security: The Formative Years*, pp. 92–103. Edited by Olav Riste. New York: Columbia University Press, 1985.

Friedberg, Aaron. "Why Didn't the United States Become a Garrison State?" *International Security* 16 (Spring 1992): 109–42.

Freud, Sigmund. *New Introductory Lectures on Psychoanalysis*. Translated by James Strachey. New York: W. W. Norton, 1964.

Fukuyama, Francis. "The End of History?" *The National Interest*, no. 16 (Summer 1989): 3–18.

Furley, Oliver. "The Humanitarian Impact." In *Britain Pre-eminent: Studies of British World Influence in the Nineteenth Century*, pp. 128–51. Edited by Christopher Bartlett. New York: St. Martin's Press, 1969.

Gadamer, Hans-Georg. *Truth and Method*. New York: Crossroad, 1988.

Gaddis, John Lewis. *The United States and the Origins of the Cold War, 1941–1947*. New York: Columbia University Press, 1972.

———. "Was the Truman Doctrine a Real Turning Point?" *Foreign Affairs* 52 (January 1974): 386–402.

———. "The Soviet Threat Reconsidered: NSC 68 and the Problems of Ends and Means." *International Security* 4 (Spring 1980): 164–70.

———. *Strategies of Containment: A Critical Appraisal of Postwar American National Security Policy*. Oxford: Oxford University Press, 1982.

———. "The Emerging Post-Revisionist Synthesis on the Origins of the Cold War." *Diplomatic History* 7 (Summer 1983): 171–90.

———. "Comments." *American Historical Review* 89 (April 1984): 382–85.

———. "The Corporatist Synthesis: A Skeptical View." *Diplomatic History* 10 (Fall 1986): 357–62.

———. *The Long Peace: Inquiries Into the History of the Cold War*. New York: Oxford University Press, 1987.

——. "The Insecurities of Victory." In *The Truman Presidency*, pp. 235–271. Edited by Michael J. Lacey. New York: Cambridge University Press, 1989.

——. *The United States and the End of the Cold War*. New York: Oxford University Press, 1992.

——. "The Cold War, the Long Peace, and the Future." *Diplomatic History* 16 (Spring 1992): 234–46.

——. "International Relations Theory and the End of the Cold War." *International Security* 17 (Winter 1992/93): 5–58.

Gallagher, John and Ronald Robinson. "The Imperialism of Free Trade." *The Economic History Review* 6 (August 1953): 1–15.

Gallie, W. B. "Essentially Contested Concepts." pp. 121–146. In *The Importance of Language*. Edited by Max Black. Englewood Cliffs, NJ: Prentice Hall, 1962.

Gardner, Lloyd. "Commentary." In *Child of Conflict: The Korean-American Relationship, 1943–1953*, pp. 57–67. Edited by Bruce Cumings. Seattle: University of Washington Press, 1983.

——. *A Covenant with Power: America and World Order from Wilson to Reagan*. New York: Oxford University Press, 1984.

——. *Spheres of Influence: From Munich to Yalta*. Chicago: University of Chicago Press, 1993.

Gardner, Richard N. *Sterling-Dollar Diplomacy in Current Perspective: The Origins and Prospects of Our International Economic Order*, 3rd ed. New York: Columbia University Press, 1980.

Garrett, Geoffrey. "International Cooperation and Institutional Choice: the European Community's Internal Market." *International Organization* 46 (Spring 1992): 533–60.

Gati, Charles. *The Bloc That Failed*. Bloomington: Indiana University Press, 1990.

Giddens, Anthony. *A Contemporary Critique of Historical Materialism*. Berkeley: University of California Press, 1981, p. 35.

——. *The Nation-State and Violence*. Berkeley: University of California Press, 1987.

Gill, Stephen, ed. *Gramsci, Historical Materialism, and International Relations*. New York: Cambridge University Press, 1993.

Gillis, John R. "Introduction." In *The Militarization of the Western World*, pp. 1–10. Edited by John R. Gillis. New Brunswick: Rutgers University Press, 1989.

Gilpin, Robert. "The Politics of Transnational Relations." In *Transnational Relations and World Politics*, pp. 48–69. Edited by Robert Keohane and Joseph Nye, Jr. Cambridge: Harvard University Press, 1972.

——. *U.S. Power and the Multinational Corporation*. New York: Basic Books, 1975.

——. "Economic Interdependence and National Security in Historical Perspective." In *Economic Issues and National Security*, pp. 19–66. Edited by Klaus Knorr and Frank N. Trager. Lawrence: University Press of Kansas, 1977.

——. *War and Change in World Politics*. New York: Cambridge University Press, 1981.

——. "The Richness of the Tradition of Political Realism." In *Neorealism and Its Critics*, pp. 301–21. Edited by Robert Keohane. New York: Columbia University Press, 1986.

——. *The Political Economy of International Relations*. Princeton: Princeton University Press, 1987.

Gimbel, John. *The Origins of the Marshall Plan*. Stanford: Stanford University Press, 1976.

——. "Cold War Historians and the Occupation of Germany." In *U.S. Occupations in Europe After World War II*, pp. 86–102. Edited by Hans Schmitt. Lawrence: The Regents Press of Kansas, 1978.

Goldgeier, James M. and Michael McFaul. "A Tale of Two Worlds: Core and Periphery in the Post-Cold War Era." *International Organization* 46 (Spring 1992): 467–91.

Goldstein, Walter. "Europe Beyond the Turn of the Century: the Limits of Economic and Security Choices." In *The Cold War Legacy in Europe*, pp. 121–38. Edited by Otto Pick. New York: St. Martin's Press, 1992.

Gong, Gerrit W. *The Standard of 'Civilization' in International Society*. Oxford: Clarendon Press, 1984.

Gourevitch, Peter. *Politics in Hard Times*. Ithaca: Cornell University Press, 1986.

Gowa, Joanne. "Anarchy, Egoism, and Third Images: *The Evolution of Cooperation* and International Relations." *International Organization* 40 (Winter 1986): 167–86.

——. "Rational Hegemons, Excludable Goods and Small Groups: An Epitaph for Hegemonic Stability Theory?" *World Politics* 41 (April 1989): 307–24.

——. "Bipolarity, Multipolarity, and Free Trade." *American Political Science Review* 83 (December 1989): 1245–56.

Gowan, Peter. "The Gulf War, Iraq and World Liberalism." *New Left Review*, no. 187 (May/June 1991): 29–71.

Green, David. "The Cold War Comes to Latin America." In *Politics and Policies of the Truman Administration*, pp. 149–97. Edited by Barton Bernstein. New York: New Viewpoints, 1974.

Greene, Owen. "Transnational Processes and European Security." In *European Security—Towards 2000*, pp. 140–62. Edited by Michael C. Pugh. Manchester: Manchester University Press, 1992.

Gray, John. *Liberalism*. Minneapolis: University of Minnesota Press, 1986.

——. *Liberalism: Essays in Political Philosophy*. New York: Routledge, 1989.

——. *Post-Liberalism: Studies in Political Thought*. New York: Routledge, 1993.

Grieco, Joseph. "Anarchy and the Limits of Cooperation: A Realist Critique of the Newest Liberal Internationalism." *International Organization* 42 (Summer 1988): 485–507.

——. *Cooperation among Nations*. Ithaca: Cornell University Press, 1990.

Grosser, Alfred. *The Western Alliance: European-American Relations Since 1945*. New York: Continuum, 1980.

Grunberg, Isabelle. "Exploring the 'Myth' of Hegemonic Stability." *International Organization* 44 (Autumn 1990): 431–77.

Gutmann, Amy. "How Liberal is Democracy?" In *Liberalism Reconsidered*, pp. 25- 50. Edited by Douglas MacLean and Claudia Mills. Totowa, NJ: Rowman & Allanheld, 1983.

Haas, Ernst B. *The Uniting of Europe*. Stanford: Stanford University Press, 1958.

——. "International Integration: The European and the Universal Process." *International Organization* 15 (Summer 1961): 366–92.

——. *Beyond the Nation-State*. Stanford: Stanford University Press, 1964.

Haas, Peter. *Saving the Mediterranean*. New York: Columbia University Press, 1990.

Habermas, Jürgen. *The Logic of the Social Sciences*. Translated by Shierry Weber Nicholson. Cambridge, MA: MIT Press, 1988.

——. *The Structural Transformation of the Public Sphere*. Translated by Thomas Burger. Cambridge: MIT Press, 1989.

——. "Three Normative Models of Democracy." *Constellations* 1 (April 1994): 1–10.

Haglund, David G. *Alliance Within the Alliance? Franco-German Military Cooperation and the European Pillar of Defense*. Boulder, CO: Westview Press, 1991.

Hall, John A. *Liberalism: Politics, Ideology and the Market*. Chapel Hill: University of North Carolina Press, 1987.

——. "Will the United States Decline as Did Britain?" In *The Rise and Decline of the Nation State*, pp. 114–45. Edited by Michael Mann. Oxford: Basil Blackwell, 1990.

Halle, Louis. *The Cold War as History*. New York: Harper & Row, 1967.

Hamerow, Theodore S. *The Birth of a New Europe: State and Society in the Nineteenth Century*. Chapel Hill: The University of North Carolina Press, 1983.

Hanrieder, Wolfram F. *Germany, America, Europe: Forty Years of German Foreign Policy*. New Haven: Yale University Press, 1989.

Harbutt, Fraser. *The Iron Curtain: Churchill, America, and the Origins of the Cold War*. New York: Oxford University Press, 1986.

Harrison, Michael M. *The Reluctant Ally: France and Atlantic Security*. Baltimore: Johns Hopkins Press, 1981.

Hart, B. H. Liddell. *Strategy: The Indirect Approach*. London: Faber and Faber, 1967.

Hartmann, Susan. *Truman and the 80th Congress*. Columbia: University of Missouri Press, 1971.

Harvey, David. *The Condition of Postmodernity*. Oxford: Basil Blackwell, 1989.

Hassner, Pierre. "Europe Beyond Partition and Unity: Disintegration or Reconstruction?" *International Affairs* 66 (July 1990): 461–76.

Hawgood, J. A. "Liberalism and Constitutional Developments." In *The New Cambridge Modern History*. Vol. 10: *The Zenith of European Power 1830–70*, pp. 192–97. Cambridge: Cambridge University Press, 1967.

Heller, Francis and Gillingham, John, eds. *NATO: The Founding of the Atlantic Alliance and the Integration of Europe*. New York: St. Martin's Press, 1992.

Henderson, W. O. *Britain and Industrial Europe 1750–1870: Studies in British Influence on the Industrial Revolution in Western Europe*. Liverpool: University Press of Liverpool, 1954.

——. *The Zollverein*. Chicago: Quadrangle, 1959.

Herf, Jeffrey. *Reactionary Modernism*. Cambridge: Cambridge University Press, 1984.

Herkin, Gregg. *The Winning Weapon: The Atomic Bomb in the Cold War, 1945–1950*. New York: Vintage Books, 1982.

Hicks, John. *A Theory of Economic History*. London: Oxford University Press, 1969.

Hilgerdt, Folke. "The Case for Multilateral Trade." *American Economic Review* 33 (March 1943): 393–407.

Hintze, Otto. *The Historical Essays of Otto Hintze*. Edited by Felix Gilbert. New York: Oxford University Press, 1975.

Hirsch, Fred and Michael Doyle. "Politicization in the World Economy: Necessary Conditions for an International Economic Order." In *Alternatives to Monetary Disorder*, pp. 11–64. Edited by Fred Hirsch, Michael Doyle, and Edward L. Morse. New York: McGraw-Hill, 1977.

Hirschman, Albert O. *National Power and the Structure of Foreign Trade*. Berkeley: University of California Press, 1969.

——. *Exit, Voice and Loyalty*. Cambridge: Harvard University Press, 1970.

——. *The Passions and the Interests*. Princeton: Princeton University Press, 1977.

Hixson, Walter. *George F. Kennan: Cold War Iconoclast*. New York: Columbia University Press, 1989.

Hobhouse, L. T. *Liberalism*. London: Oxford University Press, 1964.

Hobsbawm, E. J. *Industry and Empire*. New York: Penguin, 1968.

——. *The Age of Capital 1848–1875*. New York: Mentor, 1979.

——. *The Age of Empire 1875–1914*. New York: Vintage Books, 1987.

——. *Nations and Nationalism since 1780*. Cambridge: Cambridge University Press, 1990.

——. *The Age of Extremes: A History of the World, 1914–1991*. New York: Pantheon Books, 1994.

Hoffmann, Stanley. "Report of the Conference on Conditions of World Order - June 12–19, 1965, Villa Serbelloni, Bellagio, Italy." *Daedalus* 95 (Spring 1966): 455–78.

——. "The Crisis of Liberal Internationalism." *Foreign Policy*, no. 98 (Spring 1995): 159–77.

——. *Primacy or World Order*. New York: McGraw-Hill, 1978.

——. "Reflections on the Nation-State in Western Europe Today." *Journal of Common Market Studies* 21 (September/December 1982/1983): 21–37.

——. "Rousseau on War and Peace." In Stanley Hoffmann, *Janus and Minerva: Essays in the Theory and Practice of International Politics*, pp. 25–51. Boulder, CO: Westview Press, 1987.

——. "Liberalism and International Affairs." In Hoffmann, *Janus and Minerva*, pp. 394–419.

——. "What Should We Do in the World." *The Atlantic Monthly*, Summer 1989, pp. 719–32.

Hogan, Michael J. *The Marshall Plan: America, Britain, and the Reconstruction of Western Europe, 1947–1952*. Cambridge: Cambridge University Press, 1987.

——. "Corporatism." In *Explaining the History of American Foreign Relations*, pp. 226–36. Edited by Michael J. Hogan and Thomas G. Paterson. Cambridge: Cambridge University Press, 1991.

Hogan, Michael and Thomas G. Paterson, eds. *Explaining the History of American Foreign Relations*. Cambridge: Cambridge University Press, 1991.

Holbraad, Carsten. *The Concert of Europe: A Study in German and British International Theory 1815–1914*. New York: Barnes & Noble, 1971.

Holden, Barry. *Understanding Liberal Democracy*. New York: Philip Allan, 1988.

Hollis, Martin and Steve Smith. *Explaining and Understanding International Relations*. Oxford: Clarendon Press, 1990.

Holloway, David. *Stalin and the Bomb: The Soviet Union and Atomic Energy, 1939–1956*. New Haven: Yale University Press, 1994.

Holm, Hans-Henrik. "The Democratic Victory: What Will Happen to Foreign Policy?" *Cooperation and Conflict* 25 (December 1990): 195–206.

Holmes, Stephen. *The Anatomy of Antiliberalism*. Cambridge: Harvard University Press, 1993.

Holsti, K. J. "Governance Without Government: Polyarchy in Nineteenth-Century European International Politics." In *Governance Without Government: Order and*

Change in World Politics, pp. 30–57. Edited by James N. Rosenau and Ernst-Otto Czempiel. Cambridge: Cambridge University Press, 1992.

Howard, Michael. *War and the Liberal Conscience*. New Brunswick: Rutgers University Press, 1978.

———. "Introduction." In *Western Security: The Formative Years*, pp. 11–22. Edited by Olav Riste. New York: Columbia University Press, 1985.

Huntington, Samuel. *The Soldier and the State*. Cambridge: Harvard University Press, 1957.

———. "Transnational Organizations in World Politics." *World Politics* 25 (April 1973): 333–68.

———. *The Third Wave: Democratization in the Late Twentieth Century*. Norman, Oklahoma: University of Oklahoma Press, 1991.

———. "Democracy's Third Wave." *Journal of Democracy* 2 (Spring 1991): 12–34.

Hyde-Price, Adrian G. V. *European Security Beyond the Cold War: Four Scenarios for the Year 2010*. London: Royal Institute of International Affairs, 1991.

Ikenberry, G. John. "Rethinking the Origins of American Hegemony." *Political Science Quarterly* 104 (Fall 1989): 375–400.

———. "Creating Yesterday's New World Order: Keynesian 'New Thinking' and the Anglo-American Postwar Settlement." In *Ideas and Foreign Policy: Beliefs, Institutions, and Political Change*, pp. 57–86. Edited by Judith Goldstein and Robert Keohane. Ithaca: Cornell University Press, 1993.

Ikenberry, John G. and Charles Kupchan. "Socialization and Hegemonic Power." *International Organization* 44 (Summer 1990): 283–315.

Imlah, A. *Economic Elements in the Pax Britannica*. New York: Russell & Russell, 1958.

Ireland, Timothy P. *Creating the Entangling Alliance: The Origins of the North Atlantic Treaty Organization*. Westport, Conn.: Greenwood Press, 1981.

Iwe, Nwachukwuike S. S. *The History and Contents of Human Rights*. New York: Peter Lang, 1986.

Jackson, Robert. *Quasi-States: Sovereignty, International Relations, and the Third World*. Cambridge: Cambridge University Press, 1990.

Jackson, Scott. "Prologue to the Marshall Plan: The Origins of the American Commitment for a European Recovery Program." *Journal of American History* 65 (March 1979): 1043–68.

Jervis, Robert. *Perception and Misperception in International Politics*. Princeton: Princeton University Press, 1976.

———. "The Impact of the Korean War on the Cold War." *Journal of Conflict Resolution* 24 (December 1980): 563–92.

Johnson, Harold. *Self-Determination Within the Community of Nations*. Leyden: A. W. Sijthoff, 1967.

Johnson, Robert H. "Periods of Peril: The Window of Vulnerability and Other Myths." *Foreign Affairs* 61 (Spring 1983): 950–70.

Jessop, Bob. "Capitalism and Democracy: The Best Possible Political Shell?" In *Power and the State*, pp. 10–51. Edited by Gary Littlejohn et al. New York: St. Martin's Press, 1978.

Joffe, Josef. "Europe's American Pacifier." *Foreign Policy* 54 (Spring 1984): 64–82.

Joll, James, ed. *Britain and Europe, Pitt to Churchill, 1793–1940.* London: Nicholas Kaye, 1950.

Jones, Dorothy. "The Declaratory Tradition in Modern International Law." In *Traditions of International Ethics*, pp. 42–61. Edited by Terry Nardin and David Mapel. Cambridge: Cambridge University Press, 1992.

Jones, Howard. *"A New Kind of War:" America's Global Strategy and the Truman Doctrine in Greece.* New York: Oxford University Press, 1989.

Jones, Joseph Marion. *The Fifteen Weeks: February 21–June 5, 1947.* New York: Viking Press, 1955.

Jopp, Mathias and Wolfgang Wessels. "Institutional Frameworks for Security Co-operation in Western Europe: Developments and Options." In *Integration and Security in Western Europe*, pp. 25–76. Edited by Mathias Jopp, Reinhardt Rummel, and Peter Schmidt. Boulder, CO: Westview Press, 1991.

Kahler, Miles. "The Survival of the State in European International Relations." In *Changing Boundaries of the Political: Essays on the Evolving Balance Between State and Society, Public and Private in Europe*, pp. 287–319. Edited by Charles S. Maier. Cambridge: Cambridge University Press, 1987.

Kaldor, Mary. *The Imaginary War: Understanding East-West Conflict.* Oxford: Basil Blackwell, 1991.

——. "Warfare and Capitalism." In *Exterminism and the Cold War*, pp. 261–87. Edited by E. P. Thompson et al. London: Verso, 1982.

Kaldor, Mary and Asbjorn Eide, eds. *The World Military Order: The Impact of Military Technology on the Third World.* London: Macmillan, 1979.

Kant, Immanuel. "An Old Question Raised Again: Is the Human Race Constantly Progressing?" In *On History*, pp. 144–59. Edited by Lewis W. Beck. Indianapolis: Bobbs-Merrill, 1963.

——. "Perpetual Peace." In *Immanuel Kant: Philosophical Writings*, pp. 270–311. Edited by Ernst Behler. New York: Continuum, 1986.

——. "What is Enlightenment?" In *Immanuel Kant: Philosophical Writings*, pp. 263–69. Edited by Ernst Behler. New York: Continuum, 1986.

Kaplan, Lawrence. *A Community of Interests: NATO and the Military Assistance Program, 1948–1951.* Washington, D.C.: Office of the Secretary of Defense, 1980.

——. *The United States and NATO: The Formative Years.* Lexington: University Press of Kentucky, 1984.

Katzenstein, Peter. "International Relations and Domestic Structures: Foreign Economic Policies of Advanced Industrial States." *International Organization* 30 (Winter 1976): 1–45.

——. *Policy and Politics in West Germany: The Growth of a Semisovereign State.* Philadelphia: Temple University Press, 1987.

——, ed. *Between Power and Plenty.* Madison: University of Wisconsin Press, 1978.

——, ed. *The Culture of National Security: Norms and Identity in World Politics.* New York: Columbia University Press, 1996.

Kegley, Jr., Charles W. "The New Global Order: The Power of Principle in a Pluralistic World." *Ethics and International Affairs* 6 (1992): 21–40.

Kennan, George F. *American Diplomacy, 1900–1950.* New York: New American Library, 1951.

——. *Measures Short of War*. Washington, D.C.: National Defense University Press, 1992.

Kennedy, David. "The Move to Institutions." *Cardozo Law Review* 8 (April 1987): 841–988.

Kennedy, Paul. *The Rise and Fall of British Naval Mastery*. New York: Charles Scribner's & Sons, 1976.

Kenwood, A. G. and A. L. Lougheed. *The Growth of the International Economy, 1820–1980*. London: George Allen & Unwin, 1983.

Keohane, Robert. *After Hegemony: Cooperation and Discord in the World Political Economy*. Princeton: Princeton University Press, 1984.

——. *International Institutions and State Power*. Boulder, CO: Westview Press, 1989.

——. "International Liberalism Reconsidered." In *The Economic Limits to Modern Politics*, pp. 165–94. Edited by John Dunn. Cambridge: Cambridge University Press, 1990.

Keohane, Robert and Joseph Nye, Jr. *Power and Interdependence: World Politics in Transition*. Boston: Little, Brown, 1977.

Keohane, Robert and Stanley Hoffmann. "Institutional Change in Europe in the 1980s." In *The New European Community: Decisionmaking and Institutional Change*, pp. 1–39. Edited by Keohane and Hoffmann. Boulder, CO: Westview Press, 1991.

Kick, Edward and David Kiefer. "The Influence of the World System on War in the Third World." *International Journal of Sociology and Social Policy* No. 7 (1987): 34–48.

Kindleberger, Charles. "The Rise of Free Trade in Western Europe, 1820–1875." *Journal of Economic History* (March 1975): 20–55.

——, ed. *The International Corporation: A Symposium*. Cambridge: MIT Press, 1970.

Kirkpatrick, Jeane. "Dictatorships and Double Standards." *Commentary* 68 (November 1979): 34–45.

Kissinger, Henry. *American Foreign Policy*, 3rd ed. New York: Norton, 1977.

Klein, Bradley, *Strategic Studies and World Order: The Global Politics of Deterrence*. Cambridge: Cambridge University Press, 1994.

Klotz, Audie. *Norms in International Relations: The Struggle Against Apartheid*. Ithaca: Cornell University Press, 1995.

Kofas, Jon. *Intervention and Underdevelopment: Greece During the Cold War*. University Park: The Pennsylvania State University Press, 1989.

Kolko, Gabriel. *The Politics of War: The World and United States Foreign Policy, 1943–1945*. New York: Random House, 1968; reprint ed., 1990.

Kolko, Joyce and Gabriel Kolko. *The Limits of Power: The World and United States Foreign Policy, 1945–1954*. New York: Harper & Row, 1972.

Krasner, Stephen. "State Power and the Structure of International Trade." *World Politics* 28 (April 1976): 317–43.

——. *Structural Conflict: The Third World Against Global Liberalism*. Berkeley: University of California Press, 1985.

——, ed. *International Regimes*. Ithaca: Cornell University Press, 1983.

——. "Westphalia and All That." In *Ideas and Foreign Policy: Beliefs, Institutions, and Political Change*, pp. 235–264. Edited by Judith Goldstein and Robert Keohane. Ithaca: Cornell University Press, 1993.

Kratochwil, Friedrich. *Norms, Rules and Decisions*. New York: Columbia University Press, 1989.

——. "The Challenge of Security in a Changing World." *Journal of International Affairs* 43 (Summer/Fall 1989): 119–41.

Kruzel, Joseph ed. *1991–1992 American Defense Annual*. New York: Lexington Books, 1992.

Kuniholm, Bruce R. *The Origins of the Cold War in the Near East: Great Power Conflict and Diplomacy in Iran, Turkey, and Greece*. Princeton: Princeton University Press, 1980.

Kupchan, Charles A. and Clifford A. Kupchan. "Concerts, Collective Security, and the Future of Europe." *International Security* 16 (Summer 1991): 114–61.

LaFeber, Walter, ed. *The Origins of the Cold War, 1941–1947: A Historical Problem With Interpretations and Documents*. New York: John Wiley & Sons, 1971.

——. *America, Russia, and the Cold War, 1945–1984*, 5th ed. New York: Knopf, 1985.

——. "NATO and the Korean War: A Context." *Diplomatic History* 13 (Fall 1989): 461–78.

Lake, David A. "Powerful Pacifists: Democratic States and War." *American Political Science Review* 86 (March 1992): 24–37.

Lapid, Yosef and Friedrich Kratochwil, eds. *The Return of Culture and Identity in IR Theory*. Boulder, CO: Lynne Rienner, 1995.

Larson, Deborah. *Origins of Containment: A Psychological Explanation*. Princeton: Princeton University Press, 1985.

Lash, Scott and Jonathan Friedman. "Introduction: Subjectivity and Modernity's Other." In *Modernity and Identity*, pp. 1–30. Edited by Scott Lash and Jonathan Friedman. Oxford: Blackwell, 1992.

Latham, Robert. "Liberalism's Order/Liberalism's Other: A Genealogy of Threat." *Alternatives* 20 (Winter 1995): 114–46.

——. "Getting Out From Under: Rethinking Security Beyond Liberalism and the Level-of-Analysis Problem." *Millennium* 25 (Spring 1996): 77–108.

Leary, William, ed. *The Central Intelligence Agency: History and Documents*. Alabama: University Press of Alabama, 1984.

Lebow, Richard Ned. "The Long Peace, the End of the Cold War, and the Failure of Realism." *International Organization* 48 (Spring 1994): 249–77.

Lefebvre, Henri. *La somme et le reste*. Paris: La Nef de Paris, 1968.

Leffler, Melvyn. "The American Conception of National Security and the Beginnings of the Cold War, 1945–48." *American Historical Review* 89 (April 1984): 346–81.

——. "Strategy, Diplomacy, and the Cold War: The United States, Turkey, and NATO, 1945–1952." *Journal of American History* 71 (March 1985): 807–25.

——. "Adherence to Agreements; Yalta and the Experiences of the Early Cold War." *International Security* 11 (Summer 1986): 88–123.

——. "The United States and the Strategic Dimensions of the Marshall Plan." *Diplomatic History* 12 (Summer 1988): 277–306.

——. "Was 1947 a Turning Point in American Foreign Policy?" In *Centerstage: American Diplomacy since World War II*, pp. 19–42. Edited by L. Carl Brown. New York: Holmes & Meier, 1990.

——. "National Security." In *Explaining the History of American Foreign Relations*, pp. 202–13. Edited by Michael Hogan and Thomas G. Paterson. Cambridge: Cambridge University Press, 1991.

——. *A Preponderance of Power: National Security, the Truman Administration, and the Cold War*. Stanford: Stanford University Press, 1992.

——. "Inside Enemy Archives: The Cold War Reopened." *Foreign Affairs* 75 (July/August 1996): 120–35.

Levin, Gordon. *Woodrow Wilson and World Politics: America's Response to War and Revolution*. London: Oxford University Press, 1968.

Levy, Jack. "Long Cycles, Hegemonic Transitions, and the Long Peace." In *The Long Postwar Peace: Contending Explanations and Projections*, pp. 147–76. Edited by Charles Kegley, Jr. New York: Harper Collins, 1990.

——. "The Causes of War: A Review of Theories and Evidence." In *Behavior, Society, and Nuclear War*, vol. 1, pp. 209–333. Edited by Philip Tetlock, Jo L. Husbands, Robert Jervis, Paul C. Stern, and Charles Tilly. New York: Oxford University Press, 1989.

Lindblom, Charles E. *Politics and Markets*. New York: Basic Books, 1977.

Ling, L. H. M. "Hegemony and the Internationalizing State: A Postcolonial Critique." Paper delivered at the Annual Meeting of the International Studies Association, Washington, D.C., March 1994.

Linklater, Andrew. "The Problem of Community in International Relations." *Alternatives* 15 (1990):135–53.

——. *Men and Citizens in the Theory of International Relations*. New York: St. Martin's Press, 1982.

Lippmann, Walter. *U.S. Foreign Policy: Shield of the Republic*. Boston: Little, Brown, 1943.

——. *The Cold War: A Study in U.S. Foreign Policy*. New York: Harper, 1947.

Lipson, Charles. *Standing Guard: Protection Foreign Capital in the Nineteenth and Twentieth Centuries*. Berkeley: University of California Press, 1985.

Liska, George. *Nations in Alliance*. Baltimore: Johns Hopkins University Press, 1962.

Little, Richard. "Liberal Hegemony and the Realist Assault: Competing Ideological Theories of the State." In *State and Society in International Relations*, pp. 19–30. Edited by Michael Banks and Martin Shaw. New York: St. Martin's Press, 1991.

Locke, John. *Two Treatises of Government*. Edited by Peter Laslett. New York: The New American Library, 1965

Lodge, Juliet. "European Community Security Policy: Rhetoric or Reality?" In *European Security—Towards 2000*, pp. 49–66. Edited by Michael C. Pugh. Manchester: Manchester University Press, 1992.

Lowi, Theodore. *The End of Liberalism: Ideology, Policy, and the Crisis of Public Authority*. New York: Norton, 1969.

Lundestad, Geir. *The American Non-Policy Towards Eastern Europe, 1943–1947: Universalism in an Area Not of Essential Interest to the United States*. New York: Humanities, 1975.

——. "Empire by Invitation? The United States and Western Europe, 1945–1952." *Journal of Peace Research* 23 (1986): 262–78.

——. "Moralism, Presentism, Exceptionalism, Provincialism and Other Extravagances in American Writings on the Early Cold War Years." *Diplomatic History* 13 (Fall 1989): 527–46.

Lunn, Simon. "The Future of NATO." In *The Cold War Legacy in Europe*, pp. 7–21. Edited by Otto Pick. New York: St. Martin's Press, 1992.

Luttwak, Edward N. *The Political Uses of Sea Power*. Baltimore: John Hopkins University Press, 1974.

Macartney, C. A. *National States and National Minorities*. London: Oxford University Press, 1934.

Macdonald, Douglas J. "Communist Bloc Expansion in the Early Cold War: Challenging Realism, Refuting Revisionism." *International Security* 20 (Winter 1995/96): 152–88

Machiavelli, Niccolo. *The Prince and the Discourses*. New York: Modern Library, 1950.

MacIntyre, Alasdair. *After Virtue*. Notre Dame: University of Notre Dame Press, 1981.

Macksey, Kenneth. *Technology in War*. New York: Prentice Hall, 1986.

Macpherson, C. B. *The Life and Times of Liberal Democracy*. Oxford: Oxford University Press, 1977.

Mahan, A. T. *The Influence of Sea Power Upon History, 1660–1783*. Boston: Little Brown, 1890.

Maier, Charles S. "The Politics of Productivity: Foundations of American International Economic Policy after World War II." In *Between Power and Plenty: Foreign Economic Policies of Advanced Industrial States*, pp. 23–49. Edited by Peter Katzenstein. Madison: University of Wisconsin Press, 1978.

——. "The Two Postwar Eras and the Conditions for Stability in Twentieth-Century Western Europe." *American History Review* 86 (April 1981): 327–352.

——. "Supranational Concepts and National Continuity in the Framework of the Marshall Plan." In *The Marshall Plan: A Retrospective*, pp. 29–37. Edited by Stanley Hoffmann and Charles Maier. Boulder, CO: Westview Press, 1984.

——. "The Politics of Time: Changing Paradigms of Collective Time and Private Time in the Modern Era." In *Changing Boundaries of the Political: Essays on the Evolving Balance Between State and Society, Public and Private in Europe*, pp. 151–78. Edited by Charles S. Maier. Cambridge: Cambridge University Press, 1987.

——. "The Making of 'Pax Americana': Formative Moments of United States Ascendancy, 1945–53." Paper delivered at the Diplomatic History Workshop, Harvard University, October, 1988.

——. "Empires or Nations? Territoriality and Stabilization, 1918, 1945, 1989 . . ." Paper delivered at The New School for Social Research, March 1995.

Malinowski, Bronislaw. *A Scientific Theory of Culture and Other Essays*. Chapel Hill: University of North Carolina Press, 1944.

Manicas, Peter. *War and Democracy*. Oxford: Basil Blackwell, 1989.

Mann, Michael. "Capitalism and Militarism." In *War, State and Society*, pp. 25–46. Edited by Martin Shaw. New York: St. Martin's Press, 1984.

——. *The Sources of Social Power*, vol. 1. Cambridge: Cambridge University Press, 1986.

Manning, D. J. *Liberalism*. New York: St. Martin's Press, 1976.

Mansbach, Richard W. and John A. Vasquez. *In Search of Theory: A New Paradigm for Global Politics*. New York: Columbia University Press, 1981.

Maoz, Zeev and Nasrin Abdolali. "Regime Type and International Conflict, 1816–1976." *Journal of Conflict Resolution* 33 (March 1989): 3–35.

Maoz, Zeev and Bruce Russett. "Normative and Structural Cause of Democratic Peace, 1946–1986." *American Political Science Review* 87 (September 1993): 624–38.

Marshall, T. H. *Class, Citizenship, and Social Development*. Chicago: University of Chicago Press, 1964.

Marwick, Arthur. *War and Social Change in the Twentieth Century*. London: Macmillan, 1977.

Mastny, Vojtech. *Russia's Road to the Cold War: Diplomacy, Warfare, and the Politics of Communism, 1941–1945*. New York: Columbia University Press, 1979.

———. "Stalin and the Militarization of the Cold War." *International Security* 9 (Winter 1984/85): 109–29.

Mathias, Peter. *The First Industrial Nation: An Economic History of Britain, 1700–1914*. New York: Charles Scribner's Sons, 1969.

May, Ernest. "The American Commitment to Germany, 1949–55." *Diplomatic History* 13 (Fall 1989): 431–60.

Mayall, James. "The Institutional Basis of Post-War Economic Cooperation." In *International Institutions at Work*, pp. 53–74. Edited by Paul Taylor and A. J. R. Groom. New York: St. Martin's Press, 1988.

———. *Nationalism and International Society*. Cambridge: Cambridge University Press, 1990.

McCormick, Thomas J. *America's Half-Century: United States Foreign Policy in the Cold War*. Baltimore: Johns Hopkins University Press, 1989.

———. "World Systems." In *Explaining the History of American Foreign Relations*, pp. 89–98. Edited by Michael J. Hogan and Thomas G. Paterson. Cambridge: Cambridge University Press, 1991.

McKeown, Timothy J. "Hegemonic Stability Theory and Nineteenth Century Tariff Levels in Europe." *International Organization* 37 (Winter 1983): 73–91.

McKinlay, R. D. and R. Little. *Global Problems and World Order*. London: Frances Pinter, 1986.

McMahon, Robert J. *Colonialism and Cold War: The United States and the Struggle for Indonesian Independence, 1945–1949*. Ithaca: Cornell University Press, 1981.

McNamara, Robert S. *In Retrospect: The Tragedy and Lessons of Vietnam*. New York: Random House, 1995.

McNeill, William H. *The Pursuit of Power: Technology, Armed Force, and Society since A.D. 1000*. Chicago: University of Chicago Press, 1982.

Mearsheimer, John. "Back to the Future: Instability in Europe After the Cold War." *International Security* 15 (Summer 1990): 5–56.

———. "The False Promise of International Institutions." *International Security* 19 (Winter 1994/95): 5–49.

Mehta, Uday S. "Liberal Strategies of Exclusion." *Politics and Society* 18 (December 1990): 427–54.

Messer, Robert. "Paths Not Taken: The United States Department of State and Alternatives to Containment." *Diplomatic History* 1 (Fall 1977): 297–320.

———. *The End of an Alliance: James F. Byrnes, Roosevelt, Truman, and the Origins of the Cold War*. Chapel Hill: University of North Carolina Press, 1982.

Meyer, John W. "The World Policy and the Authority of the Nation-State." In *Studies of the Modern World System*, pp. 109–38. Edited by Albert Bergeson. New York: Academic Press, 1980.

Meyer, John W. and W. Richard Scott. *Organizational Environments: Ritual and Rationality*. Newbury Park, Calif.: Sage Publications, 1983.

Mill, John Stuart. " 'A Few Words on Non-Intervention." In *Dissertations and Discussions: Political, Philosophical and Historical*, vol. 3, pp. 238–63. New York: Henry Holt, 1874.

———. *Utilitarianism, Liberty, and Representative Government.* New York: Everyman's Library, 1951.

Miller, James. *The United States and Italy, 1940–1950.* Chapel Hill: The University of North Carolina Press, 1986.

Miller, Lynn H. *Global Order: Values and Power in International Politics.* Boulder, CO: Westview Press, 1990.

Milner, Helen. "International Theories of Cooperation Among Nations." *World Politics* 44 (April 1992): 466–96.

Milward, Alan S. *The Reconstruction of Western Europe, 1945–1951.* London: Methuen, 1984.

Miner, Steven Merritt. "Revelations, Secrets, Gossip and Lies." *The New York Times Book Review*, May 14, 1995, pp. 19–21.

Mitrany, David. *A Working Peace System.* London: London National Peace Council, 1946.

Montesquieu, Charles Louis de Secondat de. *The Spirit of the Laws.* New York: Hafner, 1966.

Moore, Barrington Jr., *The Social Origins of Dictatorship and Democracy: Lord and Peasant in the Making of the Modern World.* Boston: Beacon Press, 1967.

Moravcsik, Andrew. "Negotiating the Single European Act: National Interests and Conventional Statecraft in the European Community." *International Organization* 45 (Winter 1991): 19–56.

Morgenthau, Hans J. *Scientific Man Vs. Power Politics.* Chicago: University of Chicago Press, 1946.

———. *Politics Among Nations*, 4th ed. New York: Knopf, 1967.

Mueller, John. "The Essential Irrelevance of Nuclear Weapons." *International Security* 13 (Fall 1988): 55–79.

———. *Retreat from Doomsday: The Obsolescence of Major War.* New York: Basic Books, 1989.

Murphy, Craig N. *International Organization and Industrial Change: Global Governance Since 1850.* New York: Oxford University Press, 1994.

Nadelmann, E. A. "Global Prohibition Regimes: The Evolution of Norms in International Society." *International Organization* 44 (Autumn 1990): 472–526.

Nandy, Ashis. *Traditions, Tyranny and Utopias.* Delhi: Oxford University Press, 1987.

Nettl, J. P. "The State as a Conceptual Variable." *World Politics* 20 (1968): 559–92.

Neu, Charles. "The Rise of the National Security Bureaucracy." In *The New American State*, pp. 85–108. Edited by Louis Galambos. Baltimore: The Johns Hopkins University Press, 1987.

Niebuhr, Reinhold. *The Children of Light and the Children of Darkness.* New York: Charles Scribner's Sons, 1944.

Nietzsche, Friedrich. *The Birth of Tragedy and the The Case of Wagner.* Translated by Walter Kaufmann. New York: Vintage Books, 1967.

Nordlinger, Eric N. *Isolationism Reconfigured.* Princeton, NJ: Princeton University Press, 1995

Notter, Harley. *Postwar Foreign Policy Preparation, 1939–1945.* Washington, D.C.: G.P.O., 1950.

Nye, Jr., Joseph S. *Bound to Lead: The Changing Nature of American Power.* New York: Basic Books, 1990.

Owen, Henry and Edward C. Meyer. "Central European Security." *Foreign Affairs* 68 (Summer 1989): 22–40.

Pach, Jr., Chester. "Arming the Free World: The Origins of the United States Military Assistance Program." Ph.D. dissertation, Northwestern University, 1981.

——. *Arming the Free World: The Origins of the United States Military Assistance Program, 1945–1950.* Chapel Hill: University of North Carolina Press, 1991.

——. "The Containment of U.S. Military Aid to Latin America, 1944–1949." *Diplomatic History* 6 (Summer 1982): 225–43.

Packenham, John. *Liberal America and the Third World.* Princeton: Princeton University Press, 1973.

Park, William. "Political Change and NATO Strategy." In *European Security—Towards 2000,* pp. 33–48. Edited by Michael C. Pugh. Manchester: Manchester University Press, 1992.

Parsons, Talcott. *The Social System.* New York: Free Press, 1951.

Paterson, Thomas. *On Every Front: The Making of the Cold War.* New York: W. W. Norton, 1979.

——. *Meeting the Communist Threat: Truman to Reagan.* New York: Oxford University Press, 1988.

Patomäki, Heikki. "How to Tell Better Stories About World Politics." *European Journal of International Relations* 2 (March 1996): 105–33.

Pearton, Maurice. *Diplomacy, War and Technology Since 1830.* Lawrence: University of Kansas Press, 1984.

Perlmutter, Amos. *The Military and Politics in Modern Times.* New Haven: Yale University Press, 1977.

——. "The Presidential Political Center and Foreign Policy: A Critique of the Revisionist and Bureaucratic-Politics Orientations." *World Politics* 27 (October 1974): 87–106.

Perroux, Francois. "Economic Space: Theory and Applications." *Quarterly Journal of Economics* 64 (February 1980): 21–36.

Petras, James, Morris Morley, Peter DeWitt, and A. Eugene Havens. *Class, State, and Power in the Third World.* Montclair: Allanheld, Osmun, 1981.

Platt, D. C. M. *Finance, Trade, and Politics in British Foreign Policy 1815–1914.* Oxford: Clarendon Press, 1968.

Pocock, J. G. A. *The Machiavellian Moment.* Princeton: Princeton University Press, 1975.

Polanyi, Karl. *The Great Transformation.* Boston: Beacon Press, 1957.

Pollard, Robert A. *Economic Security and the Origins of the Cold War, 1945–1950.* New York: Columbia University Press, 1985.

Pollard, Sidney. *The Integration of the European Economy Since 1815.* London: George Allen & Unwin, 1981.

Puchula, Donald J. "The Pragmatics of International History." *Mershon International Studies Review* 39 (April 1995): 1–12.

Putnam, Robert. "Diplomacy and Domestic Politics: The Logic of Two-Level Games." *International Organization* 42 (Summer 1988): 427–60.

Rappaport, Armin. "The United States and European Integration: The First Phase." *Diplomatic History* 5 (Spring 1981): 121–49.

Rawls, John. *Political Liberalism.* New York: Columbia University Press, 1993.

Ray, James Lee. "The Abolition of Slavery and the End of International War." *International Organization* 43 (Summer 1989): 405–439.

Reiff, David. *Slaughterhouse: Bosnia and the Failure of the West*. New York: Simon & Schuster, 1995.

Revel, Jean-François. *How Democracies Perish*. New York: Harper & Row, 1983.

Ricoeur, Paul. "The Model of the Text: Meaningful Action Considered as a Text." In *Interpretive Social Science*, pp. 73–101. Edited by Paul Rabinow and William M. Sullivan. Berkeley: University of California, 1979.

Risse-Kappen, Thomas. "Collective Identity in a Democratic Community: The Case of NATO." In *The Culture of National Security*, pp. 357–399. Edited by Peter J. Katzenstein. New York: Columbia University Press.

———. "The Long-Term Future of European Security." In *European Foreign Policy*, pp. 45–60. Edited by Walter Calsnaes and Steve Smith. London: Sage, 1994.

———. *Cooperation Among Democracies: The European Influence on U.S. Foreign Policy*. Princeton: Princeton University Press, 1995.

Rohr, Donald. *The Origins of Social Liberalism in Germany*. Chicago: University of Chicago Press, 1963.

Rorty, Richard. *Contingency, Irony, and Solidarity*. Cambridge: Cambridge University Press, 1989.

Rosecrance, Richard. *The Rise of the Trading State*. New York: Basic Books, 1986.

Rosenau, James N. "Pre-theories and Theories of Foreign Policy." In *Approaches to Comparative and International Politics*, pp. 27–93. Edited by R. Barry Farrell. Evanston, Ill: Northwestern University Press, 1966.

———. *Turbulence in World Politics*. Princeton: Princeton University Press, 1990.

———. "Governance, Order and Change in World Politics." In *Governance Without Government: Order and Change in World Politics*, pp. 1–29. Edited by James N. Rosenau and Ernst-Otto Czempiel. Cambridge: Cambridge University Press, 1992.

Rosenberg, David. "American Atomic Strategy and the Hydrogen Bomb Decision." *Journal of American History* 66 (June 1979): 62–87.

Ross, Andrew L. "Dimensions of Militarization in the Third World." *Armed Forces and Society* 13 (Summer 1987): 561–87.

Ross, George. "Confronting the New Europe." *New Left Review*, no. 191 (January/February 1992): 49–68.

Rotter, Andrew. *The Path to Vietnam: Origins of the American Commitment to Southeast Asia*. Ithaca: Cornell University Press, 1987.

Rousseau, Jean-Jacques. "A Project of Perpetual Peace." In *Peace Projects of the Eighteenth Century*, pp. 1–141. New York: Garland Publishing, 1974.

Ruggie, John G. "International Regimes, Transactions, and Change: Embedded Liberalism in the Postwar Economic Order." In *International Regimes*, pp. 195–231. Edited by Stephen D. Krasner. Ithaca: Cornell University Press, 1983.

———. "Continuity and Transformation in the World Polity: Toward a Neorealist Synthesis." In *Neorealism and Its Critics*, pp. 131–57. Edited by Robert Keohane. New York: Columbia University Press, 1986.

———. "International Structure and International Transformation: Space, Time, and Method." In *Global Changes and Theoretical Challenges*, pp. 21–35. Edited by Ernst-Otto Czempiel and James N. Rosenau. Lexington, MA: Lexington Books, 1989.

———, ed. *Multilateralism Matters: The Theory and Praxis of an Institutional Form*. New York: Columbia University Press, 1993.

———. "Territoriality and Beyond: Problematizing Modernity in International Relations." *International Organization* 47 (Winter 1993): 139–74.

Ruggiero, Guido de. *The History of European Liberalism*. Boston: Beacon Press, 1959.

Rummel, R. J. *Understanding Conflict and War*. Vol. 4: *War, Power, Peace*. Beverly Hills, CA: Sage Publications, 1979.

Russett, Bruce. "Democracy and Peace." In *Choices in World Politics: Sovereignty and Interdependence*, pp. 245–60. Edited by Bruce Russett, Harvey Starr, and Richard Stoll. New York: W. H. Freeman, 1989.

———. *Controlling the Sword: The Democratic Governance of National Security*. Cambridge: Harvard University Press, 1990.

———. *Grasping the Democratic Peace*. Princeton: Princeton University Press, 1993.

Sayer, Derek. *Capitalism and Modernity*. London: Routledge, 1991.

Schelling, Thomas. *The Strategy of Conflict*. Cambridge: Harvard University Press, 1960.

Schiff, Benjamin N. "Assisting the Palestinian Refugees: Progress in Human Rights?" In *Progress in Postwar International Relations*, pp. 359–402. Edited by Emanuel Adler and Beverly Crawford. New York: Columbia University Press, 1991.

Schmitt, Carl. *The Concept of the Political*. New Jersey: Rutgers University Press, 1976.

Schmitter, Philippe. "Change in Regime Type and Progress in International Relations." In *Progress in International Relations*, pp. 89–123. Edited by Emmanuel Adler and Beverly Crawford. New York: Columbia University Press, 1991.

Schoultz, Lars. *Human Rights and United States Policy Toward Latin America*. Princeton: Princeton University Press, 1981.

Schroeder, Paul. "The 19th-Century International System: Changes in the Structure." *World Politics* 39 (October 1986): 1–26.

Schurmann, Franz. *The Logic of World Power*. New York: Pantheon Books, 1974.

Schwartz, Thomas. *America's Germany: John J. McCloy and the Federal Republic of Germany*. Cambridge: Harvard University Press, 1991.

Schwarzenberger, Georg. "The Protection of Human Rights in British State Practice." *Current Legal Problems* 1 (1948): 152–69.

———. *A Manual of International Law*, 6th ed. Abingdon: Professional Books, 1976.

Semmel, Bernard. *Liberalism and Naval Strategy: Ideology, Interests, and Sea Power During the Pax Britannica*. Boston: Allen & Unwin, 1986.

Shaw, Martin. *Post-Military Society: Militarism, Demilitarization and War at the End of the Twentieth Century*. Philadelphia: Temple University Press, 1991.

Sheehan, James. *German Liberalism in the Nineteenth Century*. Chicago: University of Chicago Press, 1978.

Sherry, Michael. *Preparing for the Next War: American Plans for Postwar Defense, 1941–1945*. New Haven: Yale University Press, 1977.

Sherwood, Elizabeth D. *Allies in Crisis: Meeting Global Challenges to Western Security*. New Haven: Yale University Press, 1990.

Shklar, Judith N. *Ordinary Vices*. Cambridge: Harvard University Press, 1984.

Shlaim, Avi. *The United States and the Berlin Blockade: a Study in Crisis Decision Making*. Berkeley: University of California Press, 1983.

Shonfield, Andrew. *Modern Capitalism: The Changing Balance of Public and Private Power.* New York: Oxford University Press, 1965.

Shoup, Lawrence H. and William Minter. *Imperial Brain Trust: The Council on Foreign Relations and United States Foreign Policy.* New York: Monthly Review Press, 1977.

SIPRI. *Yearbook 1991: World Armaments and Disarmament.* Oxford: Oxford University Press, 1991.

Siverson, Randolph M. and Juliann Emmons. "Birds of a Feather: Democratic Political Systems and Alliance Choices in the Twentieth Century." *Journal of Conflict Resolution* 35 (June 1991): 285–306.

Skinner, Quentin. "The Paradoxes of Political Liberty." In *The Tanner Lectures on Human Values,* pp. 225–250. Salt Lake City: University of Utah Press, 1986.

Skocpol, Theda. *States and Social Revolutions: A Comparative Analysis of France, Russia and China.* New York: Cambridge University Press, 1979.

Small, Melvin and J. David Singer. "The War-Proneness of Democratic Regimes, 1816–1965." *The Jerusalem Journal of International Relations* 1 (Summer 1976): 50–69.

Smith, Adam. *The Wealth of Nations.* Edited by Edwin Cannan. New York: The Modern Library, 1937.

Smith, Michael Joseph. "Liberalism and International Reform." In *Traditions of International Ethics,* pp. 201–24. Edited by Terry Nardin and David R. Mapel. Cambridge: Cambridge University Press, 1992.

Smith, Rogers M. "Unfinished Liberalism." *Social Research* 61 (Fall 1994): 631–70.

Smith, E. Timothy. "From Disarmament to Rearmament: The United States and the Revision of the Italian Peace Treaty of 1947." *Diplomatic History* 13 (Summer 1989): 359–82.

——. *The United States, Italy and NATO, 1947–52.* New York: St. Martin's Press, 1991.

Smith, Tony. *America's Mission: The United States and the Worldwide Struggle for Democracy in the Twentieth Century.* Princeton: Princeton University Press, 1994.

Snidal, Duncan. "The Limits of Hegemonic Stability Theory." *International Organization* 39 (Autumn 1985): 579–614.

——. "Cooperation Versus Prisoners' Dilemma." *American Political Science Review* 79 (December 1985): 923–42.

Snyder, Glenn H. "Alliances, Balance, and Stability." *International Organization* 45 (Winter 1991): 121–42.

Snyder, Jack. "Averting Anarchy in the New Europe." *International Security* 14 (Spring 1990): 5–41.

——. *Myths of Empire.* Ithaca: Cornell University Press, 1991.

Southgate, Donald. *'The Most English Minister . . .': The Policies and Politics of Palmerston.* London: Macmillan, 1966.

Sprout, Harold and Margaret Sprout. "Environmental Factors in the Study of International Politics." In *International Politics and Foreign Policy,* 2nd ed., pp. 41–56. Edited by James N. Rosenau. New York: Free Press, 1969.

Stambuk, George. *American Military Forces Abroad: Their Impact on the Western State System.* Columbus: Ohio State University Press, 1963.

Steel, Ronald. *Pax Americana.* New York: Viking Press, 1967.

——. *Walter Lippmann and the American Century.* Boston: Little, Brown, 1980.

Stein, Arthur. "The Hegemon's Dilemma: Great Britain, the United States, and the International Economic Order." *International Organization* 38 (Spring 1984): 355–86.

——. *Why Nations Cooperate*. Ithaca: Cornell University Press, 1990.

Steinberg, James B. "European Defense Cooperation: Why Now?" In *Europe in the Western Alliance: Towards a European Defense Entity?* pp. 41–57. Edited by Jonathan Alford and Kenneth Hunt. London: Macmillan, 1988.

Stinchcombe, Arthur. *Constructing Social Theories*. New York: Harcourt, Brace & World, 1968.

Strang, David. "Anomaly and Commonplace in European Political Expansion: Realist and Institutional Accounts." *International Organization* 45 (Spring 1991): 143–62.

Strange, Susan. "The Persistent Myth of Lost Hegemony." *International Organization* 41 (Autumn 1987): 551–75.

Stueck, William. *The Road to Confrontation: American Policy toward China and Korea, 1947–1950*. Chapel Hill: University of North Carolina, 1981.

Suganami, Hidemi. *The Domestic Analogy and World Order Proposals*. New York: Cambridge University Press, 1989.

Sunshine, Jonathan. "Economic Causes and Consequences of Democracy: A Study of Historical Statistics of the European and European-Populated English-Speaking Countries." Ph. D. dissertation, Columbia University, 1972.

Sunstein, Cass R. *The Partial Constitution*. Cambridge: Harvard University Press, 1994.

Swidler, Ann "Culture in Action: Symbols and Strategies." *American Sociological Review* 51 (April 1986): 273–86.

Tamir, Yael. "The Right to National Self-Determination." *Social Research* 58 (Fall 1991): 565–90.

——. *Liberal Nationalism*. Princeton: Princeton University Press, 1993.

Taubman, William. *Stalin's American Policy: From Entente to Detente to Cold War*. New York: Norton, 1982.

Taylor, A. J. P. *The Trouble Makers: Dissent Over Foreign Policy, 1792–1939*. Bloomington: Indiana University Press, 1958.

Taylor, Charles. "Interpretation and the Sciences of Man." In *Interpretive Social Science*, pp. 25–72. Edited by Paul Rabinow and William M. Sullivan. Berkeley: University of California, 1979.

Temperley, Harold and Lillian Penson. *Foundations of British Foreign Policy, from Pitt (1792) to Salisbury (1902)*. Cambridge: Cambridge University Press, 1938.

Tetlock, Philip E. and Aaron Belkin, eds. *Counterfactual Thought Experiments in World Politics*. Princeton: Princeton University Press, 1996.

Thee, Marek. "Militarization in the United States and the Soviet Union: The Deepening Trends." *Alternatives* 10 (Summer 1984): 93–113.

Thucydides. *The Peloponnesian War*. New York: Bantam Books, 1960.

Tilly, Charles, ed. *The Formation of National States in Western Europe*. Princeton: Princeton University Press, 1975.

——. *Coercion, Capital, and European States, A.D. 990–1990*. Cambridge: Basil Blackwell, 1990.

de Tocqueville, Alexis. *Democracy in America*, vol. 1. New York: Vintage Books, 1945.

Toulmin, Stephen. *Cosmopolis: The Hidden Agenda of Modernity*. Chicago: University of Chicago Press, 1990.

Trask, Roger. "The Impact of the Cold War on United States-Latin American Relations, 1945–1949." *Diplomatic History* 1 (Summer 1977): 271–84.

Trebilcock, Clive. *The Industrialization of the Continental Powers 1780–1914*. London: Longman, 1981.

Tucker, Robert W. *The Radical Left and American Foreign Policy*. Baltimore: Johns Hopkins University Press, 1971.

——. *The Inequality of Nations*. New York: Basic Books, 1977.

Tucker, Robert W. and David C. Hendrickson. *The Imperial Temptation: The New World Order and America's Purpose*. New York: Council on Foreign Relations Books, 1992.

Turner, Victor. *Dramas, Fields, and Metaphors*. Ithaca: Cornell University Press, 1974.

Ullman, Richard. "Redefining Security." *International Security*. 8 (Summer 1983): 129–53.

——. *Securing Europe*. Princeton: Princeton University Press, 1991.

Unger, Roberto. *False Necessity: Anti-Necessitarian Social Theory in the Service of Political Democracy*. Cambridge: Cambridge University Press, 1987.

United Nations. *Charter of the United Nations*. New York: United Nations, 1945.

U.S. Congress. House Committee on Ways and Means. *Extension of the Reciprocal Trade Agreements Act, Hearings Before a Subcommittee of the House Committee on Ways and Means on H.R.1311*, 82nd Cong., 1951.

——. Congressional Research Service Report for Congress, *Conventional Arms Transfers to the Third World, 1983–1990*, by Richard F. Grimmett. Washington, D.C.: The Library of Congress, 1991.

U.S. Department of State. *Foreign Relations of the United States, 1941*, vol. 1. Washington, D.C.: Government Printing Office, 1958.

——. *Foreign Relations of the United States, 1945*. 9 Volumes. Washington, D.C.: Government Printing Office, 1967–1969.

——. *Foreign Relations of the United States, 1946*. 11 Volumes. Washington, D.C.: Government Printing Office, 1969–72.

——. *Foreign Relations of the United States, 1947*. 8 Volumes. Washington, D.C.: Government Printing Office, 1971–1977.

——. *Foreign Relations of the United States, 1948*. 9 Volumes. Washington, D.C.: Government Printing Office, 1972–1976.

——. *Foreign Relations of the United Sates, 1949*. 9 Volumes. Washington, D.C.: Government Printing Office, 1974–1978.

——. *Foreign Relations of the United Sates, 1950*. 7 Volumes. Washington, D.C.: Government Printing Office, 1977–1980.

Vagts, Alfred. *A History of Militarism: Civilian and Military*, rev. ed. New York: The Free Press, 1959.

Vandenberg, Arthur H. Jr. *The Private Papers of Senator Vandenberg*. Boston: Houghton Mifflin, 1952.

Van Der Beugel, Ernst. *From Marshall Aid to Atlantic Partnership: European Integration as a Concern of American Foreign Policy*. Amsterdam: Elsevier, 1966.

Van Evera, Stephen. "Why Europe Matters, Why the Third World Doesn't: American Grand Strategy After the Cold War." *Journal of Strategic Studies* 13 (June 1990): 1–51.

——. "Primed for Peace: Europe After the Cold War." *International Security* 15 (Winter 1990/1991): 7–57.

Vasquez, John A. *The Power of Power Politics: A Critique.* New Brunswick: Rutgers University Press, 1983.

Vernon, Raymond. "Multinational Enterprise and National Security." In *International Politics: Anarchy, Force, Imperialism*, pp. 518–43. Edited by Robert Art and Robert Jervis. Boston: Little, Brown, 1973.

Vernon, Raymond and Debora L. Spar. *Beyond Globalism: Remaking America's Foreign Economic Policy.* New York: The Free Press, 1989.

Vincent, R.J. *Nonintervention and International Order.* Princeton: Princeton University Press, 1974.

——. *Human Rights and International Relations.* Cambridge: Cambridge University Press, 1986.

——. "The Idea of Rights in International Ethics." In *Traditions of International Ethics*, pp. 250–269. Edited by Terry Nardin and David R. Mapel. Cambridge: Cambridge University Press, 1992.

Von Hayek, F. A. *The Constitution of Liberty.* London: Routledge, 1960.

Waever, Ole. "Securitization and Desecuritization." In *On Security*, pp. 46–86. Edited Ronnie D. Lipshutz. New York: Columbia University Press, 1995.

Wagner, R. Harrison. "What was Bipolarity?" *International Organization* 47 (Winter 1993): 77–106.

Walker, R. B. J. *Inside/Outside: International Relations as Political Theory.* Cambridge: Cambridge University Press, 1993.

Wall, Irving M. *The United States and the Making of Postwar France, 1945–1954.* New York: Cambridge University Press, 1991.

Wallerstein, Immanuel. *The Modern World-System: Capitalist Agriculture and the Origins of the European World Economy in the Sixteenth Century.* New York: Academic Press, 1974.

——. *The Capitalist World-Economy.* Cambridge: Cambridge University Press, 1979.

——. *The Modern World System II: Mercantilism and the Consolidation of the European World -Economy, 1600–1750.* New York: Academic Press, 1980.

Walt, Stephen. *The Origins of Alliances.* Ithaca: Cornell University Press, 1987.

——. "Testing Theories of Alliance Formation: The Case of Southwest India." *International Organization* 42 (Spring 1988): 275–316.

Waltz, Kenneth N. *Man, the State, and War.* New York: Columbia University Press, 1959.

——. "Kant, Liberalism, and War." *American Political Science Review* 56 (June 1962): 331–40.

——. "The Stability of a Bipolar World." *Daedalus* 93 (Summer 1964): 881–909.

——. *Theory of International Politics.* Reading, MA: Addison-Wesley, 1979.

Walzer, Michael. *Spheres of Justice: A Defense of Pluralism an Equality.* New York: Basic Books, 1983.

——. "Liberalism and the Art of Separation." *Political Theory* 12 (August 1984): 315–30.

——. *Just and Unjust Wars*, 2nd ed. New York: Basic Books, 1991.

Watson, Adam. *The Evolution of International Society.* London: Routledge, 1992.

Watson, D. R. "The British Parliamentary System and the Growth of Constitutional Government in Western Europe." In *Britain Pre-eminent: Studies of British World*

Influence in the Nineteenth Century, pp. 101–27. Edited by Christopher Bartlett. New York: St. Martin's Press, 1969.

Watt, D. C. *Too Serious a Business: European Armed Forces and the Approach to the Second World War*. Berkeley: University of California Press, 1975.

Weber, Max. *The Theory of Social and Economic Organization*. Edited by Max Rheinstein. New York: The Free Press, 1947.

——. *General Economic History*. New Brunswick: Transaction Books, 1982.

Weede, Erich. "Extended Deterrence by Superpower Alliance." *Journal of Conflict Resolution* 27 (June 1983): 231–54.

——. "Democracy and War Involvement." *Journal of Conflict Resolution* 28 (December 1984): 649–64.

Wells, Jr., Samuel. "The First Cold War Buildup: Europe in United States Strategy and Policy, 1950–1953." In *Western Security: The Formative Years*, pp. 181–97. Edited by Olav Riste. New York: Columbia University Press, 1985.

Wendt, Alexander. "The Agent-Structure Problem in International Relations Theory." *International Organization* 41 (Summer 1987): 335–70.

——. "Anarchy Is What States Make of It: The Social Construction of Power Politics." *International Organization* 46 (Spring 1992): 391–425.

Wiggershaus, Norbert. "The Decision for a West German Defense Contribution." In *Western Security: The Formative Years*, pp. 198–214. Edited by Olav Riste. New York: Columbia University Press, 1985.

Wight, Martin. *Systems of States*. London: Leicester University Press, 1977.

Wilkins, Mira. *The Maturing of Multinational Enterprise: American Business Abroad from 1914 to 1970*. Cambridge: Harvard University Press, 1974.

Williams, Raymond. *Keywords*. New York: Oxford University Press, 1983.

Williams, William A. *The Tragedy of American Diplomacy*, 2nd ed. New York: Dell, 1972.

Wittgenstein, Ludwig *Philosophical Investigations*. New York: Macmillan, 1953/1968.

Wittner, Lawrence. *American Intervention in Greece, 1943–1949*. New York: Columbia University Press, 1981.

Wolfers, Arnold. *Discord and Collaboration: Essays on International Politics*. Baltimore: The Johns Hopkins University Press, 1962.

Wolfers, Arnold and Laurence W. Martin. *The Anglo-American Tradition in Foreign Affairs*. New Haven: Yale University Press, 1956.

Woods, Randall and Howard Jones. *Dawning of the Cold War: The United States' Quest for Order*. Athens: University of Georgia Press, 1991.

Yergin, Daniel. *Shattered Peace: The Origins of the Cold War*, rev. ed. New York: Penguin Books, 1990.

Zolberg, Aristide. "Moments of Madness." *Politics and Society* 1 (Winter 1972): 183–207.

INDEX

NOTE: Figures are denoted by "(fig.)" following page numbers. Notes are denoted by "n" following the page number.

Index compiled by Fred Leise.